DATE DUE

3/9/08	

DEMCO, INC. 38-2931

DESSERTS
BY THE
YARD

■ ■ ■

HOUGHTON MIFFLIN COMPANY
Boston   New York   2007

DESSERTS
BY
THE
YARD

SHERRY YARD

with Martha Rose Shulman
Foreword by Wolfgang Puck

PHOTOGRAPHS BY RON MANVILLE

FROM BROOKLYN
TO BEVERLY HILLS:
RECIPES FROM THE
SWEETEST LIFE
EVER

For information about permission to reproduce selections from
this book, write to Permissions, Houghton Mifflin Company,
215 Park Avenue South, New York, New York 10003.

Visit our Web site: www.houghtonmifflinbooks.com.

Library of Congress Cataloging-in-Publication Data

Yard, Sherry.
     Desserts by the yard: from Brooklyn to Beverly Hills: recipes
from the sweetest life ever / Sherry Yard, with Martha Rose Shulman;
photographs by Ron Manville; foreword by Wolfgang Puck.
       p. cm.
Includes index.
ISBN-13: 978-0-618-51522-6
ISBN-10: 0-618-51522-4
1. Desserts. 2. Yard, Sherry. I. Shulman, Martha Rose. II. Title.
TX773.Y37 2007
641.8'6—dc22   2007009419

Design by Anne Chalmers
Fonts: Fairplex and Meta, with some Copperplate

Food styling by Sherry Yard
Prop styling by Sherry Yard and Suzanne Griswold

Printed in the United States of America
QWV 10 9 8 7 6 5 4 3 2 1

To my mother,

ANN YARD,

who taught me that

if you can dream it,

you can do it.

And to my daddy,

BILL YARD,

who adds,

"With hard work."

Contents

Foreword

by Wolfgang Puck

IN THE FALL OF 1993 I INTERVIEWED A YOUNG WOMAN FOR the position of executive pastry chef at my West Hollywood restaurant, Spago. We sat at a sunny table by the window and talked about restaurants, desserts, and food. The morning seemed to slip away, and before I'd even seen or tasted any of her desserts, I knew she would be perfect for the job. What struck me most about this small blond woman was her love for her profession and her desire to make people happy. This was the kind of dessert chef I needed for our sometimes fickle Hollywood clientele.

I've watched Sherry evolve into a world-renowned pastry chef, author, and mentor to the many young people who work in my kitchens. Her range is tremendous; she puts as much love, effort, and attention to detail into the simplest home desserts, like apple pie and chocolate chip cookies, as she does into the extravagant, inspired desserts she creates for the biggest parties in Hollywood. And as I sensed she would, she has forged relationships with all of our regular guests. When the lady in the pink chef's jacket walks through the dining room, everybody knows that it's Sherry.

Her understanding of flavor, texture, balance, and eye appeal is unique among pastry chefs — and I have known many. Sherry has even learned the pastries of my native Austria and then taken them to a whole new level. In fact, I'm always telling her I wish she'd go back to Vienna and fix the pastries there — so many of them taste only of sugar.

At Spago, we pride ourselves in the quality of our ingredients and the way we enhance them. Sherry goes right to the source for hers. Ever since her first week at Spago, she has found the best, freshest fruits every week at our farmers' markets and turned them into unforgettable desserts, such as Passion Fruit Cheesecake, Ring of Saturn Peach "Doughnuts," and Concord Grape Soufflés.

Another thing I respect about Sherry — something that's very important to me — is that she can think on her own and be creative but remain true to the restaurant. She will always stand up for what she believes is right, even if

that means challenging a friend, or a boss. She's the only one of my many employees who's ever lodged a formal complaint against me, for telling one of her assistants to add more ladyfingers to Sherry's signature Malakofftorte, a mocha torte with ladyfingers soaked in rum syrup, without consulting her first. If I step out of line again, I could lose my job!

Dessert has always been the highlight of the meal for me, perhaps because my mother was a great baker and I grew up surrounded by delicious pastries. I've always wondered why it's served at the end. Luckily, I've never had to save the best for last when it comes to Sherry's creations. She will be the first to tell you that I'm in her bakeshop about ten times a day, reaching for a cookie, scooping up a spoonful of ice cream, or tasting her irresistible strudel. I can't help it; I'm addicted to Sherry's sweets.

It's rare to find a kindred spirit in work, somebody who understands what you do instinctively, somebody you can trust to do the best possible job, with no instructions and no questions asked. I have found that in Sherry Yard. Her reach extends far beyond Spago to my other restaurants — to Chinois on Main, Spago Las Vegas, and Wolfgang Puck Catering, and now to you, her readers.

Sherry's recipes are well suited to both the inexperienced home cook and the professional pastry chef. This collection reflects all of her baking experience, from her earliest birthday cakes to her most extravagant Oscar creations. With *Desserts by the Yard,* you will not only become a better technician but be infused with Sherry's passion.

Introduction

EVERY DAY, I MAKE A QUIET PROMISE TO THE GUESTS who flow through the doors of Spago, to fulfill their highest expectations with desserts they will never forget. It's a job that is not without its pressures, yet I am rewarded a thousand times over when I make a sweep through the dining room, and then again when the plates come back to the kitchen without a crumb.

Growing up, I had no idea that I would end up working in a restaurant, though when I look back on what I learned from my grandma, it doesn't surprise me. She was a turndown maid at the Waldorf-Astoria in New York City in the 1940s, and she taught me everything she knew—the nuances of a well-made bed, the beauty of well-pressed linens, and how to set a table. The knife belonged on the right side of the plate, blade turned in. The dessert spoon and fork were to be placed at the top of the plate, facing east and west, and were never moved until the entrée had been consumed, the plate removed, and the tablecloth crumbed.

From the time I was a very young child, I knew how to behave at a properly set table, too; Grandma had the most amazing Limoges and crystal stemware. She believed that whether you were having an egg-salad sandwich or a three-course meal, food always tasted better served on a beautiful plate and eaten with silver cutlery. She taught me that small details mattered: my sandwich cut into triangles had a better flavor than one cut into squares. Grandma liked to listen to music while she cooked; her radio sat on top of the refrigerator, and the songs that wafted high above us as she sang and danced in the kitchen set a happy tone.

Grandma was just the first of a series of incredible mentors. As I recorded the trajectory of my own career, which began in Brooklyn and New York City, then hopped west to San Francisco, Napa,

Hollywood, and Beverly Hills, I realized that my own story has a backstory. It's the story of the restaurant business in New York and California from the 1980s to the present and of the people who taught me the essential elements of the hospitality industry. They are (or were) the modern-day royalty of the restaurant world, people like Joe Baum, Jacques Pépin, Drew Nieporent, and Wolfgang Puck, and you will see their names in many of the pages that follow.

Joe, the toughest man with the softest side, taught me showmanship and the importance of detail. Jacques taught me technique and how to lead with a loving yet firm hand. Drew, who has the most amazing memory of anyone I've ever met, radiated joie de vivre. Wolfgang showed me how crucial it is to bond with guests and learn everything about them, their likes and dislikes, their birthdays and anniversaries. And *guests* is the key word. From all these teachers, I learned the most important lesson of all: in a great restaurant, the people who walk through the door are not "customers," but guests in your home.

A day never goes by in my pastry shop when I don't draw on something from my past. A favorite rainbow cookie eaten on the Brooklyn streets of my childhood, transformed into a smaller, more elegant version (page 15), adorns my cookie plate at Spago, as do minty chocolate-covered wafers (page 164) that are just like the Girl Scout thin mint cookies I worked so hard to sell. The chocolate velvet mousse that master pastry chef Albert Kumin made famous at the Rainbow Room in New York (page 74) lives on inside a domed chocolate bombe. The doughnuts I make for thousands of people every year at the Special Olympics in Santa Monica (page 314) are made with the same batter I use for Chocolate Truffle Cakes (page 80), which were all the rage in the 1980s. Even the Jell-O parfaits that Grandma used to make for us have found their counterpart on my dessert menu as the beautiful, multilayered Pussycat Café Gelée Parfaits (page 21).

I wrote this book because I wanted to share my childhood desserts with you, as well as all of the other wonderful desserts that tell my story. Some are as simple as white cupcakes with chocolate icing; others are more sophisticated finales that I make at Spago Beverly Hills. With every cake I've made over the years, every piecrust I've rolled out or chocolate truffle I've shaped, I've gained experience and learned secrets that I will share with you in these pages. No matter what your skill level in the pastry kitchen, none of these desserts will be out of your reach.

When I first began studying to be a pastry chef, I couldn't have imagined the good fortune that life had in store for me, though getting here was not easy. There have been moments of exhaustion along with those of excitement and joy. Through it all, I've been reminded that trying new things, even if it means leaving the comfort and safety of a loving family or a good job, always brings rewards.

By opening the cover of this book, you have walked through my front door. Whatever recipes you choose to make, I hope that they will leave you, your family, and your guests with sweet memories.

Notes on Ingredients and Equipment

BUTTER is *unsalted.* If the recipe calls for softened butter, it has been at room temperature long enough to cut through it effortlessly with a knife. However, it should be firm enough to hold its shape.

LEMON JUICE is always *freshly squeezed.* If it is pulpy, it should be strained.

LEMON ZEST is always *grated.* If it can't be grated on a microplane zester, it should be finely chopped.

EGGS are large and preferably hormone-free, from free-range chickens.

UNSWEETENED CHOCOLATE: I recommend Michel Cluizel Noir Infini 99% chocolate.

BITTERSWEET CHOCOLATE: I recommend 64% Cacao Barry chocolate and Valrhona Manjari.

MILK is *whole milk.*

FLOUR: I recommend King Arthur unbleached all-purpose.

SUGAR: Whereas granulated sugar will work with all of these recipes, I recommend baker's sugar, now available in supermarkets.

CREAM: Use stabilizer-free heavy cream.

BAKING SHEETS: I use 12-x-17-inch *half sheet pans* (also known as *half sheet trays*). They are available in cookware stores everywhere.

NONREACTIVE SAUCEPANS means *nonaluminum.* Aluminum reacts with acids and can change the flavor and color of acidic foods.

Brooklyn Inspirations

I GREW UP OUT IN THE FAR REACHES OF BROOKLYN, in a wonderful neighborhood called Gerritsen Beach, near Sheepshead Bay. We lived catty-corner to my grandma's house, where my mom had grown up. My dad, a New York City firefighter, had grown up in the same neighborhood. It was a safe place to be, a spit of quiet blocks bounded on two sides by Gerritsen Creek, which flowed into Rockaway Inlet, and on the third by the Brooklyn peninsula. Gaggles of kids played and ran around like street rats, unsupervised, moving freely in and out of the unlocked houses of friends and relatives. We knew the first and last names of everyone in every family. Communication between parents and kids was through the screens of open windows, not via cell phones. Even when we were little, we were allowed to cross the quiet streets by ourselves, but if we wanted to cross busy Gerritsen Avenue, where Victoria Pizzeria and Pollay's Toy Store were, we had to shout for an adult.

Our house was a two-story clapboard that sat on two lots. On the second lot, my dad built a deck and put in an aboveground pool that was the envy of the neighborhood. I shared a bedroom, and a birthday, with my older sister, Terry, and eventually we shared the same bedroom with two more sisters, Laurie and Lynne.

As in most of the Irish families on our block, meat was the focal point of our meals, and my father ruled the grill. My mom did not like to cook, and our vegetables always came out of a can. But we did sit down to a family dinner every night at a table where manners were of the utmost importance.

When we were little, if we were good, we got to help set the table. Putting out the salt and pepper shakers was what I liked to do best, until I became old enough to prepare my parents' after-dinner Chock full o'Nuts instant coffee. This was the moment I lived for each night. I memorized how each of them liked their coffee (my first recipe!), and using a special red measure, I carefully measured 1½ spoonfuls for Dad, 1 spoon for Mom. I crushed the instant powder with the back of the spoon (my own special technique) before pouring in the boiling water, and then put cream in Dad's cup but left Mom's black.

If there was any foreshadowing of my destiny as a pastry chef, the coffee ritual was it. I have almost no memory of *homemade* desserts—since my mother didn't bake. We rarely even had dessert, other than store-bought cookies. On special occasions, we were treated to cookies from Leon's Bakery and birthday cakes from Leon's or from the faraway Ebinger's Bakery, in another Brooklyn neighborhood. We loved to go to our local Carvel for ice cream, where we ate chocolate-dipped cones and, on special occasions, pistachio floats and wet walnut sundaes. On summer evenings, the only thing that could get us out of the swimming pool was the sound of Mr. Minkie's Good Humor cart, with its bells clanging, or the promise of a lemon ice from Victoria Pizzeria. I remember the sweets from my childhood so vividly that today I re-create many of them in grown-up versions, like the Rainbow Cookies that always go out on my Spago cookie plate.

*W*HEN I WAS FOUR and my sister six, we got a Susie Homemaker oven for our birthdays. It was a miniature oven—equipped with baking trays and a book of recipes—that actually worked. You would be wrong to assume that this marvelous toy marked the beginning of my career; because I was the younger sister, I was relegated to the task of assistant (read dishwasher). My older sister was in charge, and because Terry loved peanut butter, everything she chose to bake had a secret ingredient—peanut butter. I was certainly a *frustrated* baker at an early age, though not a baker. However, I always did like mixing things up. In fact, by the time I was eight, I was begging my parents not for a Barbie doll, but for a Sears chemistry set, for Christmas.

When I look back on all the jobs I had as a teenager in Brooklyn, I can see that my professional training began long before I knew what I was being trained *for*. In high school, I worked part-time as a dental assistant. I was trained to use dental tools, to be spotlessly clean and organized, and to do things in a precise way. Dr. Landesman's office was a quiet place, where I had to concentrate at all times. On my days off, I sold hamburgers at McDonald's.

The manager said they looked for not-too-tall girls with pretty smiles, and apparently I fit the bill. McDonald's was the polar opposite of the dentist's office—loud, bustling, and filled with people of all nationalities, not just the Irish and Italians I grew up with. And yet the same degree of importance was placed on precision and on systems, from making French fries to tying up a garbage bag.

I loved to draw in high school (indeed, I demonstrated a larcenous talent for making fake bus passes that looked so authentic that they were accepted as real), and my teachers said that I should apply for an art scholarship. I had my heart set on fashion school, but my mother was not one to have a "starving artist" in the family. She wanted me to have a skill that would assure some kind of employment, and she made sure I took secretarial classes like Steno and Dictaphone, along with Typing I and II.

After high school, I got a job as a receptionist in the grants department of Downstate Medical Center in Brooklyn. After five years, I had become a research grants associate, with my own office (baby blue with a royal blue swivel chair) and a hefty salary. I might have stayed at the medical center, not particularly happy in that world but unwilling to give up a good job, had a car not barreled into me one day when I was driving home from work. I landed in the hospital for a month, in traction, which provided me with a lot of time for reflection.

*W*HILE I'D BEEN DRIFTING ALONG in my workaday world, I realized that I had developed a burning passion—a love of baking. I regularly sent cookies along with our grant applications awaiting signatures. I was forever fiddling around with recipes. When I got out of traction, I decided to resign my position. For the first time in my life, I had a plan. And thanks to a fat settlement check from the insurance agency, I had the means to carry it out. I enrolled in New York City Technical College, at the foot of the Brooklyn Bridge, on the Brooklyn side.

My Favorite White Birthday Cake with Chocolate and Butter Fudge Frosting

MAKES ONE 9-INCH LAYER CAKE (2 CAKE LAYERS)

■ ■ ■

I was born on my sister Terry's second birthday. She was told that I was her birthday present—she would have preferred a doll. Every year we shared a special cake that we got from Leon's Bakery. It was a carousel cake, adorned with paper draping and studded with more than a dozen horses (which we always fought over). The white cake was filled and lathered with chocolate frosting. On my second birthday, the candle-bedecked cake burst into flames while everyone was singing "Happy Birthday" (it must have been the paper draping). We all screamed and Mom threw the cake into the backyard.

This cake is a little simpler—a white cake with a fluffy, melt-in-your-mouth chocolate frosting.

FOR THE CAKE
- 3 cups all-purpose flour
- 1 tablespoon baking powder
- ¼ teaspoon salt
- 8 ounces (2 sticks) unsalted butter, softened
- 2 cups sugar
- 6 large eggs, at room temperature
- 1 teaspoon vanilla extract
- 1 cup milk

FOR THE FROSTING
- 12 ounces bittersweet chocolate, finely chopped
- 12 ounces (3 sticks) unsalted butter, softened

1. **MAKE THE CAKE:** Place a rack in the middle of the oven and preheat the oven to 350°F. Spray two 9-inch round cake pans with pan spray and line with parchment. Spray the parchment.

2. Sift the flour, baking powder, and salt together two times and set aside.

3. Combine the butter and sugar in the bowl of a stand mixer fitted with the paddle attachment, or use a large bowl and a hand mixer, and beat together at medium speed for 4 to 5 minutes, until the mixture is very light and fluffy. Scrape down the paddle or beaters and the sides of the bowl.

4. Add the eggs one at a time, scraping down the bowl after each addition. Beat in the vanilla.

5. Beating on low speed, add the milk and the flour mixture in 3 additions, alternating wet and dry ingredients. Beat only until smooth. Scrape into the prepared pans.

6. Bake for 30 minutes, switching the position of the pans from front to back and rotating them halfway through. To test the cake for doneness, lightly touch the top with a finger—it should spring right back into place; the cake should also be beginning to pull away slightly from the sides of the pan. If necessary, bake for 5 to 10 minutes more.

7. Let the cakes cool in the pans on a rack for 15 minutes, then invert onto the rack and remove the pans and parchment. Allow to cool for at least 2 hours before frosting. (The cakes can be wrapped airtight and kept at room temperature for up to 2 days or frozen for up to 2 weeks.) If the cakes have domed, trim the domes, using a serrated knife, to create a flat surface.

8. MAKE THE FROSTING: Melt the chocolate in a microwave-safe bowl at 50 percent power for 2 to 3 minutes or in a heatproof bowl set over a saucepan of simmering water, stirring occasionally. Allow to cool until warm to the touch.

9. In the bowl of a stand mixer fitted with the paddle attachment, or in a large bowl with a hand mixer, beat the butter at medium speed until fluffy. Add the cooled melted chocolate and beat for 1 minute, until smooth.

10. Place a cake layer on a cardboard round or foam core or a plate, bottom side up. Immediately ice the cake with a metal spatula, preferably offset, using one third of the frosting for the filling. Place the other layer on top and use the balance of the frosting for the top and sides.

How to Cool and Frost a Cake

USEFUL EQUIPMENT

- For each layer and the base, a cardboard cake round or a piece of foam core, which you can find in restaurant supply stores and specialty stores. It's best to use a round that is slightly larger than the cake.
- A turntable/rotating cake stand.
- A large long metal icing spatula.
- A bench scraper.

COOLING TIPS

Once you've cooled a cake in the pan, to get it onto a rack, it's easiest to invert it onto a cardboard round, then slide it from the round onto a rack. Once the cake is cool, you can slide it from the rack back onto the round or onto a plate.

FROSTING TIPS

1. Before cutting a cake into layers, make a notch down the side of the cake so that you can easily match up the notches when assembling the layers after frosting.
2. Cut the cake into layers (see page 46).
3. Place each layer on a cardboard round, foam core, or plate. This will make the cake easier to manipulate.
4. If you've cut your cake into three layers, use the top cake layer for the bottom layer of the assembled cake. Use the middle layer for the middle, and the bottom layer, cut side down, for the top. This will give you a perfectly flat surface to frost.
5. Use a metal spatula, preferably offset, for spreading the frosting. Hold the spatula with a good grip and your pointer finger extended.
6. To smear the frosting, put your weight into the tip of the spatula and rock the spatula back and forth.
7. Scrape off the excess frosting that builds up on the spatula into a bowl or onto an unfrosted section of the cake.

FROSTING THE CAKE

1. Place a generous tablespoon of the frosting on the cardboard, foam core, or plate. This will "glue" the cake to the surface.
2. Invert the top layer of the sliced cake and center on the frosting on the cardboard.
3. Brush with Simple Syrup (page 350) if using.
4. Using a rubber spatula, scoop some of the frosting onto the cake layer.
5. Switch to a long metal spatula, preferably offset, and smear the frosting like cream cheese on a bagel, spreading it over the cake. If using a turntable, slowly turn the wheel toward you with your free hand while you rock the spatula back and forth.
6. To create an even layer of frosting, hold the spatula at a 45-degree angle and, beginning on the opposite side of the cake, drag the spatula toward you.
7. Line up the notches of the bottom and center layers and slide the center layer off the cardboard onto the bottom layer. Repeat Steps 3, 4, 5, and 6.
8. Line up the notches of the middle and remaining layer of cake and slide the remaining layer onto the middle layer.
9. Scrape out the remaining frosting onto the center of the cake. Smear over the top as in Steps 5 and 6. Let all of the excess frosting go over the edge.
10. If you have a bench scraper, hold the edge against the side of the cake and turn the turntable to spread the frosting evenly over the sides. If using a metal spatula, hold it perpendicular to the cake and rock it back and forth to coat the sides of the cake, while spinning the wheel of the turntable.
11. Gently hold the spatula at a 45-degree angle and scrape the rim of frosting around the top edge of the cake toward the center.

NO-BAKE CHEESECAKES

MAKES 24 MINI CHEESECAKES

■ ■ ■

My mom had some decidedly unusual techniques in the kitchen. Up there with the wackiest of them was warming opened cans of vegetables on a cookie sheet in the oven. She figured, "Why dirty a pot if I don't have to?" I called it Popeye cooking. We would run downstairs to the pantry every night before dinner to collect that evening's canned vegetables. Green beans were a regular (though they were more often brown by the time Mom got through with them), and creamed corn was our favorite. By now you're probably wondering why I'm prefacing a recipe for cheesecake with a story about heating cans of vegetables in the oven. It's because of what happened the time Mom and I were making no-bake cheesecakes for Thanksgiving.

Mom told Dad to put the cans of vegetables into the oven, which he dutifully did. The only problem was, no one had opened the cans. Forty-five minutes later, the oven door burst open and out flew a can of creamed corn, heading straight for the plate-glass sliding door. It flew past Grandma and the crudités, barely missing Mom and me and the cheesecakes. The cheesecakes were unharmed. Mom used whole vanilla wafers for these, but I've refined her recipe by making the little crusts out of vanilla cookie crumbs.

12 vanilla wafer cookies
8 ounces cream cheese, at room temperature
1/2 cup sugar
2 tablespoons sour cream
2 teaspoons fresh lemon juice
12 ripe strawberries, hulled and halved or quartered (depending on the size), or fraises des bois

1. Pulse the cookies in a food processor until you have crumbs. Line the cups of two mini muffin pans with paper liners and spoon a layer of cookie crumbs into the bottom of each.

2. In the bowl of a stand mixer fitted with the paddle attachment, or in a large bowl with a hand mixer, beat the cream cheese and sugar at medium speed until smooth, about 3 minutes. On low speed, beat in the sour cream and lemon juice until well combined, about 1 minute. Scrape down the sides of the bowl.

3. Spoon or pipe the filling into the cups. Refrigerate for 2 to 4 hours, until set, or overnight.

4. Before serving, top each cheesecake with a strawberry piece or two.

A & S CHEESECAKE

■ ■ ■

A & S was a department store where we shopped in Brooklyn. It had wooden escalators, which seemed massive to me. We used to ride up and down the escalators, and sometimes just before we got off the escalator, my mother would shout, "I told you kids never to steal!" and pretend to beat us. Today somebody would probably call child protective services, but back then they got the joke—at least they did when they saw us all burst out laughing. Then Mom would take us down to the basement for our reward: cheesecake. This one is a classic New York cheesecake.

- 6 ounces farmer's cheese
- 1 pound 14 ounces cream cheese, at room temperature
- 1 cup sugar
- 3 large eggs plus 2 large egg yolks, at room temperature
- 2 teaspoons fresh lemon juice
- 1½ teaspoons vanilla extract
- ¾ cup sour cream
- ¾ cup heavy cream

1. Place a rack in the middle of the oven and preheat the oven to 350°F. Spray a 9-inch springform pan with pan spray and line the bottom with a round of parchment paper. Spray the parchment. Wrap the outside of the pan with aluminum foil to prevent any water from coming in from the water bath.

2. Press the farmer's cheese through a fine-mesh strainer to ensure the curds are fine. Combine with the cream cheese and sugar in the bowl of a stand mixer fitted with the paddle attachment, or use a large bowl and a hand mixer. Beat on low speed for 2 minutes, or until smooth.

Sherry's Secrets

KEYS TO A GREAT CHEESECAKE

- Make sure the cream cheese and eggs are at room temperature.
- Blend the ingredients well, but don't whip them.
- Turn the oven off after 1 hour of baking. *Do not* open the oven door. Leave the cheesecake in the oven with the door closed for another 45 minutes to an hour.

3. Add the eggs and egg yolks one at a time, scraping down the bowl and paddle or beaters after each addition. Beat in the lemon juice and vanilla. Scrape down the bowl and paddle.

4. Still on low speed, beat in the sour cream. Slowly add the heavy cream, beating until blended; stop to scrape down the bowl and paddle every 30 seconds.

5. Pour the mixture into the prepared pan, scraping every last bit out of the bowl with a rubber spatula. Place the pan in a baking or roasting pan and place on the oven rack. Pour enough hot water into the baking pan to come halfway up the sides of the springform pan. Bake for 1 hour.

6. Turn off the oven; *do not* open the oven door. Leave in the oven for another 45 minutes to an hour; the cake will be golden and set.

7. Remove the cake from the oven, remove from the water bath to a rack, and allow to cool to room temperature, about 2 hours. Chill for at least 4 hours in the refrigerator.

8. To serve, run a knife around the inside of the rim of the springform pan and remove the rim. Allow the cake to stand at room temperature for 20 minutes before serving.

Sherry's Secrets

When making cheesecake, paddle slowly. You do not want to create air.

RAINBOW COOKIES

MAKES 80 (1½-INCH) SQUARES OR 120 (1-INCH) SQUARES

■ ■ ■

These gems are the grown-up version of the cookies that we used to buy by the pound at Leon's Bakery. They are really like little petits fours, consisting of fine layers of almond cake colored green, red, and yellow. The layers are soaked in simple syrup. At Spago we cut them into 1-inch squares. We make our own raspberry and apricot jams to sandwich the layers, but a good commercial jam will do just fine. The cookies are topped with a rich chocolate glaze.

The recipe makes a lot of cookies, and it's worth it to make this many, as the recipe is time-consuming and the cookies freeze well. You'll need a large (2-quart) food processor for this. If yours is smaller, do the cake base in 2 batches.

FOR THE CAKE

- 12 ounces almond paste
- 1½ cups sugar
- 1½ pounds (6 sticks) unsalted butter, cut into ½-inch pieces, softened
- 6 large eggs, separated
- ¾ cup almond flour (available at whole foods stores or see Sources)
- 3 cups all-purpose flour
- 1 drop red food coloring, or more as needed
- 1 drop green food coloring, or more as needed
- 2 drops yellow food coloring, or more as needed

- 1¼ cups Simple Syrup (page 350)
- ¾ cup apricot jam or Apricot Schmutz (page 367)
- ¾ cup raspberry jam

FOR THE CHOCOLATE GLAZE

- 6 ounces bittersweet chocolate, finely chopped
- 4 ounces (1 stick) unsalted butter
- 5 tablespoons light corn syrup
- 1½ tablespoons Grand Marnier

1. **MAKE THE CAKE:** Place racks in the upper and lower thirds of the oven, or if you have three racks, space them evenly. Preheat the oven to 325°F. Spray three 12-x-17-inch half sheet pans with pan spray. Line with parchment paper and spray the parchment.

2. Place the almond paste in a large food processor fitted with the steel blade and blend for 2 minutes. Add the sugar and pulse until the mixture has the consistency of coarse wet sand.

3. Add one quarter of the softened butter and pulse until it is blended with the almond paste. Blend in another quarter of the butter. Gradually add the remaining butter and blend until fluffy.

4. Scrape down the sides of the bowl. Add the egg yolks and pulse to blend. Pulse in the almond flour, then the all-purpose flour. Transfer the mixture to a large mixing bowl.

5. Using a hand mixer, beat the egg whites to soft peaks and fold into the batter.

6. Divide the batter among three bowls. Add the red food coloring to one bowl, the green food coloring to another, and the yellow food coloring to the third, and stir well to blend in each color. The batter with the red food coloring should be bright pink, the green batter should be a light green, and the yellow batter should be vibrant yellow; add a little more food coloring if necessary.

7. Scrape all of one colored batter onto one end of a prepared baking sheet and using a spatula, preferably offset, spread it evenly, turning the pan and scraping the batter off the spatula with your finger after each pass. It will take a while, but eventually the batter should be spread evenly over the baking sheet. Then slide your finger along the inside edge of the baking sheet to remove the excess batter from the edges. Repeat with the remaining 2 colored batters.

8. Place the pans in the oven (you may have to do this in 2 batches) and bake for 10 minutes. Switch the first two pans from top to bottom and rotate from front to back and continue to bake until the cake is firm to the touch, about 10 minutes more. Bake the third sheet on the middle rack, rotating from front to back after 10 minutes. The cakes should not brown. Allow to cool in the baking sheets for 10 minutes.

9. ASSEMBLE THE CAKE: Put an empty baking sheet in front of you, upside down. Spray lightly with pan spray and top with a piece of parchment (the spray will keep the parchment from slipping). Invert the yellow cake onto the baking sheet. Place a hot moist kitchen towel over the parchment on the bottom of the cake for a couple of minutes, then peel off the parchment. If it doesn't peel off neatly, then tear it off in strips. Using a pastry brush, brush evenly with one third of the simple syrup. Smear the apricot jam or apricot schmutz evenly over the cake. Top with the pink cake and remove the parch-

ment on the bottom in the same way. Brush evenly with half of the remaining syrup. Spread the raspberry jam evenly over the top. Complete with the green layer, removing the parchment and brushing with the remaining syrup. Cover with plastic wrap and refrigerate for at least 2 hours. (At this point, the cake can be stored wrapped airtight in the freezer for 3 to 4 weeks.)

10. **MAKE THE CHOCOLATE GLAZE:** Combine the chocolate with the butter in a microwave-safe bowl and melt at 50 percent power for 2 to 3 minutes, stirring once or twice. Or melt in a heatproof bowl set over a saucepan of simmering water. Stir with a rubber spatula until smooth. Stir in the corn syrup and the Grand Marnier.

11. Remove the cake from the refrigerator and unwrap it. Pour the glaze over the top and using an offset spatula, spread the glaze evenly over the top, stopping just before the edges. Allow to cool for 1 to 2 minutes, then, just as the shine disappears from the glaze, run a pastry comb or a fork in a squiggly motion over the top to make a decorative pattern (if you don't like the way it looks the first time, just run the comb or fork over the top again).

12. Refrigerate the cake for 30 minutes, or until the glaze is set. Remove from the refrigerator and cut into 1¹/₂- or 1-inch squares, using a serrated or chef's knife dipped in warm water to heat it and wiped dry. Wipe the knife clean after each cut. (The cake can be frozen, wrapped airtight, for up to 2 weeks.)

Sherry's Secrets

When lining baking sheets with parchment, first spray the sheets with pan spray, so the parchment won't slip around when you smear it with a thin layer of batter.

GRANDMA'S A&P STRAWBERRY SODAS

■ ■ ■

My grandma was a true character, and I cherished my sleepovers at her house. She would dress up like Zsa Zsa Gabor in lovely evening loungewear, complete with marabou trim and matching slippers. She seemed to have every color of the rainbow! My sisters and I got to dress up like mini Zsa Zsas, and at midnight Grandma would wake us up for snacks. First we would clip on some earrings, then she filled thin crystal glasses with ice cream. She topped the ice cream with a variety of colorful sodas from the local A&P Supermarket. For fun she would blindfold us and make us guess the flavors. "Listen to your tongue," she would say, setting a lifelong course for me. At her house, I tasted coffee soda for the first time (yuck!)—I had no trouble making the distinction between it and the strawberry.

1 quart strawberry ice cream, homemade (recipe follows) or store-bought
3 cups strawberry soda (two 12-ounce bottles or cans)
2 tablespoons Grand Marnier (optional)
1 tablespoon fresh lemon juice
Whipped cream for garnish

1. Chill six ice cream soda glasses in the freezer.

2. Place a couple of scoops of ice cream in each glass. Pour in the strawberry soda, dividing it evenly among the glasses. If desired, spoon 1 teaspoon Grand Marnier over the top of each soda. Spoon on ½ teaspoon lemon juice, garnish with whipped cream, and serve.

Strawberry Ice Cream

MAKES 1 QUART

1½ pounds ripe strawberries, hulled and halved
⅔ cup sugar
¼ cup water
2 tablespoons Grand Marnier (optional)

1½ cups heavy cream
1 cup milk
1 tablespoon fresh lemon juice
Pinch of salt

1. Place a 1-quart freezer container in the freezer.

2. Combine the strawberries, sugar, water, and Grand Marnier, if using, in a medium saucepan and bring to a simmer. Cook, stirring from time to time, until the strawberries are very soft, about 10 minutes.

3. Transfer the strawberry mixture to a blender or a food processor fitted with the steel blade and puree. Add the cream and milk and blend until smooth. Transfer to a bowl and allow to cool.

4. Stir in the lemon juice and salt, transfer the mixture to an ice cream maker, and freeze according to the manufacturer's directions. Transfer to the freezer container and freeze for at least 2 hours to firm.

PUSSYCAT CAFÉ GELÉE PARFAITS

MAKES SIX 6-OUNCE PARFAITS

■ ■ ■

When my grandpa was a bartender, he used to make a fancy cocktail with different liqueurs called the Pousse-Café, which we used to call the Pussycat Café. It was very difficult to pour and absolutely lethal. Different liqueurs were gracefully poured one on top of the other in a delicate aperitif glass. Because of their different densities, the liqueurs remained in perfect colorful layers. My grandma re-created this for us using gelatin. And I later put together both ideas. This beguiling dessert combines the vividness of fruit sorbet with the comforting attributes of Jell-O.

1. The method is the same for all of the layers, but you make them one at a time, chilling each one until set, then going on to the next. MAKE THE WATERMELON LAYER: In a medium bowl, combine the gelatin with 1/4 cup of the water and allow to bloom (soften) for 10 to 15 minutes.

2. Combine the remaining 1/4 cup water and the sugar in a saucepan and heat, stirring, until the sugar has dissolved. Pour over the gelatin mixture and stir until the gelatin has completely dissolved. Add the watermelon puree, rum, and lemon juice. Divide among six 6-ounce tumblers and refrigerate until set.

FOR THE WATERMELON LAYER
- 2 teaspoons powdered gelatin
- 1/2 cup water
- 1/4 cup sugar
- 1 1/2 cups watermelon puree (from 2 cups chopped watermelon), strained
- 2 tablespoons dark rum
- 1 tablespoon fresh lemon juice

FOR THE LEMON LAYER
- 1 tablespoon powdered gelatin
- 1 1/2 cups water
- 1/2 cup sugar
- 3/4 cup fresh lemon juice (from about 4 lemons)
- 2 tablespoons Grand Marnier

FOR THE STRAWBERRY LAYER
- 2 teaspoons powdered gelatin
- 1/2 cup water
- 3 tablespoons sugar
- 1 cup strawberry puree (from 2 cups whole strawberries)
- 1/2 cup fresh orange juice (from 1 large orange)
- 1 tablespoon fresh lemon juice
- 2 teaspoons Grand Marnier
- 1/4 teaspoon rose water (see Sources)

3. **MAKE THE LEMON LAYER:** Combine the gelatin with ¼ cup of the water in a medium bowl and allow to bloom for 10 to 15 minutes.

4. Combine the remaining water and the sugar in a saucepan and heat until the sugar has dissolved. Pour over the gelatin mixture and stir until the gelatin has completely dissolved. Add the remaining ingredients and mix well. Pour over the watermelon layer in the tumblers and refrigerate until set.

5. **MAKE THE STRAWBERRY LAYER AND THEN THE MANDARIN OR ORANGE LAYER:** Follow the directions for the lemon layer, allowing the strawberry layer to set before making the mandarin or orange layer.

6. Serve the parfaits topped with whipped cream if you wish.

FOR THE MANDARIN OR ORANGE LAYER

- 2½ teaspoons powdered gelatin
- ½ cup water
- ⅓ cup sugar
- 1 tablespoon grated mandarin or orange zest
- 1½ cups fresh mandarin or orange juice (from about 8 mandarins or 3 large or 4 medium oranges)
- ⅓ cup fresh lemon juice (from about 2 lemons)

Whipped cream for topping (optional)

Sherry's Secrets

A gelatin mixture can always be made in advance. If it sets up before you're ready to use it, gently rewarm it in a heatproof bowl set over a saucepan of simmering water to 80°F.

ITALIAN LEMON ICE

SERVES 6

■ ■ ■

Hot summer days in Brooklyn for tomboys like me meant daylong Wiffle Ball games with the guys on the street. We played at the corner and used the sewer drains as base marks, covering the holes with cardboard. Those days also meant Victoria's hot pizza and Gino's cold ices. A dollar would buy a slice and a soda or a slice and an Italian ice. The ice came in paper cups, and we'd scrape it into our mouths with a wooden spoon. The best part was flipping the cup upside down to get all the concentrated sugar at the bottom.

2½ cups water
1½ cups sugar
2 teaspoons grated lemon zest
1 cup strained fresh lemon juice (from 5–6 lemons)

6 6-ounce Dixie paper cups or ramekins

1. Combine the water and sugar in a medium saucepan and bring to a boil, stirring to dissolve the sugar. Remove from the heat and allow to cool to room temperature.

2. Stir in the lemon zest and juice and pour into the paper cups (or other containers). Freeze until solid.

3. Serve to kids on the back porch, with spoons for scraping.

VARIATION

In California I make this with Meyer lemons, and for adults I add a tablespoon of vodka or Grand Marnier to the mix.

FROZEN CHOCOLATE-COCONUT BARS

■ ■ ■

Summers also meant lazy days at Kiddie Beach. After a morning in the muddy water, we'd eat Mom's crunchy sandy bologna sandwiches, then run to the refreshment stand for frozen candy bars. I would sit and gnaw at my frozen Mounds bars for hours, saving them in their wrapper between trips back to the waves. This recipe is my take on those candy bars.

The recipe calls for ground rice, which should not be confused with rice flour. Put the rice in a food processor or spice mill (make sure the spice mill is odor-free) and process until ground, then pass through a sifter to get rid of any chunks and process one more time.

FOR THE SHORTBREAD DOUGH

- 5½ ounces (1 stick plus 3 tablespoons) unsalted butter, softened
- ¼ cup sugar
- 1 large egg
- 2 cups cake flour
- 2 tablespoons ground rice (see headnote)

FOR THE COCONUT GANACHE TOPPING

- 12 ounces bittersweet chocolate, finely chopped
- 2 tablespoons unsalted butter, softened
- 2 tablespoons sugar
- 1½ cups unsweetened coconut milk
  Toasted sweetened shredded coconut for sprinkling (optional)

1. **MAKE THE DOUGH:** In the bowl of a stand mixer fitted with the paddle attachment, or in a large bowl with a hand mixer, cream the butter and sugar at medium speed until fluffy, about 2 minutes. Beat in the egg. Scrape down the bowl and paddle. Gradually add the flour and ground rice, mixing until the dough comes together. Shape the dough into a disk, cover with plastic wrap, and refrigerate for at least 4 hours, or overnight.

2. Place a rack in the lower third of the oven and preheat the oven to 350°F. Spray a 9-x-13-inch baking pan with pan spray and line with parchment. Spray the parchment.

3. Roll out the dough to a rectangle the size of the bottom of the pan and line the pan with the dough. Pierce in several places with a fork. Cover with another

sheet of parchment and top with dried beans or rice or pie weights. Place in the oven and bake for 18 minutes. Remove the weights and top sheet of parchment and bake for another 10 to 15 minutes, until the dough is golden. Allow to cool on a rack to room temperature.

4. Clear a space in your freezer or refrigerator large enough to accommodate the pan.

5. MAKE THE GANACHE TOPPING: Combine the chocolate, butter, and sugar in a medium bowl. In a small saucepan, bring the coconut milk to a boil. Pour over the chocolate, tap the bowl against your work surface so that all of the chocolate is covered, and allow to sit for 2 minutes. Whisk the mixture until smooth.

6. Pour the ganache over the shortbread, scraping it out of the bowl with a rubber spatula. If you wish, sprinkle the top with toasted coconut. Place in the refrigerator for 4 hours or the freezer for 2 hours. (At this point the "bar" can be stored for up to 2 days in the refrigerator or 2 weeks in the freezer, wrapped airtight.)

7. Cut the bar into small squares, bars, or diamonds and return the pan to the refrigerator until ready to serve. Remove from the refrigerator 5 minutes before serving.

CHOCOLATE-COVERED CHERRIES

MAKES 48 CANDIES

■ ■ ■

My first real boyfriend, Jimmy Quinn, worked after school at the local pharmacy as a delivery boy. On Friday nights, after he got his pay, he'd stop by my front door with a box of Russell Stover chocolate-covered cherries. The dark ones were my favorite. It has become a New Year's Eve tradition for me to make these chocolate-covered cherries, using preserved cherries from last summer's crop. This recipe calls for fondant, which is essentially cooked and aerated sugar that can be poured over cinnamon buns or petits fours or hidden inside chocolates for creamy bonbons. Prepared fondant is available at specialty pastry supply shops, as are foil candy cups; preserved cherries are available at gourmet shops and Italian delis. Make sure you buy the candy fondant, such as Redi Fondant, not fondant paste for cakes.

48 1-inch foil candy cups

24 fresh cherries, halved and pitted, or 48 drained Fat Cherries (page 364)
1 cup fondant
2 tablespoons plus 1 teaspoon cognac
1 teaspoon water
12 ounces bittersweet chocolate, finely chopped

Sherry's Secrets

You can buy premade chocolate cups (see Sources) and use them instead of the foil cups. This makes for a great treat.

1. Place the foil cups on a baking sheet. Pop a cherry half or a fat cherry into each cup.

2. Heat the fondant in a heavy medium saucepan over low heat to 100°F. Stir in the cognac and water. Remove from the heat.

3. Cut a tiny tip in a disposable pastry bag (see Sherry's Secrets). Scrape the fondant into the pastry bag and pipe enough into each cup to just cover the cherry, leaving room at the top for the chocolate. Tap the baking sheet on your work surface to settle the cherries into the fondant. Refrigerate for 1 hour, or until the fondant sets and a nice skin forms on the top.

4. Temper the chocolate (see page 379). Spoon or pipe the chocolate (see Sherry's Secrets) over the fondant, filling each cup and mounding the chocolate slightly above the rim. Refrigerate until set.

5. Serve the chocolate-covered cherries in their foil cups. To eat, peel off the cup and pop the cherry into your mouth. (The chocolate-covered cherries will keep for up to 2 days, refrigerated.)

Sherry's Secrets

PIPING RUNNY INGREDIENTS, FONDANT, AND CHOCOLATE

A disposable plastic pastry bag and an office clip or a clothespin are good equipment for this somewhat delicate procedure. Cut a tiny bit off the end of a plastic pastry bag. Close the opening with an office clip or a clothespin, set the bag in a 4-cup measuring cup or a conical 2-cup measuring cup, and cuff the top over the rim. Pour the ingredient to be piped into the bag, twist the top shut, and reverse out of the cup, tip up. Remove the clip, and pipe as directed.

BISCUIT TORTONI

■ ■ ■

Our family did not go out to dinner often, but on that rare occasion when we did, we chose a local Italian place called Fra Mar. Ordering from a menu was intimidating. What to choose? Dessert always posed the biggest dilemma. The names—spumoni, tortoni, tartufo—all sounded so foreign, and so inviting. Between visits I'd forget which was which, and then I'd have to gamble. Was I ordering my favorite ice cream—crusted almond cookies? Was biscuit tortoni going to be that incredible semifrozen mousse-like almond parfait with the cherry on top, or was that spumoni? I loved the sound of *spumoni,* but the tortoni was my favorite. I now know that this frozen almond zabaglione parfait originated in the Café Tortoni in Paris and is named for the Neapolitan ice cream maker who started the café.

¼ cup hot water

¼ cup plus 2 tablespoons sugar

3 large egg yolks, at room temperature

2 tablespoons amaretto

1½ teaspoons vanilla extract

½ cup mascarpone

1½ cups heavy cream, whipped to medium peaks

½ cup crumbled Italian amaretti (or other almond cookies)

½ cup Almond Seats (page 356)

6 brandied cherries (available at gourmet stores)

1. Chill six 6-ounce glasses in the freezer. Make an ice bath by filling a large bowl with ice and water.

2. In a medium saucepan, combine the hot water with the ¼ cup sugar and bring to a simmer; remove from the heat.

3. Meanwhile, in a medium bowl, beat the egg yolks with the 2 tablespoons sugar with a hand mixer until thick and lemony. Whisk in the amaretto, vanilla, and sugar syrup. Place over a saucepan of simmering water, making sure that the bottom of the bowl is not touching the water, and whisk until the mixture is thick and foamy, 3 to 5 minutes. Remove from the heat. Immediately place the bowl over the ice bath and continue whisking until cold.

4. Beat the mascarpone in the bowl of a stand mixer fitted with the paddle attachment, or in a large bowl with a hand mixer, until smooth. Slowly add the whipped cream, a tablespoon at a time; after every 2 additions of whipped cream, scrape down the sides of the bowl. Slowly add the egg yolk mixture, beating at low speed.

5. Pour the zabaglione into the chilled glasses, leaving about $3/4$ inch at the top. Place in the freezer for 4 hours, or until frozen.

6. Mix together the crumbled cookies and almond seats. When the zabaglione is frozen, top with the cookie mixture. Return to the freezer until ready to serve. Just before serving, top with a cherry.

BLACK-AND-WHITE COOKIES

MAKES 42 SMALL COOKIES OR 24 VERY LARGE COOKIES

■ ■ ■

These cookies are iced with vanilla and chocolate fondant. Brooklyn black-and-white cookies are normally cake-like and huge, but mine are more demure. These cookies will forever symbolize Brooklyn in the 1970s to me. That was a period of racial turmoil: busing had been instituted, and every day elementary kids from what were deemed bad neighborhoods were put on school buses and taken to strange neighborhoods, where they were not welcome. One of the children I saw through the school bus window grew up to be the comedian Chris Rock. Years later at Spago, I once again saw him through a window—this time a kitchen window—and watched as he sat with three Emmy Awards on his table, accepting congratulations from everyone around.

FOR THE COOKIE DOUGH

- 1 cup cake flour
- 1 cup all-purpose flour
- 1 teaspoon baking powder
- 6 ounces ($1\frac{1}{2}$ sticks) unsalted butter, softened
- 1 cup sugar
- 1 large egg, at room temperature
- 1 teaspoon vanilla extract
- $\frac{1}{2}$ cup buttermilk

FOR THE VANILLA AND CHOCOLATE ICING

- $2\frac{1}{2}$ cups plus 1 teaspoon confectioners' sugar, plus more as needed
- 1 tablespoon light corn syrup, plus more as needed
- 2 tablespoons hot water, plus more as needed
- $\frac{1}{2}$ teaspoon vanilla extract
- 1 ounce bittersweet chocolate, finely chopped
- 2 tablespoons unsweetened cocoa powder

1. **MAKE THE DOUGH:** Place a rack in the lowest position of the oven and preheat the oven to 350°F. Line two baking sheets with parchment.

2. Sift together the cake flour, all-purpose flour, and baking powder and set aside.

3. In the bowl of a stand mixer fitted with the paddle attachment, or in a large bowl with a hand mixer, cream the butter and sugar at medium speed until fluffy, about 2 minutes. Scrape down the sides of the bowl. Add the egg and vanilla and mix at medium speed until incorporated. Scrape down the sides of the bowl and the paddle.

4. In 2 or 3 additions, beating at low speed, add the flour mixture, alternating with the buttermilk, to the butter mixture. Beat until the ingredients are incorporated.

5. **FOR SMALL COOKIES**: Spoon the batter onto the parchment-lined baking sheets by the tablespoon.

FOR BIG BROOKLYN-STYLE COOKIES: Spoon $1/4$ to $1/3$ cup batter per cookie onto the baking sheets, making sure to leave a couple of inches between each cookie.

Bake small cookies, one sheet at a time, for 8 minutes. Turn the pan and bake for another 4 to 6 minutes, until the cookies are golden around the edges. Bake Brooklyn-sized cookies, one sheet at a time, for 10 minutes, then turn and bake for another 8 to 10 minutes. Remove from the oven and allow the cookies to cool.

6. **MAKE THE ICINGS**: In a small bowl, combine the confectioners' sugar, corn syrup, water, and vanilla and stir together until smooth. Divide in half between two bowls. Melt the chocolate in a microwave-safe bowl at 50 percent power for 2 to 3 minutes or in a heatproof bowl set over a saucepan of simmering water. Stir with a rubber spatula until smooth. Scrape the chocolate into one of the bowls, along with the cocoa powder. You will have to add a little more hot water (up to 2 tablespoons) and up to 1 teaspoon more corn syrup to get a smooth, shiny mixture.

7. Brush half of each cookie with chocolate icing and allow to set. Brush the other half with vanilla icing and allow to set. If either of the icings seems too runny, add a little confectioners' sugar. You can also glaze the tops using a pastry bag fitted with a plain tip. (The cookies will keep, stored airtight, for 2 days.)

NOTE: A baby offset spatula might be easier to use for coating the cookies.

CHARLOTTE RUSSE

■ ■ ■

One summer the whole family, Grandma and Grandpa included, piled into the station wagon and drove down to Atlantic City to see Frank Sinatra. We stayed for a few days. To me it was magical. What I remember most about Atlantic City are the sweets—especially the charlotte russe, airy ladyfingers surrounding a whipped cream filling; the frozen soft-serve ice cream cones dipped in chocolate we got on the boardwalk; and the saltwater taffy we took home with us.

FOR THE LADYFINGERS

- $3/4$ cup plus 2 tablespoons cake flour
- $3/4$ cup plus 2 tablespoons all-purpose flour
- $1/4$ teaspoon salt
- 6 large eggs, separated, at room temperature
- $3/4$ cup sugar
- $1/2$ teaspoon vanilla extract
  Confectioners' sugar for dusting

- $1^1/2$ cups heavy cream
- 1 tablespoon sugar
- $1/2$ teaspoon vanilla extract
- $1/3$ cup Simple Syrup (page 350), flavored if desired
- 8 Bing or maraschino cherries

1. **MAKE THE LADYFINGERS:** Place racks in the upper and lower thirds of the oven. Preheat the oven to 350°F. Line two baking sheets with parchment paper.

2. Sift together the cake flour, all-purpose flour, and salt and set aside.

3. Combine the egg yolks with 6 tablespoons of the sugar in the bowl of a stand mixer fitted with the paddle attachment, or in a large bowl with a hand mixer. Beat at high speed until the mixture is thick and pale yellow and holds a ribbon when dropped from a spatula or the paddle, about 3 minutes. Beat in the vanilla.

4. In a large bowl, beat the egg whites on low speed with a hand mixer until they form soft peaks. Gradually add the remaining 6 tablespoons sugar and increase the speed to medium. Beat until the whites form medium-stiff peaks. Stir one quarter of the whites into the egg yolks, then one quarter of the flour mixture. Fold in the remaining whites in 3 additions, alternating with the remaining flour mixture.

5. Fit a piping bag with a #6 (½-inch) plain tip. Pipe 3-inch lengths of the batter onto the baking sheets, leaving 1 inch between them. Dust with confectioners' sugar. You should have about 48 ladyfingers.

6. Bake for 8 minutes. Rotate the baking sheets from top to bottom and from front to back and bake for another 4 to 5 minutes, until the ladyfingers are golden brown. Remove from the oven and allow to cool.

7. Whip the cream with the sugar and vanilla until stiff.

8. ASSEMBLE THE CHARLOTTE RUSSE: Line the sides of eight 8-ounce ramekins or paper cups with ladyfingers, rounded side out; the cake will rise up above the edges. Break up some of the extra ladyfingers and line the bottom of the dishes with them. Brush the ladyfingers generously with simple syrup. Fit a piping bag with a #4 star tip and pipe in the whipped cream. Top each charlotte russe with a cherry. Serve at once, or refrigerate until ready to serve. (The ramekins can be assembled up to 4 hours before serving.)

NOTE: Store leftover ladyfingers airtight at room temperature or in the freezer. They will keep for up to 5 days at room temperature and for a couple of months in the freezer.

ZEPPOLI

■ ■ ■

Zeppoli are Italian doughnuts. Brooklyn has a different Italian festival every weekend in the summer. At the Feast of San Gennaro, vats of bubbling oil are everywhere, filled with fleets of floating batter for zeppoli. Vendors fill paper bags with the warm zeppoli, then dust the zeppoli with confectioners' sugar and shake the bags to coat. When I became a pastry chef, I developed my own grown-up version, made with ricotta and milk. The tasty zeppoli are very tender.

1½ cups all-purpose flour
1 tablespoon plus 1 teaspoon baking powder
¼ teaspoon salt
2 tablespoons sugar
2 large eggs
2 cups ricotta
1 cup milk
½ teaspoon vanilla extract
¼ teaspoon freshly grated nutmeg
1 teaspoon grated lemon zest
Vegetable oil for deep-frying
¾–1 cup confectioners' sugar

6–8 paper lunch bags

1. In a medium bowl, whisk together the flour, baking powder, and salt to combine well (you can also sift the ingredients into the bowl).

2. Combine the sugar and eggs in another medium bowl and whisk until smooth. Add the ricotta and whisk to combine well. Add the milk, vanilla, nutmeg, and lemon zest and combine well. Whisk in the flour. Combine well. Cover the batter tightly with plastic wrap and refrigerate for at least 30 minutes. (The batter can be made up to 4 hours ahead.)

3. In a wide deep pot fitted with a deep-fry thermometer, heat 2 inches of oil over medium-high heat to 350°F, or heat the oil in a deep fryer. Set a wire rack over a baking sheet. Carefully spoon tablespoonfuls of the batter into the hot oil in batches. Cook for 2 to 2½ minutes, flipping over every 30 seconds, until golden brown on both sides and puffed. Using a mesh skimmer or a slotted spoon, remove the zeppoli from the oil and drain on the rack.

4. Divide the zeppoli among the paper lunch bags. Add 2 tablespoons confectioners' sugar to each bag, close up the top, and shake to coat the zeppoli. Serve hot.

BROOKLYN BLACKOUT CAKE

MAKES ONE 9-INCH LAYER CAKE (3 CAKE LAYERS)

■ ■ ■

This rich, over-the-top chocolate cake, with a chocolate pudding filling that melts in your mouth, was inspired by one from Ebinger's Bakery. You bake the layers on baking sheets, then cut them into rounds and use the left-over cake to make crumbs for the crumb layer. You will have more than enough crumbs, so let the leftovers dry out and keep in the freezer—chocolate cake crumbs come in handy!

1. **MAKE THE PUDDING FILLING:** In a large saucepan, combine the milk and ³/₄ cup of the sugar and bring to a boil over medium heat, stirring to dissolve the sugar. Remove from the heat.

2. In a medium bowl, whisk together the remaining ³/₄ cup sugar, the cocoa powder, and the cornstarch. Whisking constantly, stream this mixture into the hot milk. Return the milk to the heat and whisk constantly for 4 minutes, or until thick.

3. Remove from the heat and whisk in the chocolate, butter, and vanilla, whisking until the chocolate is melted and the mixture is smooth. Pour into a bowl and place a sheet of plastic wrap directly over the surface. Place the bowl in an ice bath to cool quickly, or refrigerate.

4. **MAKE THE CAKE:** Place racks in the upper and lower thirds of the oven, or if you have three racks, space them evenly. Preheat the oven to 350°F. Spray

FOR THE PUDDING FILLING

- 4 cups milk
- 1¹/₂ cups sugar
- ¹/₄ cup plus 2 tablespoons unsweetened cocoa powder
- ¹/₄ cup plus 2 tablespoons cornstarch
- 2 ounces unsweetened chocolate, preferably Michel Cluizel Noir Infini 99% (see Sources), finely chopped
- 2 tablespoons unsalted butter
- 1 tablespoon vanilla extract

FOR THE CAKE

- 2 cups all-purpose flour
- 1 teaspoon baking powder
- 1 teaspoon baking soda
- ¹/₂ teaspoon salt
- ¹/₂ cup unsweetened cocoa powder
- ³/₄ cup milk
- 2 tablespoons water
- 2 ounces unsweetened chocolate, preferably Michel Cluizel Noir Infini 99%, finely chopped
- 8 ounces (2 sticks) unsalted butter, softened
- 2 cups sugar
- 4 large eggs
- 2 teaspoons vanilla extract

three 12-x-17-inch half sheet pans with pan spray. Line them with parchment paper and spray the paper.

5. Sift together the flour, baking powder, baking soda, and salt, and set aside.

6. Place the cocoa powder in a medium bowl. Whisk in half the milk until a smooth paste forms. Add the remaining milk and the water and whisk until the mixture is smooth. Set aside.

7. Melt the chocolate in a micro-wave-safe bowl at 50 percent power for 2 to 3 minutes or in a heatproof bowl set over a saucepan of simmering water. Stir until smooth.

8. In the bowl of a stand mixer fitted with the paddle attachment, or in a large bowl with a hand mixer, beat the butter on high speed until it is soft and creamy, about 1 minute. Slowly add the sugar, beating until the mixture is light and fluffy and a creamy white color, about 4 minutes.

9. Stir ¼ cup of the butter mixture into the melted chocolate. Scrape the chocolate back into the mixing bowl.

10. Add the eggs one at a time, making sure that each egg is completely incorporated and scraping down the sides of the bowl before adding the next one. Add the vanilla. At low speed, add the flour ½ cup at a time, alternating with the milk and cocoa mixture. Scrape down the sides of the bowl.

Sherry's Secrets

I rarely make cakes in round cake pans. I prefer to use half sheet pans (rimmed baking sheets) for the following reasons:

1. They bake faster.
2. They cool faster.
3. The layers of the cakes you cut from the sheet cake are automatically even because you haven't had to split one cake into two or three rounds.
4. You can thicken (or pad) the layers with excess cake from the cutouts if you want a higher cake, and nobody will know once the cake is filled and frosted.
5. The cake scraps will give you lots of crumbs, which (in addition to padding your layers) can be used for cheesecake crusts, as a coating for ice cream balls and ice pops, or as a crumb coating for cakes.

When baking a cake in half sheet pans, fill them no more than three-quarters full. If there is excess batter, use it for cupcakes.

11. Divide the batter equally among the prepared half sheet pans. Place the pans in the oven (you may have to do this in 2 batches) and bake for 10 minutes. Switch the first two pans from top to bottom and rotate from front to back and bake for another 5 to 10 minutes, until the cake springs back when pressed lightly. Bake the third sheet on the middle rack, rotating from front to back after 10 minutes. Remove from the oven and immediately run a knife around the edges of each pan. Invert onto a work surface. With a metal spatula, flip each cake over onto a rack, and allow to cool completely. (The cakes can be refrigerated, tightly wrapped, for 2 days, or frozen for 2 weeks.)

12. When the cakes are cool, return them to the work surface and cut a 9-inch round from each one, using an inverted cake pan as a guide. Set the scraps aside for cake crumbs.

13. ASSEMBLE THE CAKE: Measure out 1 cup of the filling and set aside. Place the first cake round on a cardboard round or foam core or a plate. Spread half of the remaining filling on the cake round and top with another. Spread the other half of the filling on the second layer and top with the third. Spread the reserved filling over the top layer and sprinkle evenly with $1/2$ cup of cake crumbs. Freeze the remaining crumbs for another use.

NOTE: To make crumbs, rub pieces between your hands over a sheet of parchment.

Sherry's Secrets

At Spago I'm often responsible for transporting cakes on airplanes to catered events. People are always amazed that my cakes arrive intact. My secret is to line a cake pan with plastic wrap, after lightly spraying the pan to anchor the plastic, leaving a generous overhang. I assemble the cake in the pan and cover it tightly with the overlapping plastic, then wrap the entire cake again. I don't frost the cake until it arrives at its destination, when it is neatly pulled from the pan and unwrapped. I've shipped cakes across the country like this, and they've always arrived in perfect shape.

BLACK FOREST CAKE

■ ■ ■

If there was one cake that was *the* cake in the window of Leon's Bakery, this was it. Nobody made a black forest cake like the folks at Leon's. This filled, domed cake is spongy and moist, and there's no shortage of whipped cream and cherries. Bake the cake a day ahead if possible—it will be easier to slice it into thin layers without it falling apart.

1. **MAKE THE CAKE**: Place a rack in the middle of the oven and preheat the oven to 350°F. Spray an 8-inch round cake pan (see Note, page 47) with pan spray. Line with parchment paper and spray the paper.

2. Sift together the flour, baking powder, baking soda, and salt and set aside.

3. Place the cocoa powder in a medium bowl. Whisk in 3 tablespoons of the milk and stir until a smooth paste forms. Add the remaining 3 tablespoons milk and whisk until the mixture is smooth. Set aside.

4. Combine the unsweetened chocolate with the water or coffee in a heatproof bowl set over a pan of simmering water, stirring until smooth.

5. In the bowl of a stand mixer fitted with the paddle attachment, or in a large bowl with

FOR THE CAKE
- 1 cup cake flour
- 1/2 teaspoon baking powder
- 1/2 teaspoon baking soda
- 1/4 teaspoon salt
- 1/4 cup unsweetened cocoa powder
- 6 tablespoons milk
- 1 ounce unsweetened chocolate, finely chopped
- 2 tablespoons water or brewed coffee
- 4 ounces (1 stick) unsalted butter, softened
- 1 cup sugar
- 2 large eggs
- 1 teaspoon vanilla extract

FOR THE SYRUP
- 1/2 cup sugar
- 1/2 cup water
- 1 teaspoon fresh lemon juice (optional)

FOR THE WHIPPED CREAM FILLING AND TOPPING
- 3 cups heavy cream
- 2 tablespoons sugar
- 1 cup Bing or Garnet cherries, pitted and quartered, or 1/2 cup Fat Cherries (page 364)

FOR GARNISH
- 2 tablespoons pistachio nuts, lightly toasted and finely chopped
- 1 maraschino cherry

a hand mixer, beat the butter on high speed until soft and creamy, about 1 minute. Slowly add the sugar, beating until the mixture is light, fluffy, and a creamy white color, about 4 minutes.

6. Turn the mixer down to medium speed. Add the eggs one at a time, making sure that the first egg is completely incorporated and scraping down the sides of the bowl before adding the second one. Add the vanilla and the melted chocolate. At low speed, add the flour $\frac{1}{2}$ cup at a time, alternating with the milk and cocoa mixture. When the ingredients are smooth, scrape down the sides of the bowl.

7. Scrape into the prepared pan. Tap the pan lightly on the work surface three times to eliminate air bubbles, then, using the same jerking wrist action you would use to throw a Frisbee, swing the pan around on the counter so that the batter is forced up the sides of the pan (this prevents a dome from forming in the middle). Bake, rotating the pan after the first 20 minutes, for 30 to 35 minutes, until the top springs back when lightly pressed with your finger and the cake pulls away from the sides of the pan. Remove from the oven and allow to cool for 15 minutes in the pan, set on a rack. Invert onto the rack, remove the parchment, and allow to cool completely. Wrap in plastic wrap and leave overnight at room temperature.

Sherry's Secrets

I like to add a little bit of lemon juice to cut the sweetness in sugar syrup. You can also use orange juice, depending on the flavors in the cake.

8. **MAKE THE SYRUP:** Combine the sugar and water in a small saucepan and bring to a boil, stirring to dissolve the sugar. Reduce the heat and simmer until the sugar has dissolved completely. Stir in the lemon juice, if using. Remove from the heat and allow to cool.

9. Using a long serrated knife, cut the cake into 5 thin layers. Spray a deep 2-quart bowl with pan spray and line the bowl with plastic wrap, leaving a generous overhang. Line the bowl with a layer of the cake, pushing the cake up the sides of the bowl. Brush the cake lightly with sugar syrup.

10. **MAKE THE FILLING AND TOPPING:** Rub pieces of one of the cake layers between your hands over a sheet of parchment to make cake crumbs.

Beat the cream and sugar together with a hand mixer to medium-stiff peaks. Spread ¾ cup in an even layer over the cake in the bowl. Distribute one third of the cherries over the cream and press them in. Top with another layer of cake. Brush the cake with syrup. Spread 1 cup of whipped cream over the cake, top with one third of the cherries, and press them in. Press the third layer of cake over the cream, brush with syrup, and top with another cup of whipped cream and the remaining third of the cherries, pressing them in. Cover with the remaining layer of cake and brush with the remaining syrup. Don't worry if the cake breaks up as you assemble it. Patch the pieces together and use the cake crumbs to fill the spaces if you need to, reserving ½ cup for garnish.

11. Pull the overhanging edges of the plastic wrap over the cake, then cover tightly with another sheet of plastic. Refrigerate for 2 hours. Cover and refrigerate the remaining whipped cream.

12. Remove the cake from the refrigerator, uncover, and lay an 8-inch cardboard round or foam core or a plate on top of the

---

HOW TO CUT A ROUND CAKE INTO LAYERS

I bake the cake a day ahead, wrap it in plastic wrap, and leave it overnight. To cut it into thin rounds, I use my favorite offset serrated knife. It's got a great grip and the teeth to cut thin layers from a round.

Place the cake on a cardboard or foam cake round. This will enable you to turn the cake as you cut. The key here is to let the knife do the work by rotating the cake against it. Grip the handle of the knife with your pinkie, ring finger, and middle finger. Extend your pointer finger over the back of the knife blade. Place your other hand on top of the cake, and holding the knife horizontally against the cake, cut into the cake only about 2 inches. Then rotate the cake against the knife, sawing ever so gently as you turn it, to get a level cut 2 inches in all the way around. Once you've cut the cake all the way around, rotate it once more while you gently saw through the center.

cake. Invert onto the round and remove the plastic. Set the cake on a cake plate or platter. Cover the domed top with the remaining whipped cream. Using the reserved cake crumbs, make a border around the bottom of the dome. Sprinkle the top with the chopped pistachio nuts. Put the maraschino cherry on the summit. Chill until ready to serve.

NOTE: You can also bake the cake in two 12-x-17-inch half sheet pans. Bake for about 15 minutes. Cut out the layers using an 8-inch round cake pan for a template.

DEEP-FRIED APPLE DUMPLINGS

MAKES 6 DUMPLINGS

■ ■ ■

It's my conviction that all fine-dining professionals would benefit from some fast-food training. When I started working at McDonald's, I was taught to work quickly and to count and tally money and stack it in a drawer, all the bills facing the same way. Mickey D's fifteen-minute videos on making French fries, searing hamburgers, prepacking order bags, and tying up garbage taught me the value of precision and systems, and that has stood me in very good stead as I have put pastry teams in place in restaurants all over the United States and in Japan.

When we took an order, we were trained to say, for example, "Can I get you a hot apple pie with your order?" If somebody answers yes to that question today, this is what they might get from me.

2 ounces (1/2 stick) unsalted butter
1 vanilla bean, split, seeds scraped out and reserved
2 Granny Smith apples, peeled, cored, and cut into 3/4-inch pieces
1/4 cup sugar
1/4 teaspoon ground cinnamon
1 large egg white
6 egg roll wrappers
    Vegetable oil for deep-frying
    Creamy Caramel Sauce (page 354)

1. Heat a large heavy skillet over medium-high heat and add the butter and the scraped seeds from the vanilla bean. When the butter begins to brown lightly, add the apples and cook without stirring to sear on one side, 2 to 5 minutes. Then toss in the pan for a few minutes until the apples are golden and just tender. Add the sugar and cinnamon and toss with the apples until the sugar has dissolved. Remove from the heat and allow the mixture to cool.

2. Beat the egg white in a small bowl until foamy. Lay an egg roll wrapper on your work surface with a point facing you. Brush the edges with the beaten egg white. Place 1/4 cup of the filling on the lower third and fold the point up over the filling. Fold in the sides to lock in the filling and roll up the egg roll wrapper. Repeat with the remaining wrappers and filling.

3. In a wide deep pot fitted with a deep-fry thermometer, heat 3 inches of oil over medium-high heat to 350°F, or heat the oil in a deep fryer. Set a wire rack over a baking sheet. Deep-fry the dumplings, turning frequently, for about 3 minutes, until golden and crisp. Remove from the oil with a wire skimmer or a slotted spoon and drain on the rack. Serve hot, with the creamy caramel sauce for dipping.

CHOCOLATE-DIPPED
FROZEN CUSTARD CONES

MAKES 8 CONES

■ ■ ■

On the boardwalk in Atlantic City, we ate frozen soft-serve ice cream cones dipped in chocolate. I used to love to watch the ice cream man dip the filled cones, one after another. Frozen custard looks like soft-serve ice cream, but it has more body. Made with egg yolks, milk, and a small amount of cream, this version has a dense, rich taste and a satiny texture.

2 cups milk
2–3 tablespoons honey (to taste), preferably a mild honey like clover
4 large egg yolks
3/4 cup sugar
1/4 teaspoon salt
1/2 cup heavy cream
1 tablespoon vanilla extract

FOR THE CHOCOLATE DIP
8 ounces bittersweet chocolate, finely chopped
1/3 cup vegetable oil

8 store-bought ice cream cones

1. Place a 1-quart freezer container in the freezer. Prepare an ice bath: fill a large bowl halfway with ice, add a little water, and nestle a medium bowl inside the ice.

2. In a medium nonreactive saucepan, combine the milk and honey. Place the pan over medium heat and bring it to a simmer; do not boil.

3. Meanwhile, whisk together the egg yolks and sugar in a medium bowl. Remove the hot milk from the heat and slowly add 1/2 cup of the milk to the egg yolks, whisking constantly. Once the milk is incorporated into the egg yolks and the eggs are warmed (tempered), pour the mixture back into the hot milk, whisking constantly; use a rubber spatula to scrape all the eggs into the pan.

4. Place the pan over low heat, insert an instant-read thermometer, and immediately begin stirring the custard sauce with a heat-resistant rubber spatula. Stir in figure eights all around the edge of the pan and into the center, until the con-

sistency is like thick cream; the temperature should reach 180°F. To test for readiness with the spatula, dip it into the sauce, pull it out, and run your finger across the back of the spatula—your finger should leave a clear trail.

5. Immediately remove the pan from the heat and pour the custard through a fine-mesh strainer into the bowl in the ice bath. Stir in the salt. Stir the custard occasionally for 5 to 10 minutes to cool evenly, until the temperature drops to 40°F. The custard will become thicker as it cools. Cover tightly and place in the refrigerator to chill. (The custard can be made a day in advance.)

6. Stir the heavy cream and vanilla into the cold custard and freeze in an ice cream maker according to the manufacturer's directions. Transfer to the chilled container and place in the freezer for at least 2 hours to firm.

7. MAKE THE CHOCOLATE DIP: Shortly before serving, combine the chocolate with the vegetable oil in a microwave-safe bowl and melt at 50 percent power for 2 to 3 minutes or melt in a heatproof bowl set over a saucepan of simmering water. Stir until the mixture is smooth. Remove from the heat and cool to 80°F. The chocolate will still be runny.

8. At least 2 hours before serving, scoop the frozen custard into the cones. Hold in the freezer. At serving time, dip into the chocolate and serve immediately.

NOTE: If you have leftover chocolate dip, keep it refrigerated. Reheat in the microwave at 50 percent power or over a saucepan of simmering water when you want chocolate sauce for ice cream.

MOM'S CUISINART CHOCOLATE MOUSSE

■ ■ ■

The invention of the food processor inspired my mom to make her first homemade dessert. I was about fourteen, and it was the most exciting culinary event that had ever occurred in our kitchen.

8 ounces bittersweet chocolate
1/4 cup brewed espresso
2 tablespoons Grand Marnier
1 cup heavy cream
2 large eggs, separated, plus
    6 large egg whites, at room temperature
Pinch of cream of tartar
2 tablespoons sugar
Whipped cream and chocolate shavings for serving (optional)

1. Place the chocolate in the bowl of a food processor fitted with the steel blade and pulse to chop the chocolate very fine.

2. Combine the espresso, Grand Marnier, and 2 tablespoons of the cream in a small saucepan and bring to a boil. Turn on the food processor and add the hot liquid with the processor running. Process until the chocolate has melted. Stop the processor and scrape down the sides. Continue to process until smooth. Add the egg yolks and process until blended. Scrape into a large bowl.

3. In the bowl of a stand mixer fitted with the whisk attachment, or in a large bowl with a hand mixer, beat the egg whites on medium speed. When they foam, add the cream of tartar and continue to beat on medium speed while you slowly stream in the sugar. Beat until the egg whites form medium peaks. Fold into the chocolate base, in 2 additions.

4. In the same mixer, beat the remaining 3/4 cup plus 2 tablespoons cream until it forms soft peaks. Fold into the mousse. Spoon into six 8-ounce ramekins or other serving cups and refrigerate for 2 hours, or until set. Serve with whipped cream and chocolate shavings, if desired.

Sherry's Secrets

I serve this in small portions at Spago, prepared three ways: chilled, semifrozen, and hot, with whipped cream and chocolate sauce. To serve hot, place the ramekins in a 350°F oven for 10 minutes. They will be slightly set on the outside and molten in the middle. Serve immediately. To serve semifrozen, place the ramekins in the freezer for 2 hours before serving.

PRETZELS

■ ■ ■

When I was growing up, one of the things I loved best about New York was smelling the chestnuts roasting and sharing the street-vendor pretzels with my sisters. One January we went to Rockefeller Center for my birthday. We couldn't afford the skating rink, but we could afford the pretzels. These surpass any I ever ate on a New York City street.

FOR THE DOUGH

1¼ teaspoons active dry yeast
½ cup warm (90°F) water
¼ cup buttermilk
2 tablespoons light brown sugar
¾ teaspoon sugar
1½ teaspoons vegetable oil, plus more as needed
2 cups bread flour
1½ teaspoons salt

FOR THE SIMMERING LIQUID

2 quarts water
¼ cup amber beer
¼ cup baking soda
¼ cup packed light brown sugar
3 tablespoons vegetable oil for glazing
1–2 tablespoons pretzel salt or coarse sea salt (to taste)

1. **MAKE THE DOUGH:** In a medium bowl or a Pyrex measuring cup, dissolve the yeast in the water and let sit for 5 minutes, or until cloudy. Add the buttermilk, brown sugar, sugar, and vegetable oil and mix well.

2. Place the flour and salt in the bowl of a food processor fitted with the steel blade. With the motor running, add the liquid mixture and process for 2 minutes.

3. Spray a large bowl with pan spray. Scrape out the dough and place in the bowl. Cover with sprayed plastic wrap and refrigerate for 1 hour.

4. Line four half sheet pans with parchment paper and spray the parchment. Lightly oil your work surface and your hands. Remove the dough from the refrigerator and press into a 6-inch square. Cut into 1½-x-3-inch rectangles. One at a time, shape each piece into a pretzel. (Cover the pieces you aren't working with, with plastic or a damp kitchen towel.) Roll each piece out into a 24-inch-long rope, slightly tapered at the ends. Shape into a U, then crisscross the ends halfway up, twist them together twice like a twist-tie, and pull the legs down over the bottom of the U. Place the shaped pretzels on two of the lined baking

sheets. Cover with lightly oiled plastic wrap and allow to rise in the refrigerator for 30 minutes, or until not quite doubled.

5. While the pretzels are rising, place racks in the upper and lower thirds of the oven and preheat the oven to 450°F. Cut the parchment the pretzels are on into squares to facilitate lifting and transferring the pretzels into the water bath.

6. SIMMER THE PRETZELS: In a 10-inch-wide stainless-steel pot, combine the water, beer, baking soda, and brown sugar and bring to a simmer. Two at a time, lift a parchment square with a pretzel and carefully reverse the pretzel off the parchment into the simmering water. Cook for 10 seconds and flip, using a skimmer or slotted spoon. Cook for another 10 seconds, and with the skimmer, lift above the pan to drain. Then transfer to the other two baking sheets, rounded sides up. Brush with vegetable oil. Dust with pretzel salt or coarse salt.

7. Bake, switching the sheets from top to bottom and rotating from front to back halfway through, for 15 minutes, or until the pretzels are chestnut brown. Remove from the oven and serve warm.

BAGELS

■ ■ ■

Bagels have become common throughout the United States now, but nothing you get at your local coffee shop can measure up to the H&H bagels I grew up on. I still get my bagels shipped frozen from H&H when I'm not making them myself, and I can't eat them without becoming a Catholic school kid in knee socks and loafers.

I like making my bagel dough in a food processor, but I give methods for both the food processor and a stand mixer here.

Malt syrup, also known as malt extract, is a grain extract that enhances the shiny crust of any yeast bread. You can find it at whole foods stores and baking supply stores.

FOR THE DOUGH

- 2 teaspoons active dry yeast
- 1 1/2 cups warm (90°F) water
- 2 teaspoons malt syrup (see headnote) or light brown sugar
- 4 cups bread flour
- 2 1/2 teaspoons salt
- Cornmeal for sprinkling

FOR THE SIMMERING LIQUID

- 2 quarts water
- 1/4 cup malt syrup or light brown sugar

1 . MAKE THE DOUGH. FOOD PROCESSOR METHOD: Whisk together the yeast, water, and malt syrup or brown sugar in a Pyrex measuring cup and let stand for 5 to 10 minutes, until cloudy. Place the bread flour and salt in the bowl of a food processor fitted with the steel blade. Pulse a few times to combine, then, with the machine running, add the liquid in a steady stream. Process just until the dough comes together.

STAND MIXER METHOD: In the bowl of a stand mixer fitted with the paddle attachment, whisk together the yeast, water, and malt syrup or brown sugar. Let stand for 5 to 10 minutes, until cloudy. In a separate bowl, mix together the bread flour and salt. Add 1 cup of the flour to the yeast mixture and mix together on medium speed. Scrape down the bowl and paddle. Add another cup of the flour and mix together. Scrape down the bowl and paddle. Add another cup of the flour and mix on medium speed for 4 minutes. Turn the

speed to low and slowly add the remaining 1 cup of flour. Change to the dough hook and mix for 8 minutes on medium-low. The dough should be elastic and silky.

2. Remove the dough from the food processor or mixer and divide into 8 equal pieces. Roll the pieces into balls, cover them with a damp kitchen towel, and allow them to rest for 15 minutes.

3. Roll the balls into eight 12-inch-long sausages and join the sausages at the ends, overlapping the ends slightly. Pinch together on the bottom of the overlap.

4. Line a 12-x-17-inch half sheet pan with parchment paper and spray the parchment with pan spray or dust with cornmeal. Place the bagels on the pan, spray them lightly with pan spray, and cover with plastic wrap. Refrigerate for 10 to 12 hours or overnight, until they double in volume.

5. Remove the bagels from the refrigerator. Place a baking stone on the middle rack of the oven and preheat the oven to 450°F for 30 minutes. Sprinkle a baking peel or a sheet pan generously with cornmeal.

6. SIMMER THE BAGELS: Bring the water to a simmer and add the malt syrup or brown sugar. Cut the parchment between the bagels. Lift 2 bagels, one after another, with their parchment and carefully invert off the paper into the simmering water. Cook for 20 seconds, then flip the bagels over and cook for another 20 seconds. Remove from the water and place on the cornmeal-sprinkled baking peel or sheet pan. Repeat with another 2 bagels.

7. Quickly slide the 4 bagels from the peel or sheet pan onto the baking stone and bake for 12 minutes, or until golden brown. Transfer to a wire rack. Repeat with the remaining bagels, 2 at a time in the water bath and 4 at a time on the baking stone. Serve warm or at room temperature, toasted if desired.

New York City
FROM CIGARETTE GIRL
TO PASTRY CHEF

I KNEW I WAS HEADED FOR NEW YORK CITY AS SOON as I began my classes at Brooklyn's New York City Technical College. My first job was as a waitress at the American Festival Cafe at the ice-skating rink at Rockefeller Center, but I set my ambitions sixty-five floors higher when I read an article in *Cue* magazine about the newly renovated Rainbow Room, the celebrated restaurant at the top of the RCA Building. The owner, Joe Baum, employed three full-time costume designers to help maintain the look of art deco opulence that was all the rage in the 1980s. The Rainbow Room had an elaborate bar with a rotating dance floor on the sixty-fourth floor, and on the next floor, a full restaurant. At the time, I was enthralled with deco and with Erté, the Russian fashion designer who had given the Ziegfeld Follies their look, and when I saw the big magazine spread showing the Rainbow Room, with its sumptuous decor and incredible costumes—the uniforms that everyone in the front of the house would wear—I knew I had to work there. I applied and was promptly hired as a . . . cigarette girl.

Being a cigarette girl at the Rainbow Room was all about pageantry. We wore pink pillbox hats, fitted pink spencers (short jackets) with sheer pink-polka-dotted puffed black sleeves, and long black skirts slit up to the thigh. Our black heels had to be a minimum of two inches high, and our earrings could be no larger than a nickel. We were trained to have perfect posture; to "serve the guest with the arm, not the body;" and to make eye contact with each guest as we served our cigarettes from silver trays held aloft on our perfectly manicured fingertips.

Within a month of landing this exciting job, though, a law was passed that banned the selling of cigarettes in dining establishments. I have the surgeon general to thank for my first promotion in my restaurant career. I was immediately made a cocktail waitress and front waiter, trading in my pink spencer for a sexy black fitted jacket and my pink pillbox hat for a slicked-back hairdo. We worked in teams of three: the captain taking orders and attending to the guests, the front waiter (me) getting drinks and managing the checks, and the back waiter, or runner, picking up the food. We all bused tables.

It was a heady time. Every night, right after my last class at college, I took the Q train from Brooklyn into Manhattan. Emerging from far below Rockefeller Center, I rode the service elevator up to the Rainbow locker room and changed from culinary school whites into a newly pressed uniform. Some nights I would work "the Room," with its revolving dance floor and two bands. Other nights I worked in the Promenade, a cocktail space that looked out on the Empire State Building, serving the most amazing cocktails made by master mixologist Dale DeGroff.

I've never seen a company holiday party like the one Joe Baum threw for us. He closed the restaurant for the evening, having placed a full-page ad in the *New York Times* stating he was doing so, and engaged the Rockettes, the Shirelles, and the Moscow State Circus to come and perform on his rotating floor.

ALL THE WHILE, I HAD MY EYE ON THE KITCHEN. In culinary school, I was focused on pastry. After a year of waitressing, I went to human resources and asked for a transfer. An opening had come up on the pastry line, and I took it. It was only a matter of weeks before I found myself working in the pastry kitchen alongside Albert Kumin, one of the most gifted pastry chefs I have ever met and my first true mentor.

We served more than 800 people a night—300 pretheater dinners, 400 dinners, and 100 after-theater suppers. Six hundred covers was considered a slow night. (I never left work before 2 A.M.) The volume was daunting at first, but I adjusted to it soon enough. I had questions about everything. Why did the chocolate sauce break this time but not yesterday? Why did the Grand Marnier soufflé rise higher than the chocolate soufflé? Why did my caramel seize? Albert always took the time to explain things to me, and I became increasingly enamored of the intricacies of pastry.

I was finishing up at the technical college, and I was dating a *poissonnier/* line cook whose father happened to be an instructor at the Culinary Institute of America (CIA) in upstate New York. He offered me a room in his house there, and suddenly the Culinary Institute became affordable. I gave my notice at the Rainbow Room and entered the CIA's Master of Baking and Pastry Arts program.

The CIA was and is the Harvard of culinary schools. Although my teachers included such amazing pastry chefs as Joe Amendola, CEPC; Jean-Pierre LeMasson of La Côte Basque in Manhattan; Helmut Loibel, certified master pastry chef; Walter Schreyer; Markus Farbinger; and Joe McKenna, I missed the city, and I had burning questions that could be answered only by working in restaurants. So before I completed my degree, I took a year's sabbatical and returned to Manhattan.

*N*EW YORK RESTAURANTS THRUMMED with excitement in the 1980s. Great young chefs like Daniel Boulud, Jean-Georges Vongerichten, David Bouley, Michael Romano, and Charlie Palmer were just getting started. Pastry chefs like Bill Yosses, Richard Leach, and Jacques Torres were leaving guests spellbound with their sweet finales. I sent my résumé around to a number of places and heard back right away from David Blom, a hot young chef who was doing pastry at Montrachet, Drew Nieporent's beautiful, intimate restaurant in Tribeca. David hired me to be his assistant in Montrachet's closet-sized kitchen.

If the Rainbow Room was about service and pageantry, Montrachet was about perfection and over-the-top dining pleasure. We knew our guests' tastes, and we would do anything to please them. With David I learned about intimate fine dining. I began to hone my skills in the art of plating desserts, which we did *à la minute* in our tiny corner of the kitchen. And no matter how busy we were, we always had fun doing it. That training transformed me from a pastry chef into a dessert chef, a distinction that is defined by one's skill in presenting desserts on the plate.

RAINBOW ROOM CHOCOLATE SOUFFLÉS

SERVES 6

■ ■ ■

It was an honor to learn the restaurant trade with Joe Baum, the owner of the Rainbow Room, a detail man who was not above sending home a waiter if he could not rattle off six champagnes by the glass at a moment's notice. He was quintessential old-school New York, always in a pinstripe suit with his cigar and his cane, edgy yet refined, quiet and a little Godfather-esque. "Never let anyone know what you're thinking," he used to tell me.

The dining room was one floor up from the kitchen, which was challenging for the waitstaff. All orders had to be run up an escalator! Imagine getting a soufflé from oven to table, one floor up, before it fell. These can withstand being assembled several hours before they are baked, which is handy even if you don't have to run up a long flight of stairs to serve them.

2 tablespoons unsalted butter, plus 1 tablespoon melted, for the ramekins

2/3 cup sugar, plus 1 tablespoon for dusting the ramekins

1/4 cup all-purpose flour

1/4 cup unsweetened cocoa powder

3/4 cup milk

3 large eggs, separated, plus 4 large egg whites

1 tablespoon dark rum

1/8 teaspoon cream of tartar

Confectioners' sugar for dusting (optional)

1. Place a rack in the lowest position of the oven and preheat the oven to 425°F. Brush six 8-ounce ramekins with the 1 tablespoon melted butter, using upward strokes for the sides. Dust with the 1 tablespoon sugar, turning the ramekins and tapping out any excess sugar that doesn't stick.

2. Make the soufflé base. Place a piece of parchment paper on your work surface. Sift together the flour, 1/4 cup of the sugar, and the cocoa powder onto the parchment.

3. In a wide heavy saucepan, combine the milk and the 2 tablespoons butter and bring to a boil over medium heat. Remove from the heat and quickly whisk in the sifted dry ingredients. Place back on the heat and cook, whisking, for 2 to 3 minutes, until the mixture pulls away from the sides of the pan and has a pudding-like consistency. Remove from the heat.

4. Beat the egg yolks in a small bowl and stir in the rum. Beat this mixture into the cocoa mixture with a hand mixer. Set aside.

5. In the bowl of a stand mixer fitted with the whisk attachment, or in a large bowl with the clean hand mixer, beat the egg whites on low speed until they are foamy. Add the cream of tartar and 1 tablespoon of the sugar. Turn the mixer to medium speed and beat until soft peaks form. Slowly stream in the remaining sugar, a tablespoon at a time. Continue to beat until the egg whites reach the medium-peak stage (the peaks will stand up and then flop over).

6. Using a whisk, preferably a balloon whisk, fold one third of the egg whites into the soufflé base. Fold in the balance of the whites with a rubber spatula.

7. Fill the ramekins to just below the rim and slide a knife around the inside perimeter of the ramekins. Set them on a baking sheet. Bake for 12 to 14 minutes, until the soufflés are puffed. The center should remain pudding-like. Dust with confectioners' sugar, if using, and serve immediately.

BAKED ALASKA

MAKES ONE 9-INCH CAKE, SERVING 8 GENEROUSLY

■ ■ ■

All restaurant professionals, no matter how experienced, no matter how exclusive or elite their restaurant, find themselves "in the weeds" from time to time. "In the weeds" means being so overwhelmed that you can't see through the work, as if you were caught in a tangle of undergrowth. The people in the front are out there waiting, and you are in total disarray in the back. There is no way to prepare for it; you just have to be a quick, creative thinker.

My quintessential in-the-weeds experience happened at the Rainbow Room. We were doing a huge wedding, and somehow nobody in the pastry department had checked the party sheets that were always posted so that the kitchen could plan. Two hundred and sixty guests were ready for their baked Alaska, and there was not a meringue in sight. I stalled them with cookies while the prep cooks and I madly beat egg whites and unmolded ice cream. Meringue flew everywhere, the kitchen looked like a Jackson Pollock painting, and I piped like a whirling dervish. But the guests had no idea, and they left ecstatic.

3 cups vanilla ice cream, slightly softened

3 cups raspberry sorbet, slightly softened

3 cups chocolate sorbet, slightly softened

A 1/2-inch-thick layer cut from 1 layer of My Favorite White Birthday Cake (page 7) or White Chocolate–Buttermilk Cake (page 266) (freeze the rest and use for another recipe)

6 large egg whites, at room temperature

1/4 teaspoon cream of tartar

1 1/3 cups superfine sugar

1/2 recipe Strawberry Sauce (page 223) for serving (optional)

1. Spray a 9-x-3-inch springform pan with pan spray. Line the pan with plastic wrap, letting it hang over the sides. Spread the vanilla ice cream over the bottom of the pan in an even layer. Top the vanilla ice cream with the raspberry sorbet and spread evenly. Top with the chocolate sorbet and spread in an even layer. Cover with the overhanging plastic and then another sheet of plastic wrap and freeze for 4 hours, or until firm.

2. Remove the pan from the freezer and remove the plastic from the top. Place the cake layer on the chocolate sorbet, then invert the cake pan onto an ovenproof plate and remove the pan. Return the ice cream to the freezer, still covered in plastic wrap.

3. Make the meringue. Place the egg whites in the bowl of a stand mixer or in a large stainless-steel bowl and heat over a pan of simmering water until the egg whites are 90°F; the mixture will feel barely warm on your lips. Remove from the heat and beat on medium speed, either with the stand mixer fitted with the whisk attachment or with a hand mixer, until the egg whites begin to foam. Add the cream of tartar and 1 tablespoon of the sugar and continue to beat the egg whites at medium-low speed until they form soft, slightly drooping peaks when the whisk or beaters are lifted out.

4. Turn the speed to medium and continue to beat the egg whites as you gradually add the remaining sugar, a tablespoon at a time. Beat until the meringue is shiny and holds stiff, upright peaks when the whisk or beaters are lifted out.

5. As soon as the meringue is ready, remove the ice cream from the freezer, remove the plastic, and use an icing spatula or the back of a large spoon to spread the entire batch of meringue evenly over its surface. This is done most easily if you spoon the meringue onto the top of the ice cream and spread it down the sides. I also like to pipe lines of meringue side by side up the sides of the cake with a star tip and pipe spiky rosettes around the edge. The more spikes, the more crunch you get. (At this point, you can freeze the Alaska overnight, uncovered.) Return the dessert to the freezer once more, until serving time.

6. Brown the meringue. **USING THE OVEN**: Place a rack in the lowest position of the oven (a convection oven works best) and preheat the oven to 500°F. Remove the Alaska from the freezer and place in the oven for no more than 5 minutes, until the meringue is nicely caramelized and browned. Remove from the oven and serve at once.

   USING A PROPANE OR BUTANE TORCH: Light a small kitchen torch, following the manufacturer's directions, setting its flame to medium. Holding the flame about 1 inch from the surface of the meringue, move it slowly across the surface to lightly brown the peaks. (The kitchen torch is not my favorite method, as the flavor doesn't compare to the flavor you get using a hot convection oven, which also gives you more crunch.)

   TO SERVE: Use a long serrated bread knife to cut the baked Alaska, placing a hand on each end of the knife. Each time you cut, dip the knife in hot water, then wipe dry with a clean kitchen towel. Or heat the knife with a kitchen torch. Serve with strawberry sauce, if you'd like.

ARLETTES

■ ■ ■

These sugar-coated cookies made from swirls of puff pastry look like galaxies. At the Rainbow Room, we loved to sit on the fire escape and throw them up in the air like Frisbees. They can be tricky, but this method is pretty foolproof. If you have a sheet of puff pastry in your freezer, these swirls make a dazzling way to use it up. They were beloved by Joe Baum.

The cookies can be made with puff pastry scraps from pastry that you've used for something else.

1 8-x-6- or 8-x-8-inch sheet all-butter puff pastry (see Sources), ⅛ inch thick, chilled
1 large egg white, lightly beaten
½ cup sugar
1 cup confectioners' sugar

1. Place the sheet of puff pastry on a work surface and brush with the beaten egg white. Dust evenly with the granulated sugar. Roll up the dough lengthwise (starting from the 6-inch side if working with a rectangle) very tightly, like a jelly roll, and place in the freezer for at least 30 minutes, until firm, or overnight.

2. Place a rack in the middle of the oven and preheat the oven to 375°F. Line two baking sheets with parchment paper. Remove the rolled-up puff pastry from the freezer and cut into very thin slices, about ⅛ inch thick. Place the slices on the baking sheets and return to the freezer. Chill for 15 minutes.

Sherry's Secrets

If you are using a convection oven, layer the cookies between silicone mats, then weight the top with a half sheet pan. Bake as directed, and when done, remove the sheet pan and the top mat, remove the arlettes from the bottom mat, and allow to cool on a rack.

3. Place the confectioners' sugar in a bowl and use some of it to dust your work surface. Dip a pastry disk into the confectioners' sugar and roll out into an oval shape, pressing down firmly with your rolling pin. Flip the disk and roll out again to a paper-thin 4-inch-long oval. Place on

the parchment-lined baking sheet, and when the tray is filled, place a second piece of parchment over the arlettes.

4. Bake, one sheet at a time, for 12 minutes, or until the cookies begin to look golden. Remove the pan from the oven, lift off the top parchment and discard, and using a metal spatula, flip over each arlette. Rotate the pan from front to back, return to the oven, and bake for another 6 minutes, or until the arlettes are a deep golden color. Remove from the oven and slip the parchment off the baking sheets onto a rack to cool the cookies. (The arlettes can be stored airtight for up to 2 days.)

SOUR CREAM TART ROYALE

■ ■ ■

At lunchtime, the sixty-fifth floor of the Rainbow Room became the Rockefeller Center Club, a private members-only club. Executives from the building, much of which was occupied by NBC, loved this tart, topped with fresh fruit. Red currants are my favorite.

2 large eggs

3 tablespoons sugar

1/2 cup plus 2 tablespoons sour cream

1/2 cup heavy cream

1 10-inch tart shell made with Pâte Sucrée (page 373), prebaked

1 pint red currants or raspberries

1. Place a rack in the middle of the oven and preheat the oven to 325°F.

2. In the bowl of a stand mixer fitted with the whisk attachment, or in a large bowl with a hand mixer, gently beat the eggs until broken up. Beat in the sugar and combine well. Beat in the sour cream, then slowly add the heavy cream. Beat until smooth.

3. Line the prebaked pastry shell with the red currants or raspberries. Pour the custard over the top. Let sit for a minute, then lightly tap the pan against your work surface to eliminate air pockets.

4. Bake for 35 to 40 minutes, until the custard is set (the top should not brown). Remove from the heat and allow to cool on a rack. (The tart can be refrigerated at this point, if desired, for up to 1 day, tightly wrapped.) Serve chilled or at room temperature.

CHOCOLATE VELVET

■ ■ ■

The master pastry chef Albert Kumin created this grand dome-shaped, dark-chocolate-glazed mousse, which has the texture of velvet inside. Kumin was in many ways the father of American pastry. He opened many of Joe Baum's big New York City restaurants, including Windows on the World, and he was White House pastry chef during the Carter administration. He had hands like leather and could reach into the oven and pull out soufflés and baking sheets without wearing oven mitts.

We used to make these chocolate bombes for big Rainbow Room parties. The morning pastry assistants would set up the breast-like bombes and their rococo garnishes, then go home, leaving the evening staff to run the show. One evening an apprentice accidentally guillotined twelve giant Velvets with a sheet pan. They were completely beyond repair, but we did our best to patch and glaze them—to fake the master's work in the ten minutes left before service.

At the restaurant, we always mounted the bombes on thin rounds of cake, then set them on a rack to glaze before transferring them to serving plates. With the cake base, the bombe is easy to lift and transfer. When you are making this at home, you might not have cake on hand the way we do in restaurants, so you can unmold the bombe directly onto your serving plate before glazing it.

FOR THE MOUSSE

- 5 ounces bittersweet chocolate, finely chopped
- 2 ounces milk chocolate, finely chopped
- 2 ounces (½ stick) unsalted butter
- ¼ cup Hazelnut Praline Paste (page 357)
- ½ cup sugar
- ¼ cup water
- 6 large eggs, at room temperature
- 2 tablespoons dark rum (I prefer Myers's)
- 2 tablespoons Kahlúa
- 1 cup heavy cream

FOR THE CHOCOLATE GLAZE

- 6 ounces bittersweet chocolate, finely chopped
- 4 ounces (1 stick) unsalted butter
- 5 tablespoons light corn syrup

A ½-inch-thick layer cut from 1 layer of white cake, such as My Favorite White Birthday Cake (page 7; optional)

1. **MAKE THE MOUSSE:** Melt the chocolates with the butter in a microwave-safe bowl at 50 percent power for 2 to 3 minutes or in a heatproof bowl set over a saucepan of simmering water, stirring with a rubber spatula until smooth. Stir in the praline paste.

2. Combine the sugar and water in a small saucepan and bring to a boil. Stir to dissolve the sugar. Insert a candy thermometer and bring the syrup to 235°F (soft-ball stage).

3. Meanwhile, beat the eggs on high speed in the bowl of a stand mixer fitted with the whisk attachment, or in a large bowl with a hand mixer, until light and fluffy, about 5 minutes. Stream in the hot sugar syrup and continue to beat on high speed until the eggs have tripled in volume, about 5 minutes. Scrape down the bowl and the whisk or beaters. Beat in the rum and Kahlúa.

4. Stir one third of the egg mixture into the chocolate to lighten it, then using a rubber spatula, fold the chocolate into the eggs, turning the bowl and scraping the bottom with your spatula to incorporate all the chocolate.

5. With a hand mixer, beat the cream to just under soft peaks. It should form a thick coating on the beaters but should not stand up. Fold into the chocolate mixture.

6. Spray a 2-quart bowl, the more dome-shaped the better, with pan spray and line it with plastic wrap, leaving an overhang. Pour in the mousse mixture. Cover the bowl with plastic and freeze until set, 4 to 6 hours.

7. **MAKE THE GLAZE:** Combine the chocolate with the butter and melt in a microwave-safe bowl for 2 to 3 minutes at 50 percent power or in a heatproof bowl set over a saucepan of simmering water. Stir with a rubber spatula until smooth. Stir in the corn syrup. Allow to cool to 90°F (the mixture will feel barely warm on your lips).

8. **UNMOLD THE BOMBE:** Remove the mousse from the freezer, uncover, and warm the bowl by wrapping a hot moistened kitchen towel around it for a few seconds. If you are using the cake base, cut the round of cake to fit just inside the rim of the bowl. Place it on the mousse, invert the bowl onto a rack set over a sheet of parchment paper and remove the plastic. If you do not have a cake base, invert the bombe onto your serving plate.

9. Pour the glaze over the top of the bombe and let it run down the sides. Transfer to a serving plate if necessary and return to the freezer until ready to serve. You won't use all of the glaze. Allow the remaining glaze to cool and thicken, and pipe through a small star or round tip to decorate the bombe.

CHOCOLATE HOT-AND-COLD

■ ■ ■

This extraordinary, decadent dessert is incredibly easy to make. Chocolate-raspberry ganache is poured over a pastry base set into individual ring molds. Just before serving, I pop the desserts out of the ring molds, sprinkle them with sugar, caramelize the tops, then heat them very briefly in a 350°F oven. The insides remain cold, but the outsides are warm and oozy. You'll need eight 3-x-½-inch ring molds, which you can buy at kitchen supply stores.

8 3-inch rounds ¼-inch-thick Pâte Sucrée (from 1 recipe; page 373), prebaked
3 pints raspberries
8 ounces bittersweet chocolate, finely chopped
¾ cup heavy cream
¼ cup sugar, plus 6 tablespoons plus 2 teaspoons for caramelizing
½ cup strained raspberry puree (from 1 pint of the raspberries above)
1 tablespoon Chambord

1. Prepare the bases. Arrange eight 3-inch ring molds on a baking sheet and line the molds with the pâte sucrée. Top each with 4 or 5 of the raspberries.

2. Place the chocolate in a heatproof bowl. Combine the cream and the ¼ cup sugar in a small saucepan and bring to a boil, stirring to dissolve the sugar. Pour over the chocolate. Tap the bowl against your work surface to settle the chocolate into the cream and allow to sit for 1 minute. Using a whisk, stir the mixture until the chocolate has melted and the ganache is smooth. Stir in the raspberry puree and the Chambord.

3. Pour the chocolate-raspberry ganache into the lined ring molds, filling the molds right to the top. Transfer to the refrigerator and chill until firm, 4 hours to overnight.

4. Shortly before serving, place a rack in the middle of the oven and preheat the oven to 350°F.

5. Remove the desserts from the refrigerator and remove from the molds. You can do this by running a knife around the inside or by heating the outside with a kitchen torch and lifting off the rings. Caramelize the tops: Sprinkle 1 teaspoon

sugar over the top of each dessert, and using a propane or butane kitchen torch according to the manufacturer's directions, set its flame to medium and just melt the sugar, being careful not to burn the chocolate. Add another teaspoon sugar and melt it using the torch, again being careful not to burn the chocolate. Sprinkle with $\frac{1}{2}$ teaspoon sugar and caramelize with the torch.

6. Place the desserts on a 12-x-17-inch half sheet pan and place in the oven for 3 to 5 minutes, until the outsides are hot and beginning to melt. Remove from the oven, set on plates, garnish with the remaining raspberries, and serve immediately.

CHOCOLATE TRUFFLE CAKES

■ ■ ■

If crème brûlée was the most popular dessert of the 1980s, chocolate truffle cake was the favorite of the nineties. The first time I tried chocolate truffle cake was at the Lafayette in New York City. Jean-Georges Vongerichten had brought it to America from Europe. He called these almost-flourless cakes (they're really more like molten chocolate) Valrhona chocolate cupcakes. The recipe is now a secret weapon in my pastry arsenal—the batter comes up in many of my creations: I use it for the Chocolate Purses (page 173) I developed for Spago, for the chocolate doughnuts I make for the Special Olympics (page 314), and for the chocolate crème brûlée I made for the Oscars (page 338). It's a great recipe to have in your repertoire.

Spray the molds very generously and make sure the melted chocolate and butter are hot when you add them to the egg and sugar mixture.

8 ounces bittersweet chocolate, finely chopped

8 ounces (2 sticks) unsalted butter, cut into 1-inch pieces

6 large eggs, at room temperature

¾ cup sugar

¼ cup all-purpose flour, sifted

1. Place a rack in the middle of the oven and preheat the oven to 375°F. Spray eight 4-ounce aluminum molds or ramekins generously with pan spray.

2. Place the chocolate in a medium heatproof bowl. Place the butter in a saucepan over medium heat. Place the bowl with the chocolate over the saucepan to warm the chocolate as the butter melts.

3. When the butter has melted, pour over the chocolate. Stir until the chocolate has melted and has reached 100°F. Set aside on top of the oven or in another warm place to keep the mixture hot.

4. In the bowl of a stand mixer fitted with the whisk attachment, or in a large bowl with a hand mixer, combine the eggs and sugar and beat on medium speed until just lemony yellow and doubled in volume, about 3 minutes.

5. Whisk the flour into the chocolate mixture. Turn the mixer to low speed and add the hot chocolate mixture to the eggs all at once. Scrape down the bowl and continue to mix for 30 seconds, until well combined. Scrape down the bowl. (At this point the batter can be refrigerated, tightly wrapped, for up to 5 days or frozen for up to 1 month.)

6. Fill the aluminum molds or ramekins three-quarters full and place on a 12-x-17-inch half sheet pan. Bake for 12 minutes. Rotate the pan from front to back and bake for an additional 2 minutes, or until the cakes are just set on the sides. Remove from the oven and allow to sit for 5 minutes. Run a knife around the inside of the molds and invert the cakes onto plates.

    NOTE: These can be prebaked and left in the molds, then reheated shortly before serving. Reheat at 350°F for 4 to 5 minutes.

CHOCOLATE DEVIL'S FOOD CAKE WITH CHOCOLATE FILLING

MAKES ONE 9-INCH LAYER CAKE (2 CAKE LAYERS)

■ ■ ■

This super deep, dark, moist, sexy cake was one of the most popular desserts at Tribeca Grill, another exciting downtown restaurant where I worked after my stint at Montrachet, alongside executive sous-chef/pastry chef Gerry Hayden, who is certainly one of the country's best pastry chefs. It's characteristic of the dark, rich chocolate cakes that were very fashionable in the eighties. This cake requires high-alkaline black cocoa, which you can find in the King Arthur Flour catalog (see Sources). It's essential for achieving its dark, Oreo-like color.

1. **MAKE THE CAKE:** Place a rack in the middle of the oven and preheat the oven to 350°F. Prepare two 9-x-2-inch round cake pans. Spray only the bottoms with pan spray. Line them with a circle of parchment paper and spray the paper.

2. Sift together the all-purpose flour, cake flour, baking soda, baking powder, and salt and set aside.

3. Place the chocolate in a bowl with the cocoa. Bring the espresso or coffee to a boil and pour over the chocolate. Tap the bowl once on your work surface and then

FOR THE CAKE

- 1 cup all-purpose flour
- 1 cup cake flour
- 2 teaspoons baking soda
- 1/2 teaspoon baking powder
- 1/2 teaspoon salt
- 4 ounces unsweetened chocolate, preferably Michel Cluizel Noir Infini 99% (see Sources), finely chopped
- 1/4 cup unsweetened cocoa powder (see headnote)
- 1 cup brewed espresso or coffee
- 3/4 cup buttermilk
- 3/4 cup vegetable oil
- 1 cup packed light brown sugar
- 1 cup sugar
- 1 teaspoon vanilla extract
- 3 large eggs, at room temperature

FOR THE FILLING

- 8 ounces milk chocolate, preferably Valrhona Jivara (see Sources), finely chopped
- 2 cups heavy cream

FOR THE CHOCOLATE GLAZE

- 3 ounces bittersweet chocolate, finely chopped
- 2 ounces (1/2 stick) unsalted butter
- 2 1/2 tablespoons light corn syrup

whisk until the chocolate has melted and the mixture is smooth. Whisk in the buttermilk and set aside.

4. In the bowl of a stand mixer fitted with the paddle attachment, or in a large bowl with a hand mixer, mix together the vegetable oil, brown sugar, sugar, and vanilla and beat for 2 minutes, until well blended. Add the eggs one at a time, scraping down the bowl after each addition. In 3 additions, add the flour and the chocolate mixture, alternating the two and scraping down the bowl and paddle after each addition.

5. Divide the batter between the two pans, filling the pans two thirds of the way up. Tap each pan lightly on your work surface three times to eliminate air bubbles. Then, using the same jerking wrist action you would use to throw a Frisbee, swing each pan around on the counter so that the batter is forced up the sides of the pan. This will prevent a dome from forming in the middle of the cake. Bake for 25 minutes, then switch the pans from front to back and rotate them 180 degrees. Bake for another 5 to 10 minutes. Test the cake for doneness by lightly touching the top of it with a finger. The finger indentation should spring right back into place. If it doesn't, continue baking for 5 to 10 more minutes. The cake is also done when it begins to pull slightly away from the sides of the pan. Remove the cakes from the oven, allow to cool in the pans for 15 minutes, then invert onto a rack, remove the pans and parchment, and allow to cool for at least 2 hours.

Sherry's Secrets

Your chocolate is a very important ingredient in your baking arsenal. One thing I'll never compromise on is my 99% bitter chocolate. I use Michel Cluizel Noir Infini 99%, which is now widely stocked in specialty stores. It has a powerful chocolate flavor with hints of jasmine and a texture that is never chalky, as Baker's unsweetened chocolate often is.

6. MEANWHILE, MAKE THE FILLING: Place the chocolate in a heatproof bowl. Bring 1 cup of the cream to a boil and pour over the chocolate. Tap the bowl against your work surface and let sit for 1 minute, then using a heatproof spatula, stir until smooth. Let cool to room temperature.

7. With a hand mixer, beat the remaining 1 cup cream to medium peaks. Fold half into the chocolate mixture to lighten it, then fold in the rest. Refrigerate for 2 hours or more, until set.

8. ASSEMBLE THE CAKE: Place one of the cake layers on a cardboard round or foam core or a plate, bottom side up. Spread the chocolate filling over the cake in an even layer, and top with the second round. Refrigerate while you make the glaze.

9. MAKE THE GLAZE: Combine the chocolate with the butter and melt in a microwave-safe bowl at 50 percent power for 2 to 3 minutes or in a heatproof bowl set over a saucepan of simmering water. Stir with a rubber spatula until smooth. Stir in the corn syrup. Allow to cool to 90°F (the glaze will feel barely warm on your lips).

10. Place the cake on a rack on a parchment-lined work surface. Pour the glaze over the top and allow it to run down the sides of the cake, then use a spatula, preferably offset, to cover the sides evenly, turning the cake as necessary. Transfer the cake to a serving plate or platter and refrigerate until ready to serve.

CARAMELIZED BANANA TARTS

MAKES FOUR 4-INCH TARTS

■ ■ ■

These banana tarts, which I learned from Gerry Hayden, who is now an executive chef and restaurateur on Long Island's North Fork with his wife, Claudia Fleming, are one of the easiest and tastiest desserts I've ever served, and they were a favorite at Tribeca Grill. The tarts are big linzer cookies, spread with banana schmutz or apple compote, and the bananas are meticulously arranged in a floral swirl on top, then caramelized. The tarts are served with caramel swirl ice cream. You'll need a propane or butane kitchen torch for caramelizing the tops.

½ batch Linzer Dough (page 368)
½ cup Banana Schmutz (page 366) or Apple Compote (page 365)
4 ripe but firm bananas (less ripe is better than fully ripe)
2 tablespoons plus 2 teaspoons sugar
2 cups vanilla ice cream mixed with ¾ cup Creamy Caramel Sauce (page 354)
¼ cup Croquante (page 355), pulverized
Spun Sugar (page 352) for topping (optional)

1. Place a rack in the lowest position of the oven and preheat the oven to 375°F. Line a baking sheet with parchment paper.

2. Roll out the linzer dough into a 9-inch square, ¼ inch thick. Cut into four 4-inch round disks with a cookie cutter and place on the baking sheet.

3. Bake the disks for 12 minutes. Rotate the baking sheet from front to back and bake for another 6 to 8 minutes, until golden. Remove from the oven and allow to cool slightly or completely. (The disks can be baked up to 2 days ahead.)

4. To assemble the tarts, spread each tart crust with a layer of banana schmutz or apple compote. Place a banana on a cutting board so that it is smiling at you. Cut thin slices on the bias. Fan the banana over the schmutz or compote like the petals of a flower, overlapping the slices. Repeat with the remaining bananas and tarts.

5. Place a rack over a 12-x-17-inch half sheet pan and place 2 tarts on the rack. Sprinkle each tart with a heaping teaspoon of sugar, making sure to dust the

CARAMELIZING WITH A KITCHEN TORCH

Whether it's a crème brûlée or a caramelized tart like this one, the trick to caramelizing the top of a dessert is to layer the sugar. The first layer protects the top of the dessert. Sprinkle the sugar on and melt it with the torch. If you try to caramelize it, you will burn the top of the dessert. Once this first layer has melted, add a second layer of sugar. Now you can begin to lightly caramelize the sugar. You can add a third and even a fourth layer of sugar if you wish, caramelizing each subsequent layer a little more.

bananas evenly. Using a propane or butane kitchen torch, following the manufacturer's directions, set on a medium flame and holding it 1 inch from the bananas, begin to caramelize the sugar, moving the torch in a circular motion. When the sugar has melted, add another teaspoon of sugar and lightly caramelize with the torch. Repeat with the other 2 tarts. Let sit for 5 minutes.

6. Place a scoop of ice cream in the middle of each tart, sprinkle with croquante, and serve immediately. Top with spun sugar if desired.

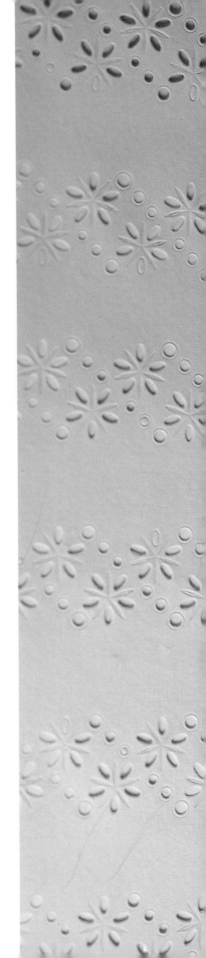

London Interlude

I HAD READ THAT NEW YORK CITY TECHNICAL COLLEGE offered a scholarship for an internship in London. I dreamed of going abroad, and the scholarship would be my ticket. There were only four places available for twenty applicants. We would be selected on the basis of our grades, an interview, and a practical exam. I knew I'd have to do well on all three. I was thrilled when I found out I'd been accepted.

My parents and my best friend, Stephanie, who had worked at McDonald's with me, took me to the airport, where I joined the three other students from our school. Julie, a beautiful girl from Queens, could have just as easily come from the Upper West Side of Manhattan. Chain-smoking Josh, now a restaurateur, was confident and assertive, the Jewish counterpart to Thomas, a tall, good-looking Irish ladies' man who is now a club owner. In many ways, we were not alike, but we all liked to have a good time. Okay, that's an understatement: we were trouble. That semester the four of us (five of us, really, since Julie's English boyfriend was soon adopted by the group) blew off a lot of steam at restaurants and clubs all over London.

In London I was exposed to the European hospitality industry. At Ealing Technical College, I took a class taught by Professor Halsey, a famous English confectioner who had invented the Twix candy bar for the Mars candy company. Professor Halsey, who looked like a small Santa Claus, turned me on to the alchemy of pastry and especially confectionery. When he had us make Twix bars from scratch, I began to explore the intricacies of candy, one of the most difficult areas not just of pastry but of cooking in general. When he took me on a guided tour of Harrod's pastry kitchens,

I began to understand just how far one could go with confectionery.

At first I was puzzled by the fact that in England all desserts, be they cakes, tarts, trifles, or actual puddings, were called puddings. At any rate, I soon began to understand that the words *pudding* and *dessert* were interchangeable and finally understood what Pink Floyd meant by "no meat, no pudding."

It was imperative that I, still the struggling student, work. I soon discovered a little restaurant called Charlotte's Place, across Ealing Common from the school. I befriended the owner, Charlotte, a fun-loving six-foot-tall pear-shaped South African who was not averse to paying me off the books to wait tables and make desserts for her restaurant. Every night after school, I would traipse across the common to Charlotte's Place, where I not only honed my pastry-making skills but also learned a lot about running a small restaurant. And I acquired a good friend in the bargain.

Although Grandma had always served tea in Brooklyn, in London I experienced the joys of tea beyond Lipton. Never a coffee drinker, I sipped magnificent teas from former British colonies like Sri Lanka and Assam. I learned the proper ways of tea service and delighted in making terrific scones and crumpets. My palate was maturing, developing more depth by the day.

When I got on a Pan Am flight in December 1988 to go home (two days later, that same flight would be blown up by terrorists), I knew I would become a serious pastry chef. I had one more semester of college to go and the whole New York City restaurant world ahead of me.

TRADITIONAL ENGLISH CRUMPETS

■ ■ ■

Crumpets are griddle-baked yeasted pancakes reminiscent of English muffins, one of my childhood favorites. They're spongy in the middle and nicely browned on each side. You ladle the batter into rings set on a griddle and let the first side brown, then flip the crumpets over. Once they're cool, you remove the rings. Serve them with thick Devonshire Cream (page 93) and berries or preserves.

1 teaspoon fast-rising yeast
1 tablespoon light brown sugar
2¼ cups all-purpose flour, preferably Gold Medal Better for Bread flour
1 teaspoon salt
¾ cup warm (90°F) water
1½ cups warm (90°F) milk
¾ teaspoon baking soda
1 tablespoon water

1. In a medium bowl, whisk together the yeast, brown sugar, flour, and salt. Add the warm water and milk and whisk vigorously for 2 minutes. Cover and set aside at room temperature for 1½ hours, or until doubled and bubbly.

2. Shortly before the end of the rise, preheat a griddle, preferably an electric griddle, to 300°F or medium. Lightly grease the griddle and twelve 3-inch metal rings (or crumpet rings, or you can use clean tuna fish cans with the tops and bottoms removed) with pan spray. Place the rings on the griddle to preheat.

Sherry's Secrets

Do not overfill the molds, or the crumpets will be too dense.

3. When the batter has doubled, dissolve the baking soda in the 1 tablespoon water. Stir into the crumpet batter.

4. Cooking in batches if necessary, scoop a scant ¼ cup of batter into each ring. Cook, without disturbing, for 9 to 10 minutes. When bubbles in the batter rise to the top and break, making honeycomb-like holes through the crumpet from top to bottom, the top is no longer shiny, and the crumpets are beginning to shrink away from the edges, flip over in the rings and cook for an additional 4 to 5 minutes, until a crumpet springs back when gently pressed with a finger. Remove from the heat and allow to cool in the rings, then remove the rings. Wrap the crumpets in a clean kitchen towel and serve at once.

TRADITIONAL ENGLISH SCONES

MAKES SIXTEEN 2-INCH SQUARES OR 32 SMALL TRIANGLES

■ ■ ■

Nothing is as perfect with tea as a traditional English scone, but here in the States, scones have ballooned into big cloyingly sweet doughy pastries, when they should be small, dainty, and flaky like a biscuit, with only a bit of sweetness. One of the keys to success with scones is not to handle the dough too much. Serve with your favorite jam and Devonshire Cream (page 93).

2 cups all-purpose flour

1/4 cup sugar, plus more for sprinkling (optional)

1/2 teaspoon baking soda

1/2 teaspoon cream of tartar

1/8 teaspoon salt

4 ounces (1 stick) cold unsalted butter, cut into 1/2-inch pieces

1 tablespoon grated orange zest

1 large egg

1/4 cup heavy cream, or more as needed

1/4 cup milk, or more as needed

1/3 cup Fat Raisins, drained (page 364; optional)

Milk for brushing

1. Place racks in the upper and lower thirds of the oven. Preheat the oven to 400°F. Line two 12-x-17-inch half sheet pans with parchment paper.

2. Sift together the flour, sugar, baking soda, cream of tartar, and salt into the bowl of a stand mixer fitted with the paddle attachment. Add the butter and orange zest and mix on low speed for 1 minute, until the butter and flour are broken down into pieces the size of walnut meats. Use your thumb and forefinger to flatten the "walnuts." (You can also mix this by hand by rubbing the butter into the flour between your thumbs and fingers.) Then take up the mixture and rub briskly between your hands.

3. In a separate bowl, whisk together the egg, cream, and milk. Add to the flour mixture along with the fat raisins, if using, and blend at low speed just until the dough comes together, about 10 seconds. If it seems dry, add a bit more cream or milk, a tablespoon at a time.

4. Line your work surface with parchment, dust the parchment with flour, and scrape out the dough. Shape into an 8-inch square, about 1 inch thick. You can use a rolling pin for this. Cut the dough into 2-inch squares. If making triangles, cut the squares in half on the diagonal. Flip the scones over and place on the parchment-lined pans. Brush with milk, and sprinkle with sugar if desired.

5. Bake for 15 to 20 minutes, until dark golden brown and puffed.

Sherry's Secrets

Flipping scone and biscuit doughs over before baking gives them an even puff. The pastry will rise evenly and have a flatter, more finished looking surface. Using parchment on your work surface makes folding the dough easier and cleanup a snap.

VARIATIONS

LEMON: Substitute 2 tablespoons grated lemon zest for the orange zest and add 1 additional tablespoon sugar.

BUTTERMILK: Substitute ½ cup buttermilk for the cream and milk, and add 1 additional tablespoon sugar.

NUT: Substitute ¾ to 1 cup toasted nuts, such as chopped walnuts or almonds, for the fat raisins.

CHOCOLATE CHIP: Substitute 1 cup coarsely chopped bittersweet chocolate for the fat raisins.

DEVONSHIRE CREAM

■ ■ ■

This thick, slightly sweet cream, known also as clotted cream, is a traditional English accompaniment to scones or crumpets at afternoon tea. The luscious cultured cream balances the sweetness of the jam that is also served with the scones or crumpets. You can find it at some specialty stores. Here is my improvised version. I prefer it made with mascarpone, but if you can't find mascarpone, it will work fine with the cream cheese.

$1/2$ cup mascarpone or cream cheese, at room temperature
2 teaspoons sugar
$1/4$ teaspoon cream of tartar
1 teaspoon vanilla extract
$1/2$ cup heavy cream

Place the mascarpone or cream cheese in the bowl of a stand mixer fitted with the paddle attachment, or use a large bowl and a hand mixer. Add the sugar, cream of tartar, and vanilla and blend well on low speed. Without stopping the machine, stream in the heavy cream. When well blended, scrape into a bowl or ramekin, cover with plastic wrap, and refrigerate until ready to use. (The cream will keep, covered and refrigerated, for 2 days.)

LEMON TEA BISCUITS

■ ■ ■

You can make these rich, moderately sweet shortbread cookies a little sweeter if you brush them with the lemon icing. Either way, they go wonderfully with a nice "cuppa" tea.

8 ounces (2 sticks) unsalted butter, softened
1 tablespoon grated lemon zest
$\frac{1}{2}$ teaspoon vanilla extract
$\frac{1}{2}$ cup confectioners' sugar
$\frac{1}{4}$ teaspoon salt
$2\frac{1}{2}$ cups all-purpose flour
$\frac{1}{2}$ cup cornstarch
$\frac{1}{2}$ cup crystallized ginger, finely chopped

FOR THE LEMON ICING (OPTIONAL)

1 tablespoon fresh lemon juice
$\frac{1}{2}$ cup confectioners' sugar

1. Place the butter, lemon zest, vanilla, confectioners' sugar, and salt in the bowl of a stand mixer fitted with the paddle attachment, or use a large bowl and a hand mixer. Cream together on medium speed for 4 minutes, or until the mixture is light and fluffy. Scrape down the sides of the bowl and the paddle or beaters.

2. Sift together the flour and cornstarch. On low speed, add the flour mixture to the butter mixture a cup at a time, scraping down the bowl after each addition, and beat until the dough comes together. Beat in the crystallized ginger at low speed. The dough will be firm.

3. Scrape out the dough onto a sheet of parchment paper and use the parchment to roll it into a log about 3 inches wide and 6 inches long. Wrap the paper-covered log tightly in plastic wrap and refrigerate for about 4 hours, until firm enough to slice, or overnight.

4. Place a rack in the lowest position of the oven and preheat the oven to 350°F. Line two 12-x-17-inch half sheet pans with parchment.

5. Slice the dough into $\frac{1}{4}$-inch-thick disks and place on the lined baking sheets. Bake, one sheet at a time, rotating the pan from front to back halfway through, for 15 to 20 minutes, until the cookies are golden around the edges. Remove from the oven and allow to cool on racks. (The biscuits will keep, stored airtight, for 2 days.)

6. Make the lemon icing if using. When the biscuits have cooled, mix together the lemon juice and confectioners' sugar. Brush the cookies with the icing and allow the icing to dry before serving.

Sherry's Secrets

You can save a step (and parchment paper) if you slice the dough on the parchment you used for rolling up the log of dough. Unroll the parchment, slice the dough, and transfer the parchment to the baking sheet. Then re-arrange the disks on the pan if they need to be spaced farther apart.

HOMEMADE TWIX COOKIES

MAKES ONE 9-X-13-INCH PAN; 100 SMALL COOKIES OR 24 LARGE COOKIES

■ ■ ■

This is based on the Twix candy bar, with a shortbread bottom, a caramel center, and a chocolate glaze topping. You can cut these smaller for a buffet or larger for individual desserts.

FOR THE SHORTBREAD

- 5½ ounces (1 stick plus 3 tablespoons) unsalted butter, softened
- ¼ cup sugar
- 2 cups cake flour
- 2 tablespoons ground rice (see headnote, page 26)

FOR THE CARAMEL TOPPING

- 2 cups sugar
- ¾ cup Lyle's Golden Syrup (available at most supermarkets and at whole foods stores)
- ½ cup water
- 1 teaspoon fresh lemon juice
- 1 cup heavy cream
- 1 cup sweetened condensed milk

FOR THE CHOCOLATE GLAZE

- 6 ounces bittersweet chocolate, finely chopped
- 2 tablespoons unsalted butter

1. MAKE THE SHORTBREAD: Place a rack in the lowest position of the oven and preheat the oven to 350°F. Spray a 9-x-13-inch baking pan with pan spray and line with parchment paper. Spray the parchment.

2. In the bowl of a stand mixer fitted with the paddle attachment, or in a large bowl with a hand mixer, cream the butter and sugar at medium speed until fluffy, about 2 minutes. Gradually add the flour and ground rice and allow the dough to come together.

3. Remove from the bowl and press the dough evenly into the bottom of the pan. Place in the oven and bake for 12 minutes. Rotate the pan from front to back and bake for another 8 minutes, until the shortbread is a deep golden brown. Remove from the oven and allow to cool on a rack to room temperature.

4. MAKE THE CARAMEL: In a large saucepan, combine the sugar, golden syrup, water, and lemon juice. Brush down the inside of the pan with a little water, using your hand to feel for stray granules of sugar. Cover the saucepan and place it over medium heat for 4 minutes. After 4 minutes, remove the lid,

increase the heat, and bring to a boil. Do not stir from this point on. Keep an eye on the pan. The mixture will be very bubbly. When stray sugar crystals appear on the sides of the pan, brush them down with a clean wet pastry brush. As the sugar cooks, the bubbles will get larger.

5. In a small saucepan, bring the heavy cream to a boil. Remove from the heat and set aside.

6. After 5 to 6 minutes, the sugar will turn golden brown. Insert a candy thermometer and when the temperature reaches 300°F, remove the pan from the heat and let it sit for 1 minute, or until the bubbles subside. Carefully whisk in the heavy cream. Stir until smooth, then whisk in the condensed milk. Whisk until smooth.

7. Return the pan to the heat and stir constantly over medium heat until the caramel reaches 240°F. Remove from the heat and pour over the shortbread. Allow to set.

8. MAKE THE CHOCOLATE GLAZE: Melt the chocolate and butter in a microwave-safe bowl at 50 percent power for 2 to 3 minutes or in a heatproof bowl set over a saucepan of simmering water. Stir with a rubber spatula until smooth. Pour over the caramel and smear evenly. Let sit at room temperature or in the refrigerator until set.

9. Cut into the desired size and serve. (The cookies will keep, stored airtight, for 1 day.)

FLOURLESS CHOCOLATE CAKE
WITH MERINGUE TOPPING

MAKES ONE 9- OR 10-INCH TORTE

■ ■ ■

If there is one recipe in this book that you *must* make, this cake is the one. The first time I saw it on the dessert cart at Charlotte's Place, I wanted to plunge into it. It's a dense, decadent, gooey chocolate cake that is lightened by an angelic meringue topping.

FOR THE CAKE
8½ ounces bittersweet chocolate, finely chopped
4 ounces (1 stick) unsalted butter
5 large eggs, at room temperature
1 cup plus 2 tablespoons sugar
½ cup unsweetened cocoa powder

FOR THE MERINGUE TOPPING
8 large egg whites, at room temperature
¼ teaspoon cream of tartar
1½ cups sugar

1. **MAKE THE CAKE:** Place a rack in the middle of the oven and preheat the oven to 350°F. Butter a 10-inch fluted tart pan or a 9-inch springform pan. The pan must be at least 1 inch deep or the batter will overflow.

2. Melt the chocolate and the butter in a microwave-safe bowl for 2 to 3 minutes at 50 percent power or in a heatproof bowl set over a saucepan of simmering water. Stir together with a rubber spatula until smooth.

3. In the bowl of a stand mixer fitted with the whisk attachment, or in a large bowl with a hand mixer, beat together the eggs and the sugar on medium speed until pale and the mixture forms a ribbon when lifted from the bowl with a spatula, about 2 minutes. On low speed, beat in the cocoa powder and the chocolate mixture and combine well. Pour into the prepared pan.

4. Bake for 15 minutes. Rotate the pan from front to back and continue to bake for another 8 minutes, or until the cake is slightly firm to the touch. Remove from the oven and allow to cool on a rack to room temperature.

5. **MAKE THE MERINGUE:** Place a rack in the middle of the oven and preheat the oven to 375°F. In the bowl of a stand mixer fitted with the whisk attachment, or in a large bowl with a hand mixer, beat the egg whites on low speed

until foamy. Add the cream of tartar and increase the speed to medium. Continue beating while you gradually add the sugar, a tablespoon at a time. Beat the mixture to stiff, satiny peaks.

6. Spoon the meringue over the chocolate cake, creating lots of wisps and peaks. Bake for 12 to 15 minutes, until the meringue is golden brown. Serve from the pan. Refrigerate leftovers.

ORANGE "BUTTER" CAKE

■ ■ ■

I traded one of my chocolate cake recipes for this gem of a cake, served at the Fifth Floor Café at Harvey Nichols department store in Knightsbridge. I call it a butter cake because the texture is so buttery, even though there's no butter in it. Almond flour is the secret. The cake just gets better overnight, and it's great sliced and toasted, served with marmalade and (of course) tea.

2 medium navel oranges (about 1 pound)
2 tablespoons peeled and chopped fresh ginger
1 cup sugar
2 cups almond flour (available at whole foods stores, or see Sources), lightly toasted (see Sherry's Secrets) and cooled
2 tablespoons cake flour
1 teaspoon baking powder
6 large eggs, at room temperature
Confectioners' sugar for dusting

1. Place the whole oranges in a medium saucepan, cover with water, and bring to a boil. Reduce the heat, cover, and simmer for 1½ hours.

2. Meanwhile, place the ginger and ¼ cup of the sugar in a food processor fitted with the steel blade and pulse until you have a paste.

3. Drain and cut the oranges into quarters. Remove and discard any seeds and allow the oranges to cool. Place the oranges, skin and all, in the food processor with the ginger paste and process until smooth.

4. Place a rack in the middle of the oven and preheat the oven to 375°F. Spray a 9-inch springform pan with pan spray and line with parchment paper. Spray the parchment.

5. Sift together the almond flour, cake flour, and baking powder. Set aside.

6. Combine the eggs and the remaining ¾ cup sugar in the bowl of a stand mixer fitted with the whisk attachment, or in a large bowl with a hand mixer, and beat at medium speed until the eggs have tripled in volume, are thick and lemon-

colored, and form a ribbon when lifted with a spatula, 10 to 12 minutes. Stir in one third of the pureed oranges.

7. Fold the flour mixture into the eggs in 3 additions, alternating with the remaining orange mixture.

8. Scrape the batter into the cake pan. Tap the pan on your work surface. Using the same jerking wrist action you would use to throw a Frisbee, swing the pan around on the counter so that the batter is forced up the sides of the pan (this prevents a dome from forming in the middle). Bake for 60 minutes, or until the cake springs back lightly when pressed gently with a finger. Remove from the oven and allow to cool in the pan on a rack for 10 minutes, then remove the springform pan and allow to cool completely.

9. Dust with confectioners' sugar before serving.

Sherry's Secrets

Toasting almond flour brings out the rich flavor of the almonds. Place in a baking pan and toast in the middle of a 350°F oven for 5 to 10 minutes, stirring after 5 minutes. The flour should be golden brown and smell toasty and fragrant.

ENGLISH TRIFLE

■ ■ ■

This is a decidedly grown-up dessert. The cake, a simple sponge cake, is smeared with blackberry preserves and cut into squares, then doused with cream sherry and topped with pastry cream and whipped cream, both of which are also spiked with sherry. Trifle is sometimes made with vanilla custard sauce, but I prefer the pastry cream (I fold in whipped cream, which makes it crème baumanière), as it gives more body to the pudding. Make the cake a day ahead.

1. **MAKE THE SPONGE CAKE:** Place a rack in the middle of the oven and preheat the oven to 350°F. Spray a 9-inch round cake pan with pan spray and line with parchment paper. Spray the parchment.

2. Sift together the all-purpose flour, cake flour, and salt.

3. In the bowl of a stand mixer fitted with the whisk attachment, or in a large bowl with a hand mixer, beat the egg whites on low speed until they form soft peaks. Add the cream of tartar and increase the speed to medium while you gradually add ¼ cup of the sugar, 1 tablespoon at a time. Beat until the whites form medium-stiff peaks.

4. In a separate clean bowl, using the whisk attachment, or with the hand mixer, beat together the egg yolks and the remaining ¼ cup sugar on high speed until

FOR THE SPONGE CAKE
- ½ cup plus 1 tablespoon all-purpose flour
- ½ cup plus 1 tablespoon cake flour
- ¼ teaspoon salt
- 4 large eggs, separated
- ⅛ teaspoon cream of tartar
- ½ cup sugar
- ½ teaspoon vanilla extract

- ½ cup blackberry preserves
- ⅓ cup cream sherry

FOR THE CRÈME BAUMANIÈRE
- 2½ cups milk
- ½ cup sugar
- 1 vanilla bean, split, seeds scraped out, seeds and bean reserved
- 3 tablespoons all-purpose flour
- 5 large egg yolks
- 2 tablespoons cream sherry
- 1 cup heavy cream, whipped to stiff peaks

FOR ASSEMBLING THE TRIFLE
- 1 cup heavy cream
  Cream sherry to taste
- 2 pints blackberries for garnish

the mixture is thick and pale yellow and holds a ribbon when drizzled from a spatula, about 3 minutes. Beat in the vanilla. Stir in one quarter of the beaten egg whites.

5. Fold the flour mixture into the egg yolks in 4 additions, alternating with the remaining egg whites.

6. Scrape the batter into the prepared cake pan. Tap once against your work surface to deflate any large air bubbles. Bake for 15 minutes and rotate the pan from front to back. Bake for another 10 to 15 minutes, until the cake is firm to the touch and a cake tester inserted in the center comes out clean. Remove from the oven and allow to cool in the pan on a rack for 15 minutes, then invert onto another rack, remove the pan, peel off the parchment, and invert again on the rack to cool. Wrap airtight in plastic wrap if not using right away.

7. The day before, or the morning of the night you wish to serve the trifle, spread the top of the cake with the preserves. Cut the cake into 2-inch pieces. Line a flat wide bowl (a trifle dish is a lovely stemmed glass bowl with a flat bottom and straight sides) with the cake, in one layer. Douse the cake with the 1/3 cup cream sherry. Cover with waxed paper or plastic wrap, set a plate on top, and place a weight, such as a large can of tomatoes, on top of the plate. Cover and refrigerate for at least 12 hours, or overnight.

8. MAKE THE CRÈME BAUMANIÈRE: In a medium nonreactive saucepan, combine the milk, 1/4 cup of the sugar, and the vanilla seeds and bean and bring to a boil over medium heat. Turn off the heat, cover tightly with plastic wrap, and let steep for 15 minutes. Remove and discard the vanilla bean.

9. Sift together the remaining 1/4 cup sugar and the flour onto a piece of parchment paper. In a medium bowl, whisk the egg yolks. Add the sifted dry ingredients. Whisk until fluffy.

10. Bring the milk back to a simmer, uncovered. Remove from the heat and slowly ladle 1/2 cup into the eggs while whisking. Once the milk is incorporated into the eggs, whisk them back into the hot milk. Be sure to scrape all the eggs into the milk with a rubber spatula. Place the saucepan back over the heat. Immediately begin to rapidly whisk the pastry cream. In under a minute, it will boil and begin to thicken. Continue to whisk for about 3 minutes, until it reaches pud-

ding consistency. To test the cream for doneness, tilt the saucepan to one side. The pastry cream should pull away from the pan completely.

11. Immediately remove the pan from the heat and pour the pastry cream through a fine-mesh strainer into a clean bowl. Allow to cool to room temperature. (To cool pastry cream quickly, spread it out on a baking sheet lined with plastic wrap.) To prevent a skin from forming as it cools, place a sheet of plastic wrap directly on the surface. (The pastry cream can be refrigerated for up to 3 days.)

12. Fold in the sherry and the stiffly whipped cream.

13. ASSEMBLE THE TRIFLE: Spoon the crème baumanière over the cake. Chill for at least 1 hour more in the refrigerator.

14. With a hand mixer, beat the 1 cup cream until it forms soft peaks. Flavor it with cream sherry to taste. Spoon over the trifle and refrigerate until ready to serve. Serve, garnishing each helping with berries.

NOTE: You can also use ladyfingers (page 35) for this dessert. You will need about thirty-six 3-inch-long ladyfingers.

BANANA BRÛLÉE

■ ■ ■

This is like an eggless crème brûlée, a thick cream loaded with bananas and topped with caramelized sugar. The dessert always makes me think of my friend Charlotte, who made it in big crocks at her restaurant in Ealing. Charlotte loved to drink pink champagne, as did I. When we'd had a few glasses of champagne, we liked to challenge each other to say the name of this dessert three times quickly. One of the great things about this dessert is that, unlike crème brûlée, you can make it, topping and all, in advance.

FOR THE BRÛLÉE
- 1/4 cup fresh orange juice
- 3 tablespoons plus 1 teaspoon sugar
- 2 tablespoons light brown sugar
- 1 tablespoon fresh lemon juice
- 1 vanilla bean, split, seeds scraped out and reserved
- 2 tablespoons Tia Maria or other coffee liqueur
- 3 ripe but firm bananas
- 2 cups heavy cream
- 1/2 cup crème fraîche

FOR THE CARAMEL TOPPING
- 1 1/2 cups sugar

1. **MAKE THE BRÛLÉE:** Combine the orange juice, 2 tablespoons of the sugar, the brown sugar, lemon juice, seeds from the vanilla bean, and the liqueur in a medium bowl. Peel and slice the bananas and toss with the mixture. Let the bananas macerate for 30 minutes.

2. Divide the bananas and their liquid evenly among six 6-ounce ramekins. Whip the cream and crème fraîche with the remaining 1 tablespoon plus 1 teaspoon sugar until the mixture forms stiff peaks. Spoon over the bananas, piling the cream up higher than the tops of the ramekins, then smoothing the tops with a spatula, preferably offset, so that the surface of each ramekin is flat.

3. **MAKE THE CARAMEL TOPPING:** Place the sugar in a medium saucepan and stir over medium-high heat until it has melted and become golden. Insert a candy thermometer and cook, without stirring, until the caramel reaches 325°F and is dark amber. Remove the pan from the heat and let sit for 2 minutes, or until the bubbles subside.

4. Line a 12-x-17-inch half sheet pan with aluminum foil and place the ramekins on top. Pour the hot caramel over the tops of the brûlées, allowing it to run down the sides of the ramekins. At first the cream will bubble up from underneath and the surface will look mottled with caramel and cream, then the caramel will harden. Place the brûlées in the refrigerator until ready to serve. (The brûlées can be made up to 4 hours in advance.)

SNAKE BITE SORBET

■ ■ ■

The idea for this sorbet came from a drink that was served at the Nelson Mandela Pub in London. Snake Bite was a popular college cocktail made with lager, hard cider, and a shot of cassis that flowed down the center of the drink like venom. Technically, it is unlawful for pubs to serve drinks with three kinds of alcohol mixed together, but the Snake Bite got away with it. A group of us students, 100 or more, danced so hard one rainy night that when we opened all the double doors, steam literally came off our bodies. Years later I still associate the drink with the heat in that pub. I've taken the concept and turned it into a cooling beautiful pink sorbet. If you want to use this recipe for a punch rather than a sorbet, eliminate the simple syrup in Step 3.

1 cup Framboise Lambic (Belgian raspberry beer; available at wine and beer stores)
1 cup sparkling apple juice
2 tablespoons crème de cassis
½ cup water
⅓ cup sugar
2 tablespoons fresh lemon juice
Pinch of salt

Sherry's Secrets

The higher a sorbet's sugar content, the softer it will be. Too much sugar, and it will "bleed"— there will be melted rivulets in the mixture. Alcohol can act as an antifreeze just as well; a small addition will add flavor and contribute to a softer sorbet. But just as for sugar, too much, and your sorbet will bleed.

1. Place a 9-x-12-inch baking dish or a 1-quart freezer container in the freezer.

2. Combine the Framboise Lambic, sparkling apple juice, and crème de cassis in a bowl.

3. Combine the water and sugar in a small saucepan and bring to a boil. When the sugar has dissolved, pour the syrup into the alcohol mixture. Allow to cool. Stir in the lemon juice and salt.

4. Freeze in an ice cream maker according to the manufacturer's directions. Transfer to the cold baking dish or freezer container, cover tightly, and freeze for 2 hours.

5. Scrape into chilled wineglasses and serve.

TREACLE TART

■ ■ ■

There is nothing quite like the flavor of this tart. It's reminiscent of pecan pie, but with a much sharper flavor, sweet, but not cloyingly so.

Treacle is known as golden syrup in some parts of England. It has a marvelous flavor, somewhere between honey and molasses. You can find Lyle's Golden Syrup at most supermarkets and at whole foods stores; it comes in a distinctive white, green, and gold can.

1 cup Lyle's Golden Syrup (see headnote)
½ cup fresh white bread crumbs
¼ cup almond flour (available at whole foods stores, or see Sources), lightly toasted (see page 101)
1 large egg, beaten
½ cup heavy cream
1 teaspoon grated lemon zest
1 teaspoon fresh lemon juice or orange juice
1 9-inch tart shell made with Pâte Sucrée (page 373), prebaked Devonshire Cream (page 93) or crème fraîche

1. Place a rack in the middle of the oven and preheat the oven to 375°F.

2. Place the golden syrup in a medium saucepan and bring to a boil. Stir in the bread crumbs and almond flour and remove from the heat. Let sit for 5 minutes, then stir in the egg, heavy cream, lemon zest, and lemon juice or orange juice.

3. Pour into the tart crust. Bake for 10 minutes, then turn the oven down to 325°F and bake for an additional 30 to 40 minutes, or until set. Remove from the oven and allow to cool completely before slicing, or serve warm. Serve with Devonshire cream or crème fraîche.

PEACH MELBA

■ ■ ■

When our semester at Ealing Technical College was over, my classmates and I treated ourselves to a wonderful feast at London's most expensive restaurant, Tante Marie, a Michelin two-star in Chelsea. The dessert is what I remember most vividly about that meal. Peach Melba is one of my favorite flavor, texture, and temperature combinations. The room-temperature peaches are served with warm raspberry compote and cold ice cream. Today I'm fortunate to have the most wonderful California peaches to work with.

FOR THE PEACHES

- 3 ripe but firm freestone peaches
- 2 cups sugar
- 2 cups water

FOR THE RASPBERRY SAUCE

- 12 ounces fresh raspberries
- 1/4 cup sugar
- 1/2 cup water
- 1 tablespoon fresh lemon juice
- 1/4 cup dry red wine
- 2 tablespoons Chambord

- 1 quart Seven-Bean Vanilla Ice Cream (page 340) or store-bought vanilla ice cream

Sherry's Secrets

As an apprentice, I was taught to make a cross in the bottom of a peach before blanching it, then afterward peel the skin back from the bottom. I prefer to forget about the cross and peel from the stem end. The skin comes away naturally when the peach is blanched, and there's no tearing of the flesh at the end of the peach.

1. TO PEEL THE PEACHES: Bring a large saucepan of water to a boil. Fill a bowl with ice water. Blanch the peaches in the boiling water for 1 minute, then transfer to the ice water and let sit for a minute or two. Peel away the skins, cut the peaches in half, and remove the pits.

2. In a heavy nonreactive saucepan, combine the sugar and water and bring to a boil. When the sugar has dissolved, remove from the heat and drop in the peaches. Allow to cool to room temperature. Refrigerate if not using right away. (The peaches can be poached and refrigerated, covered, up to 2 days ahead. Bring to room temperature before serving.)

3. **MAKE THE RASPBERRY SAUCE:** In a heavy nonreactive saucepan, combine two thirds of the raspberries, the sugar, water, lemon juice, red wine, and Chambord. Bring to a simmer and cook for 5 minutes, or until the raspberries burst. Stir and continue to simmer until the sauce is thick enough to coat the back of a spoon. Pour through a fine-mesh strainer into a bowl and stir in the remaining raspberries.

4. To serve, place a peach half, cut side up, in a glass bowl or a wineglass. Top with 1 large or 2 small scoops of vanilla ice cream and drizzle with the raspberry sauce.

Go West, Young Gal

SAN FRANCISCO AND NAPA

IN 1989 I WAS VERY BUSY, FINISHING UP MY DEGREE at the CIA and working at the Tribeca Grill in pastry prep and at Montrachet as pastry assistant. In California lots of women chefs were making names for themselves: not only Chez Panisse founder Alice Waters but also other important women chef/restaurateurs, like Joyce Goldstein (Square One), Barbara Tropp (China Moon Cafe), and Judy Rodgers (Zuni Café). In pastry there was Alice Medrich at Cocolat, Lindsey Remolif Shere at Chez Panisse, Emily Luchetti at Stars, Mary Cech at Cypress Club, Janet Rikala Dalton at Cypress Club, and Elizabeth Falkner at Elka.

So when Michael Mina, a young chef I'd worked with at Tribeca Grill, suggested I come out to be his assistant in a restaurant called Aqua that was slated to open in a few months, I decided to move. I didn't know a soul in San Francisco; I'd been to Europe, but I'd never been west of New Jersey. Nonetheless, I sold my car and most of my belongings and bought a round-trip ticket.

Two weeks before my departure date, Michael called and told me that there wasn't going to be enough work for me to have more than a part-time job, about twelve or at most eighteen hours a week. "That's okay," I said. "That'll give me the chance to look around, get to know the place, find out what's happening."

Then, the night before I was due to leave, Michael called and said, "Sorry, Sherry, there's no job at all for you." I hit the ceiling. "Well, you just meet me at the airport anyway and get your couch ready for me, because I'm coming, and I'm staying with you."

I didn't tell my family. They knew I'd sold all my stuff, and I didn't want to worry them. I figured that with my round-trip ticket and New York chutzpah, I'd get through. So with $500 in my pocket and two suitcases, I boarded a plane to San Francisco.

Michael reluctantly let me stay on his couch for a night, then I found an apartment to house-sit for a couple of weeks. I arrived on a Monday night, and on Tuesday I hit the ground running. I called every place I could think of.

*M*Y FIRST STOP was the Campton Place Hotel, a landmark four-star luxury boutique hotel with an award-winning restaurant, located right off Union Square in San Francisco's toniest shopping district. The chef, Jan Birnbaum, had just taken over the ovens from chef Bradley Ogden, and he needed a pastry cook. "Can you come in and try out?" he asked, and I was in there the next morning at 9 A.M. This place had a great reputation. By noon I was in his office, negotiating my salary as swing assistant to the pastry chef.

Pastry chefs in restaurants always work long shifts; in hotels like Campton Place, the hours are extraordinary. We catered to sophisticated travelers and were responsible for breakfast, lunch, afternoon tea, dinner, and twenty-four-hour room service. I even decided to make dog biscuits for the pets guests were allowed to bring! I began two of my five weekly shifts at 3 A.M., preparing all of the doughs for the viennoiserie (rich layered doughs for pastries such as croissants and Danish) and the breads, for the biscuits and the corn sticks, and for the other shifts at 10. Unlike the Rainbow Room and Tribeca Grill, we didn't make a million of one item—we made a million *different* pastries and baked goods, all from scratch.

One day, within three weeks of my being hired, the cab I took to work at 3 A.M. had a head-on collision. I was knocked out. When I came to, rather than go to the hospital, I went to work, so worried was I about being late and not getting my breakfast doughs ready for the 7 A.M. breakfast. As I finished my shift, the pastry chef, who had not made my life easy during those three weeks, turned to me and said, "I'm quitting. If you want my job, it's yours." And before I knew it, I was in Jan Birnbaum's office, once again negotiating my deal. I was now pastry chef at Campton Place Hotel, and I remained there for four years, a record.

I joined a group of bakers called the Baker's Dozen, who met regularly to talk about the wonders of baking, ask questions, and share information. Whereas desserts in New York had been about technique, refinement, and flash, here pastry was about flavor, thanks to the fresh ingredients that farmers' markets made available. At Campton Place, I began to create my own style of pastry, inspired by the fruit I found at the markets.

*F*OUR YEARS INTO MY STINT at Campton Place, Jan moved up to Napa and opened a restaurant in Calistoga called Catahoula. He asked me (*coerced* might be a more accurate word for it) to come and work with him, enticing me by granting me full autonomy to create all the breads and pastries I wanted. So I took the job and moved to Napa—without a car!

Sometimes it was tough, being so far away from home, but Mom and Dad sent letters and telegrams of encouragement that kept me going. Slowly I was becoming a Californian. I rode everywhere on my bicycle. The Napa seasons enthralled me. I had arrived after the harvest, and I watched the reddening vines go to sleep, the air peaceful and calm. I loved the cold winter nights. In February the bright yellow mustard began to flower, and in no time it was spring, with flowers everywhere and the vineyards bursting into bright green leaf. Summer in Napa was blazing hot and busy with tourists. I learned to make pastry work in a kitchen with no air-conditioning, where the temperature often reached 100°F. In the fall the whole valley lived and breathed the grape harvest. I learned about grapes, wine, and wine regions from the wine people who came to the restaurant. Calistoga became a time of discovery, of learning to pair food and wines, of experiencing new flavors, and of making homey, comforting desserts.

A native of Louisiana, Jan had named Catahoula after his home state's dog, a unique, hardworking hunting dog known to be "worth its salt." The restaurant was in the Mount View Hotel, the oldest hotel in Napa. I decided that historic desserts would be the perfect sweet endings for such a restaurant, and before I began my job, I spent two weeks in the archives of the San Francisco Public Library, researching recipes in cookbooks from the 1800s and the turn of the twentieth century. In this chapter, you'll find many of the desserts I developed at the Mount View Hotel.

CAMPTON PLACE COFFEE CAKE

MAKES 1 BUNDT CAKE

■ ■ ■

This is the densest, moistest coffee cake you'll ever eat, made of alternating layers of rich sour-cream cake and a filling consisting of peaches mixed with cinnamon-cocoa sugar. We always served it in our breakfast basket.

FOR THE CAKE

- 3 cups all-purpose flour
- 2 teaspoons baking powder
- 1 teaspoon baking soda
- 1/2 teaspoon salt
- 6 ounces (1 1/2 sticks) unsalted butter, softened
- 1 1/4 cups sugar
- 3 large eggs, at room temperature
- 2 cups sour cream

FOR THE FILLING

- 1/4 cup sugar
- 1/4 cup packed light brown sugar
- 1 tablespoon ground cinnamon
- 1 tablespoon unsweetened cocoa powder
- 1/4 cup slivered almonds, toasted and finely chopped (optional)
- 12 ounces peaches (4 small or 2 large), peeled, pitted, and cut into 1/2-inch pieces (12 ounces of frozen are fine)

1. **MAKE THE CAKE:** Place a rack in the middle of the oven and preheat the oven to 350°F. Spray a Bundt or Kugelhopf pan with pan spray.

2. Sift together the flour, baking powder, baking soda, and salt three times and set aside.

3. In the bowl of a stand mixer fitted with the paddle attachment, or in a large bowl with a hand mixer, cream the butter and sugar together on medium speed for 5 minutes, or until light and fluffy. Add the eggs one at a time. Scrape down the bowl and paddle after each addition. In 3 additions of each, add the sour cream and the sifted dry ingredients, alternating the wet and dry ingredients, and beat on low speed until all of the ingredients are blended.

4. **MAKE THE FILLING:** In a medium bowl, mix together the sugar, brown sugar, cinnamon, cocoa powder, and almonds, if using.

5. Scoop 1 1/2 cups of the cake batter into the prepared Bundt pan, and using a small metal spatula, spread it evenly to cover the bottom. Sprinkle on 1/4 cup of

the sugar mixture and dot with one third of the peach chunks. Scoop in 2 cups of the batter and spread evenly. Sprinkle with ¼ cup of the sugar mixture and dot with another third of the peach chunks. Add another 2 cups of batter, spreading it evenly. Sprinkle with the remaining sugar mixture and dot with the remaining peaches. Spoon in any remaining batter and spread over the peaches.

6. Bake for 35 minutes. Rotate the pan from front to back and bake for another 20 to 25 minutes, until a tester inserted into the center of the cake comes out clean. Allow to cool in the pan on a rack for 30 minutes, then invert, remove the pan, and allow the cake to cool completely upside down on the rack.

CAMPTON CORN STICKS

■ ■ ■

This is a rich, sweet version of old-fashioned corn bread, baked in corn stick pans. We would heat the pans in the oven until very hot before spooning in the batter. Make sure your pans are well seasoned, or the corn sticks will stick.

1 cup yellow cornmeal

1 cup cake flour

¼ cup sugar

2 teaspoons baking powder

1¼ teaspoons salt

2 large eggs

2 cups heavy cream, right from the refrigerator

4 ounces (1 stick) unsalted butter, melted and still warm (90°F)

1 cup fresh or frozen (not thawed) corn kernels

1 cup finely diced red and green bell peppers (optional)

1. Place a rack in the middle of the oven and preheat the oven to 475°F for 20 minutes. Place corn stick pans on a baking sheet and place in the oven while you mix the batter (or if you have only one pan, bake the corn sticks in batches).

2. Sift together the cornmeal, cake flour, sugar, baking powder, and salt. Set aside.

3. In a separate bowl, whisk together the eggs and cream. Stream in the warm melted butter. Add the dry ingredients and whisk together, being careful not to overmix. Fold in the corn and the diced peppers, if using.

4. Check your pans: They should be very hot and sizzle when you drop batter onto them. If they don't, return them to the oven for a few minutes, then fill. Protect your work surface by putting an upside-down half sheet pan on it. Place the hot corn stick pans on the inverted sheet pan and spray them with pan spray. Either spoon the batter into the molds or cut an inch off the end of a disposable pastry bag, insert a #6 tip, and pipe in the batter. Fill almost full. The pans should sizzle as soon as the batter hits them. Return the pans to the oven and bake the corn sticks until brown around the edges and slightly puffed, 12 to 15 minutes. Carefully remove from the oven and invert onto a rack. Serve hot. If baking in batches, place the pans back in the oven for 10 minutes to reheat before baking the next batch.

CAMPTON PLACE MUFFINS

■ ■ ■

A good breakfast menu must have a great muffin on it. Mine can be filled with any type of fruit—blueberries or chopped peaches, sliced bananas, chopped apples or figs. If you want them to be sweeter and cakier, add another ¼ cup sugar.

1 cup cake flour
1 cup all-purpose flour
¾ cup sugar
1 teaspoon baking powder
½ teaspoon salt
2 large eggs, at room temperature
1 cup sour cream
¼ cup milk
1½ teaspoons vanilla extract
3 ounces (¾ stick) unsalted butter, melted and still warm (90°F)
1½ cups fruit, such as blueberries (fresh or frozen; see Sherry's Secrets), chopped apples, or chopped figs

1. Place a rack in the middle of the oven and preheat the oven to 375°F. Spray a muffin tin with pan spray or line with paper liners.

2. Sift together the cake flour, all-purpose flour, sugar, baking powder, and salt. In a bowl, whisk together the eggs, sour cream, milk, vanilla, and melted butter. Whisk in the flour mixture, then fold in the fruit. Spoon the batter into the muffin cups, filling the cups three-quarters full.

3. Bake for 15 minutes. Rotate the tin from front to back and bake for another 10 to 15 minutes, until the muffins are lightly browned, firm to the touch, and a tester inserted in the center comes out clean. Remove from the oven and allow to cool in the tin on a rack for 15 minutes, then remove the muffins from the tin and allow to cool completely on the rack.

VARIATIONS

Fold in with the fruit:
½ cup unsweetened shredded coconut
2 cups shredded carrots
½ cup chopped walnuts or pecans
½ cup Fat Raisins (page 364), drained

Sherry's Secrets

When using frozen blueberries, toss them first in a very small amount of flour—just enough to coat them—to prevent them from bleeding into the batter.

CAMPTON PLACE PANCAKES

MAKES 12 TO 15 PANCAKES

■ ■ ■

I always tell young chefs that they can get very good training working on a breakfast line. I have the utmost respect for these cooks: eggs are not forgiving, and people always want everything fast and fresh. Watching our amazing chefs, Jim Dowling and Scotty Lenau, pump out 120 meals a morning was like watching a beautifully choreographed dance. It's no wonder we were known for our breakfasts at Campton Place. For eight years running, the hotel was voted first in the city for its food. These pancakes are easy to make and foolproof, as long as your griddle is hot enough. Serve with the apple cider butter and sautéed apple, or be traditional and top them with maple syrup.

FOR THE TOPPING
- 4 ounces (1 stick) unsalted butter, softened
- 1 Fuji, Braeburn, or Granny Smith apple, peeled, cored, and cut into 1/2-inch cubes
- 1/4 cup apple cider

FOR THE PANCAKES
- 1 cup all-purpose flour
- 1 cup cake flour
- 1/4 cup whole wheat flour
- 3 tablespoons sugar
- 2 teaspoons baking powder
- 1 teaspoon baking soda
- 1/4 teaspoon salt
- 1/4 teaspoon ground cinnamon
- 2 large eggs
- 2 cups buttermilk
- 1 teaspoon vanilla extract
- 2 ounces (1/2 stick) unsalted butter, melted

1. **MAKE THE TOPPING:** Melt 2 tablespoons of the butter in a medium nonstick skillet over medium-high heat. Add the apple and sauté until softened and slightly caramelized, about 8 minutes. Add the cider and cook, stirring, for 3 minutes, until the apples are tender and the sauce is slightly thick.

2. Remove from the heat and transfer to a food processor fitted with the steel blade. Process until smooth and allow to cool to room temperature.

3. Beat the remaining 6 tablespoons butter until fluffy. Add the apple mixture and stir well to combine. Set aside.

4. **MAKE THE PANCAKES:** Sift together the flours, sugar, baking powder, baking soda, salt, and cinnamon. In a separate bowl, whisk the eggs, then

whisk in the buttermilk, vanilla, and melted butter. Whisk in the flour mixture and combine well, but do not overmix.

5. Heat a griddle until hot. Ladle the batter onto the hot griddle, about $1/3$ cup per pancake. The batter should sizzle quietly when it hits the surface. Cook until bubbles break through, a couple of minutes, and turn the pancakes over. Cook for another minute, until the pancakes are nicely browned on both sides. Transfer to plates and serve hot, or if making all at once, keep warm in a low oven. Serve with the apple topping.

CAMPTON SHORTCUTS
WITH BERRIES AND CREAM

■ ■ ■

With so few of us on staff and so little time, I had to be creative. These are called shortcuts because the dough is like an easy version of puff pastry. It's a super-rich biscuit dough that is folded and turned like puff pastry, but without the traditional block of butter that is layered into the dough. You can mix the dough in advance and store it in the refrigerator or freezer, ready to cut into squares or triangles, which makes it great for the home cook. I also use the dough as a topping for my Nectarine Cobbler (page 189).

FOR THE DOUGH

- 1½ cups all-purpose flour, plus 6 tablespoons for dusting
- ⅓ cup sugar, plus ⅓ cup for dusting
- 2 teaspoons baking powder
- ¼ teaspoon salt
- 4 ounces (1 stick) cold unsalted butter, cut into ½-inch pieces and frozen for 15 minutes
- 1 large egg
- ½ cup heavy cream
- 2 tablespoons crystallized ginger, cut into ½-inch dice (optional)
- 1 egg beaten with 1 egg yolk, for egg wash

FOR THE BERRIES AND CREAM

- 1 cup heavy cream
- ½ cup crème fraîche
- 2 tablespoons sugar
- 1 pint blueberries or ripe strawberries, hulled and halved

1. **MAKE THE DOUGH:** Sift the 1½ cups flour, the ⅓ cup sugar, the baking powder, and salt into the bowl of a stand mixer fitted with the paddle attachment. Add the partially frozen butter and mix on low speed for 1 to 2 minutes, until the butter is broken down into large lumps that are still visible in the mix. Stop the machine and flatten out any round lumps of butter with your thumb and forefinger. Continue beating on low speed for about 30 seconds. The butter should resemble flattened walnut pieces. (You can also mix this by hand by rubbing the butter into the flour between your thumbs and fingers.)

2. In a separate bowl, whisk together the egg and heavy cream. Pour into the dry ingredients along with the crystallized ginger, if using, and pulse the mixture on and off for 20 to 30 seconds to mix (or mix with your hands or a wooden spoon). The dough should be crumbly and tacky when you take it out of the bowl.

3. Place a piece of parchment paper on your work surface, flour it with 2 table-spoons flour, and scrape out the dough. Begin the three-fold process. Fold the edges of the parchment over, using them to press the dough into a 1-inch-thick square. The dough will be tacky in places. Peel back the paper. Lightly dust the top of the dough with 1 tablespoon flour and flip the dough over. Lightly press it into an even 1-inch-thick 6-x-8-inch rectangle. With the side of your hand, make a crease through the middle of the dough, parallel to the bottom edge. Using the parchment to lift the dough, fold it over at the crease. Peel back the parchment and dust the top of the dough with 1 tablespoon flour. Lightly press out the dough again and turn it 90 degrees. Make a crease in the middle and fold and turn again. Lightly dust the dough again with 1 tablespoon flour. If any pieces have crumbled off the dough and fallen onto the parchment, place them on top of the dough. Crease, fold, and turn one more time. The dough will now be a uniform block. Dust with the remaining 1 tablespoon flour and gently roll out into a 1-inch-thick 6-x-8-inch rectangle. Cover with plastic wrap and place in the freezer for 30 minutes. (At this point, you can refrigerate the dough for 1 day or freeze for up to 1 week. When you are ready to cut the dough, defrost just until the dough is soft enough to cut, and cut while it is semifrozen.)

Sherry's Secrets

The trick to making this act like puff pastry, not like scones, is to be sure not to overmix the dough—you want to be able to see chunks of flattened butter in it. Those little chunks within the dough will act like butter in puff pastry; the dough will puff out, rather than be dense and cake-like.

4. Place a rack in the middle of the oven and preheat the oven to 400°F. Line a baking sheet with parchment paper.

5. Unwrap the dough and place it in front of you so that the smoother side is down. Cut crosswise on the diagonals to make 4 long triangles, then cut from top to bottom and crosswise through the middle to create 8 triangles in all. Flip the triangles over and place them on the baking sheet. You will have scraps at each end that you can use for irregularly shaped shortcuts. Brush the triangles with the egg wash. Generously dust with the 1/3 cup sugar: grab a handful of

the sugar and let it fall through your hand over the dough, from one end of the triangles to the other. Then, with your finger, smooth the sugar evenly over the surface of the dough.

6. Bake for 15 minutes. Rotate the sheet from front to back and bake for another 5 to 8 minutes, until the shortcuts are golden brown.

7. **PREPARE THE BERRIES AND CREAM:** Whip the cream and crème fraîche with the sugar to soft peaks.

8. Serve the shortcuts with a spoonful of whipped cream and berries on the side.

GINGERSNAP TOASTER-OVEN TARTS
WITH PEACH FILLING

MAKES 8 TARTS

■ ■ ■

Here's another one of the magical desserts our tiny staff of three was able to turn out, thanks to a small toaster oven and a shelf in the refrigerator that was large enough to keep the peach filling. We'd pop the tart rectangles into the toaster oven, and then off they'd go, with peach ice cream on the side. You will have more dough than filling here. Make cookies with the leftovers.

FOR THE GINGERSNAP DOUGH
- 2 cups all-purpose flour, plus more for dusting
- 1 teaspoon baking soda
- 4 ounces (1 stick) cold unsalted butter, cut into 1/2-inch pieces
- 2 tablespoons sugar
- 1/2 cup packed light brown sugar
- 1/4 teaspoon salt
- 1 tablespoon ground ginger
- 1 1/2 teaspoons ground cinnamon
- 1/2 teaspoon ground allspice
- 1/8 teaspoon ground cloves
- 1 large egg, at room temperature
- 3 tablespoons blackstrap molasses

FOR THE PEACH FILLING
- 2 tablespoons unsalted butter
- 3 fresh peaches or nectarines, pitted and sliced into eighths, or 24 frozen slices, thawed and drained
- 3 tablespoons sugar
- 1/8 teaspoon ground cinnamon

Sugar for dusting

1. **MAKE THE GINGERSNAP DOUGH:** Sift together the all-purpose flour and baking soda and set aside.

2. In the bowl of a stand mixer fitted with the paddle attachment, or in a large bowl with a hand mixer, cream the butter on medium speed until lemony yellow, about 2 minutes. Scrape down the sides of the bowl and the paddle or beaters. Mix together the sugars, salt, and spices and add to the butter. Continue creaming the mixture on medium speed until it is smooth and lump-free, about 1 minute. Stop the mixer and scrape down the sides of the bowl and the paddle.

3. Add the egg and molasses and beat on medium speed for 1 minute, until they are fully incorporated. Do not overbeat. Scrape down the sides of the bowl. On low speed, add the sifted flour. Beat slowly, until all the dry ingredients are incorporated. Scrape down the sides of the bowl.

4. Remove the dough from the bowl and press it into a ½- to 1-inch-thick disk, wrap it in plastic wrap, and chill in the freezer for 30 minutes or in the refrigerator for 2 hours. (At this point, the dough will keep nicely, well wrapped, in the refrigerator for up to 3 days, or up to 1 month in the freezer.)

5. Remove the dough from the freezer or refrigerator. Roll out the dough between two sheets of parchment or waxed paper to a 12-inch square (the dough will be very moist). Dust with flour if necessary. Place, still between the pieces of paper, in the freezer for 30 minutes.

6. MEANWHILE, MAKE THE FILLING: Heat a large heavy skillet over high heat, add the butter, and allow it to melt and turn light brown, about 5 minutes. Add the peaches or nectarines in a single layer and cook for 1 to 2 minutes, then sprinkle with the sugar and cinnamon. Cook, stirring, until the peaches are tender, 3 to 5 minutes. Remove from the heat and allow to cool. Cut the fruit into ½-inch pieces.

7. Place a rack in the middle of the oven and preheat the oven to 350°F. Line two baking sheets with parchment paper.

8. Remove the dough from the freezer. Pull back the top piece of parchment or waxed paper and dust the dough with flour. Replace the paper, flip the dough over, peel back the paper, and dust on the other side. Cut the dough into sixteen 3-inch squares. Place 1½ tablespoons of filling over 8 of the squares and cover the filling with another square. Pinch the edges of the dough together like ravioli and dust the tarts generously with sugar. Place in the oven and bake for 12 to 18 minutes, until crisp and fragrant. Serve warm (you can rewarm them in a toaster on a low quick setting or in a toaster oven).

Sherry's Secrets

SUGAR AND SPICE

Most recipes instruct the cook to add the spices with the flour. Whenever I am creaming a mixture that contains butter, sugar, and spice, I prefer to add the spice to the fat with the sugar first. Combining the sugar and spice distributes the spice better, and then when the mixture hits the butter, creaming releases the fragrant spice oils.

GIANT GINGERBREAD COOKIES

MAKES 16 LARGE COOKIES

■ ■ ■

The actor-producer-director Henry Winkler stayed at Campton Place for a month while he was filming. Every night when he returned from the set, I sent up a plate of warm cookies. On his last day, I gave him a bag to take home. That night, I happened to be watching *The Tonight Show,* and there was Henry—giving the cookies to Jay Leno! Years later, when I was working at Spago, we catered Henry's fiftieth birthday party at his house. I showed up with these cookies. Henry, who didn't know that I'd been the pastry chef at Campton Place but had never forgotten the cookies, was flabbergasted. All I said, as I presented them to him, was "Jay Leno."

2¼ cups all-purpose flour
2 teaspoons baking soda
¼ teaspoon salt
6 ounces (1½ sticks) unsalted butter, softened
¾ cup packed light brown sugar
¼ cup sugar, plus ⅓ cup for dusting
1¼ teaspoons ground ginger
½ teaspoon ground cinnamon
Pinch of ground cloves (optional)
1 large egg
¼ cup blackstrap molasses
½ cup crystallized ginger, chopped

1. Place a rack in the middle of the oven and preheat the oven to 350°F. Line two baking sheets with parchment paper.

2. Sift together the flour, baking soda, and salt and set aside.

3. In the bowl of a stand mixer fitted with the paddle attachment, or in a large bowl with a hand mixer, cream together the butter, brown sugar, the ¼ cup sugar, the ginger, cinnamon, and cloves, if using, for 1 minute at medium speed. Stop the machine, scrape down the sides of the bowl and the paddle or beaters, and add the egg and molasses. Blend at medium speed for 1 minute, then scrape down the bowl and paddle. On low speed, add the sifted dry ingredients and then the crystallized ginger. Mix for 30 seconds.

4. Place the ⅓ cup sugar in a bowl. Lightly flour your hands. Divide the dough into 16 pieces and roll into balls about 2 inches in diameter. Roll in the sugar and place on the prepared baking sheets about 2 inches apart.

5. Bake, one sheet at a time, for 12 minutes. Rotate the sheet from front to back and bake for another 5 to 7 minutes, until the cookies are light brown around the edges. Remove from the oven and transfer to a rack to cool. (The cookies will keep, stored airtight, for 2 days.)

COFFEE AND DOUGHNUTS SHERRY'S WAY

MAKES SIXTEEN 2½-INCH DOUGHNUTS AND 16 DOUGHNUT HOLES

■ ■ ■

I was at home, relaxing into my one and only day off, when the phone rang. Julia Child had decided to have an impromptu dinner at Campton Place! I raced to the hotel to make a dessert, barely making it to the kitchen before the guests began to arrive. What would I want to serve Julia if she came to see me at home? Looking around the pastry shop, I spotted a bowl of sourdough starter I'd made up the day before. Wow! Sourdough doughnuts! Perfect! With coffee ice cream—coffee and doughnuts! We printed menus and I went to work. Here buttermilk stands in for the sourdough starter, so you don't need to prepare that. Julia was very happy and sat me down for a late-night chat. I would have traded my day off for that moment any time.

FOR THE COFFEE ICE CREAM

- 2 cups milk
- 1 cup heavy cream
- ½ cup plus 1 tablespoon sugar
- 5 large egg yolks
- ¾ cup strong brewed espresso (regular or decaf)
- 2 tablespoons amaretto
- 1½ teaspoons fresh lemon juice

FOR THE DOUGHNUTS

- ½ ounce fresh yeast or 2 teaspoons active dry yeast
- 1 cup milk, heated to lukewarm (80°F)
- ⅓ cup sugar
- 4 cups all-purpose flour
- 1 cup buttermilk, heated to lukewarm (80°F)
- 1 teaspoon freshly grated nutmeg
- 1 teaspoon grated lemon zest
- 1½ teaspoons salt
- 2 ounces (½ stick) unsalted butter, cut into tablespoon-sized pieces, softened
  Vegetable or peanut oil for deep-frying
- 1 cup Vanilla Sugar (page 349) for dusting

1. **MAKE THE COFFEE ICE CREAM:** Place a 1-quart freezer container in the freezer. Prepare an ice bath for quickly cooling the finished custard: fill a large bowl halfway with ice, add a small amount of water, and nestle a medium bowl inside the ice. The hot custard will be strained into the medium bowl to cool.

2. In a medium nonreactive saucepan, combine the milk, cream, and ¼ cup of the sugar. Place the pan over medium heat and bring the mixture to a simmer. Meanwhile, whisk together the egg yolks and the remaining ¼ cup plus 1 table-

spoon sugar in a medium bowl. Slowly whisk 1 cup of the hot milk into the eggs. The eggs are now warmed, or tempered. Whisking constantly, pour the eggs back into the hot milk. Be sure to scrape all the egg mixture into the pan with a rubber spatula.

3. Place the pan over low heat and insert an instant-read thermometer. Using a heat-resistant rubber spatula, immediately stir the custard. Stir in figure eights around the edge of the pan and into the center. Keep stirring until the temperature reaches 180°F. Remove from the heat. Test for readiness with your spatula: Dip it into the custard, pull it out, and run your finger across the back of the spatula. Your finger should leave a clear trail and the rest of the spatula should remain coated with sauce. If the custard does not run into the finger trail, it is thick enough. If it does run, cook the custard for another minute, or until the consistency is right. Stir in the espresso, amaretto, and lemon juice.

4. Immediately pour the mixture through a fine-mesh strainer into the medium bowl in the ice bath. Stir the custard occasionally for 10 minutes, until cool (40°F) and thickened. It will become thicker as it cools. If there is time, place the custard in the refrigerator and chill for 4 hours. Transfer to an ice cream maker and freeze according to the manufacturer's directions. Once ready, pack in the freezer container and store in the freezer.

Sherry's Secrets

Whenever you are deep-frying pastries, to eliminate the risk of spattering oil, cut the parchment paper under the risen pastry into squares, gently lift a square, and slowly slide the pastry into the oil.

5. MAKE THE DOUGHNUTS: In the bowl of a stand mixer, whisk together the yeast and ½ cup of the milk until the yeast has dissolved. Let stand for 5 minutes, then stir in 1 tablespoon of the sugar and ½ cup of the all-purpose flour, forming a thin batter. Cover this sponge with plastic wrap and let rest at room temperature for 20 to 30 minutes, until bubbles form.

6. Reheat the remaining ½ cup milk to lukewarm. Stir the warm milk, buttermilk, nutmeg, lemon zest, and the remaining ¼ cup plus 1 teaspoon sugar into the sponge. Place the remaining 3½ cups flour and the salt on top of the sponge. Put the bowl on the mixer fitted with the paddle attachment. Mix on low speed

for 2 minutes, or until the dough comes together. Scrape down the bowl and the paddle and change to the dough hook. Increase the speed to medium and knead the dough for 5 minutes. The mixture will be tacky.

7. Turn the speed down to medium-low and add the softened butter, 1 tablespoon at a time. Stop the mixer and scrape down the sides. Mix for 5 minutes, or until the dough is smooth. Scrape the dough from the sides of the bowl, cover the bowl with plastic wrap, and set it aside to rise at room temperature (70°F) until doubled in volume, 1½ to 2 hours.

8. Line two 12-x-17-inch half sheet pans with parchment paper and lightly flour the parchment. When the dough has doubled in volume, turn it out onto a lightly floured work surface, and using a rolling pin, roll it out to a 10-inch square with a thickness of ½ inch. Wrap the dough in plastic wrap and place in the freezer for 20 minutes. Using a 2½-inch doughnut cutter, cut out the doughnuts. Dip the cutter in flour each time to make it easier. Place the doughnuts and the holes on the parchment-covered half sheet pans. Cover with lightly sprayed plastic wrap and let rise for 30 minutes.

9. In a deep heavy skillet or wide deep saucepan fitted with a deep-fry thermometer, heat 3 inches of oil over medium heat to 350°F (or heat the oil in a deep fryer). Cut the parchment that the doughnuts are sitting on into squares, each square holding a doughnut or hole, and carefully slide 4 doughnuts off their parchment squares into the oil. After 30 seconds, use a slotted spoon to carefully flip them over. Brown the other side for 1 minute, then flip the doughnuts once more and cook for another 30 seconds. Remove the doughnuts from the oil and drain them on paper towels for 30 seconds. Coat the tops of the doughnuts with the vanilla sugar while they are still hot and wet with oil. If the doughnuts cool down and dry, the sugar will not stick. Repeat with the remaining doughnuts and the holes.

10. Serve immediately, with the coffee ice cream. Fried doughnuts stay fresh for only about 2 hours.

    NOTE: The doughnuts can be cut out and stored in the freezer for up to 1 week. Place in the freezer on the half sheet pans until frozen hard, then wrap each doughnut tightly in plastic wrap, transfer to a freezer container or freezer bags, and return to the freezer. Remove the plastic, defrost in the refrigerator for about 3 hours, and let sit at room temperature for 10 to 15 minutes before frying.

BRAZIL WET WALNUT SUNDAE WITH ROASTED BANANA ICE CREAM

SERVES 6

■ ■ ■

My friend and colleague Jim Dodge came to Campton Place one day with executives from the California Walnut Marketing Board. I made this dessert, and they liked it so much that they sent me on a trip to Brazil. What a trip! I'll never forget my first sight of Rio, flying in over the water after a twenty-two-hour flight and seeing the statue of Christ the Redeemer towering above the city, welcoming me to Rio with outstretched arms. I got to see the beach at Ipanema and the jungle around Manaus. You'll have ice cream left over here; all the better for your freezer, where it will keep well for a few weeks.

FOR THE ICE CREAM
- 2 ripe but firm bananas, unpeeled
- 2 cups milk
- 3/4 cup heavy cream
- 4 large egg yolks
- 1/2 cup sugar
- 3 tablespoons packed light brown sugar
- 1 1/2 tablespoons dark rum
- 2 teaspoons fresh lemon juice

FOR THE WET WALNUT SAUCE
- 1 cup maple syrup
- 1/4 cup honey
- 2 tablespoons blackstrap molasses
- 1/4 cup packed light brown sugar
- 2 tablespoons dark rum
- 1 teaspoon grated orange zest
- 2 cups walnuts, toasted (see page 378)

FOR THE WHIPPED CREAM
- 1 cup heavy cream
- 1/4 cup crème fraîche
- 2 tablespoons sugar

Cherries for garnish

1. **MAKE THE ICE CREAM**: Place a 1 1/2-quart freezer container in the freezer. Place a rack in the middle of the oven and preheat the oven to 350°F.

2. Roast the bananas. Poke the unpeeled bananas in a few spots with the tip of a paring knife and place on a baking sheet. Roast until they turn black, 10 to 12 minutes. Remove from the oven and allow to cool until you can handle them.

3. Make the ice cream custard. Prepare an ice bath for quickly cooling the finished custard: fill a large bowl halfway with ice, add a small amount of water, and nestle a medium bowl inside the ice. In a medium saucepan, combine the milk

and cream. Place the pan over medium heat and bring the milk to a simmer. At the simmer, remove the pan from the heat.

4. Meanwhile, whisk together the egg yolks, sugar, and brown sugar in a medium bowl. Ladle out ½ cup of the hot milk and drizzle it slowly into the eggs while whisking. Once the ½ cup of milk is incorporated into the eggs and the eggs are warmed, pour the mixture back into the hot milk, whisking constantly. Be sure to scrape all the eggs into the pan with a rubber spatula. Place the pan over low heat and insert an instant-read thermometer. Immediately stir the custard with a heat-resistant rubber spatula. Stir in figure eights around the edge of the pan and into the center. Keep stirring until the consistency is like thick cream. The custard is done when the temperature reaches 180°F. Test for readiness with your spatula: dip it into the custard, pull it out, and run your finger across the back of the spatula. Your finger should leave a clear trail and the rest of the spoon should remain coated. If the custard does not run into the finger trail, it is thick enough and can be taken off the heat. If it does run, cook the custard for another minute, or until the consistency is right.

5. Remove the pan from the heat and immediately pour the mixture through a fine-mesh strainer into the bowl in the ice bath. Stir in the rum and lemon juice. Peel and mash the bananas. Whisk 1 cup of the custard into the mashed bananas, then pour the bananas into the custard and blend into the custard with a handheld blender. To cool evenly, stir the custard occasionally for 5 to 10 minutes, until the temperature drops to 40°F. The custard will become thicker as it cools. If possible, chill the mixture in the refrigerator before freezing in an ice cream maker, following the manufacturer's directions. You will have about 1 quart.

6. MAKE THE WET WALNUT SAUCE: In a large saucepan, combine all of the ingredients for the sauce except the walnuts and bring to a boil. (The saucepan should be at least double the volume of the ingredients because they boil up and can easily overflow.) Boil gently until the mixture is thick, then stir in the walnuts. Remove from the heat.

7. MAKE THE WHIPPED CREAM: Combine the heavy cream, crème fraîche, and sugar and whip to medium peaks.

8. To serve, place 2 or 3 scoops of ice cream in each bowl. Top with the warm sauce, then with the whipped cream. Serve at once. Any leftover sauce will keep for up to a week in the refrigerator.

TRIPLE SILKEN PUMPKIN PIE

MAKES ONE 9-INCH TORTE, SERVING 8 TO 10

■ ■ ■

This incredible triple-layer creation is a grown-up twist on pumpkin pie. It consists of one layer of pumpkin custard, one layer of whipped cream, and one layer of caramel-pumpkin mousse. The pie does require some thinking ahead and a bit of work, but what you end up with for Thanksgiving is well worth the effort. It became a tradition at Campton Place. (For a simpler version, you can also double the pumpkin custard layer and omit the other layers.)

Dough for single-crust Pâte Brisée (page 371)

FOR THE PUMPKIN CUSTARD LAYER
- 2 tablespoons sugar
- 1/4 teaspoon ground ginger
- 1/4 teaspoon ground cinnamon
- 1 large egg
- 1/2 cup packed dark brown sugar
- 6 tablespoons plain canned pumpkin (not pie filling)
- 1/4 cup sour cream
- 6 tablespoons heavy cream
- 1 tablespoon brandy

FOR THE WHIPPED CREAM LAYER
- 3/4 cup heavy cream
- 1/2 cup crème fraîche
- 2 teaspoons sugar
- 2 teaspoons maple sugar (available at whole foods stores, or see Sources)

FOR THE CARAMEL-PUMPKIN MOUSSE LAYER
- 1/2 cup heavy cream
- 3 tablespoons water
- 2 1/4 teaspoons (1 package) powdered gelatin
- 2 tablespoons light brown sugar
- 1/2 teaspoon ground cinnamon
- 1/2 teaspoon ground ginger
- 3/4 cup plus 3 tablespoons sugar
- 1/2 teaspoon fresh lemon juice
- 3/4 cup plain canned pumpkin (not pie filling)
- 3 large egg whites
- 1/8 teaspoon cream of tartar

Whipped cream for garnish (optional)

1. Roll the dough out to a 16-inch circle, 1/4 inch thick; you will need only about two thirds of the pastry. Freeze the rest for later use. Press the pastry into the bottom and up the sides of a 9-x-2 1/2-inch springform pan. The extra dough on the sides will compensate for shrinkage. Place in the freezer for 30 minutes. Re-

move from the freezer and trim away the excess dough from the rim of the pan. Prebake, following the directions on page 372, until golden brown. Allow to cool completely on a rack.

2. **MAKE THE PUMPKIN CUSTARD LAYER:** Place a rack in the middle of the oven and preheat the oven to 325°F.

3. In a medium bowl, whisk together the sugar, ginger, and cinnamon. Add the egg and whisk until smooth. Whisk in the brown sugar, pumpkin, sour cream, heavy cream, and brandy. Pour the mixture into the springform pan. Cover the pan with a sheet of buttered aluminum foil (buttered side down) and bake until the custard is just set, about 1 hour. Remove from the oven and allow to cool completely. (The recipe can be prepared to this point up to 2 days in advance and refrigerated.)

4. **MAKE THE WHIPPED CREAM LAYER:** Combine the cream and crème fraîche in a large bowl, and using a hand mixer, beat until it starts to thicken. Add the sugar and maple sugar and continue beating until stiff. Spread in an even layer on top of the cooled or chilled pumpkin custard and refrigerate.

5. **MAKE THE CARAMEL-PUMPKIN MOUSSE LAYER:** Whip the cream until it forms soft peaks. Chill in the refrigerator until ready to use. Place 2 tablespoons of the water in a small bowl and sprinkle the gelatin over the top. Stir, then let it bloom (soften) while you prepare the caramel.

6. Combine the brown sugar, cinnamon, and ginger in a bowl and set aside. In a heavy saucepan, combine the ¾ cup sugar, the remaining 1 tablespoon water, and the lemon juice and cook over high heat until the mixture turns a deep amber color, at about 335°F on a candy thermometer. This will take 4 to 5 minutes. Remove from the heat.

7. Remove the caramel from the stove and wait until the bubbles subside. Stir in the brown sugar mixture. Add the softened gelatin and stir to dissolve. Whisk in the canned pumpkin and set aside.

8. Using the hand mixer, beat the egg whites until they foam. Add the cream of tartar and 1 tablespoon of the remaining sugar and beat. Continue to beat, adding the remaining 2 tablespoons sugar in a slow, steady stream. Beat until the egg whites are stiff and shiny, about 2 minutes.

9. Lighten the warm caramel-pumpkin mixture by folding in one third of the beaten egg whites, using a whisk, preferably a balloon whisk. Pour the remaining egg whites over the top and carefully fold them into the pumpkin mixture using a rubber spatula. Fold in the chilled whipped cream.

10. Carefully pour the caramel-pumpkin mousse mixture over the whipped cream layer and smooth the top. Refrigerate for 2 hours, or until set. (The pie can be made up to a day in advance.)

11. To serve, gently remove the springform ring from the pie and set the pie on a plate. Garnish with additional whipped cream if desired.

BANANA CRÈME BRÛLÉE "PIE"

SERVES 6

■ ■ ■

Here's a banana cream pie with a twist: the pastry is puff pastry, the filling is crème brûlée that is baked in a pan, and the bananas, marinated in a heavenly spiced citrus marinade, are hidden beneath a thick layer of sweet whipped cream.

1/2 cup fresh orange juice (from 1 large orange)
1 tablespoon fresh lemon juice
2 tablespoons sugar
2 tablespoons light brown sugar
1 vanilla bean, split, seeds scraped out and reserved
2 tablespoons Tia Maria or other coffee liqueur
2 ripe but firm bananas, sliced
1 sheet all-butter puff pastry (see Sources), cut to 4 x 8 inches, 1/8 inch thick
2 ounces bittersweet chocolate, finely chopped
Crème Brûlée (page 359), made through Step 4 but baked in a 9-x-13-inch baking dish lined with a silicone mat and frozen overnight

FOR THE TOPPING
1 cup heavy cream
1/2 cup crème fraîche
2 tablespoons sugar

1. Combine the orange juice, lemon juice, sugar, brown sugar, seeds from the vanilla bean, and liqueur in a medium bowl and stir to combine. Add the bananas to the bowl. Toss to coat thoroughly and let macerate while you bake the pastry.

2. Place a rack in the middle of the oven and preheat the oven to 375°F. Line a baking sheet with parchment paper.

3. Place the piece of puff pastry on the parchment, top with another sheet of parchment, and top with another baking sheet. Place in the middle of the oven and bake for 20 minutes. Reduce the heat to 350°F. Remove the top baking sheet and parchment and continue to bake for another 20 to 25 minutes, until the puff pastry is dry and dark golden brown. Remove from the oven and allow to cool; place the puff pastry on a cookie sheet or transfer to a platter.

4. Melt the chocolate in a microwave-safe bowl at 50 percent power for 2 to 3 minutes or in a heatproof bowl set over a saucepan of simmering water. Stir until smooth, then, using a spatula, smear evenly over the top of the pastry. Allow to cool. Line a cutting board with parchment paper.

5. Invert the frozen crème brûlée onto the cutting board, remove the silicone mat, and trim to a 4-x-8-inch rectangle. Using a wide spatula, place it on top of the pastry. Drain the bananas and layer them over the crème brûlée.

6. **MAKE THE TOPPING:** Whip the cream, crème fraîche, and sugar together until very stiff. Spread over the bananas in a thick, even layer. Refrigerate the "pie" for at least 30 minutes, or up to 4 hours.

7. Just before serving, using a serrated knife dipped in hot water and wiped dry between cuts, cut into 6 pieces. Serve at once.

CAMPTON PLACE BAR NUTS

MAKES 4 CUPS

■ ■ ■

In addition to all the desserts, the pastry kitchen was responsible for the bar nuts that were consumed by the pound every night. We used a mix of nuts and roasted them with rosemary, salt, pepper, and olive oil. Since each type of nut bakes at a slightly different rate (it has to do with their fat content), you need to bake them on separate baking sheets. Then combine when they're all nicely browned.

1 cup almonds
1 cup cashews
1 cup walnuts
1 cup hazelnuts
1/2 cup olive oil
1/4 cup dried rosemary, finely chopped
1 tablespoon freshly ground black pepper
3 tablespoons coarse salt or fleur de sel (see Sources)

1. Place racks in the upper and lower thirds of the oven and preheat the oven to 325°F.

2. Place each type of nut in a different bowl. Toss each type with 2 tablespoons of the olive oil and sprinkle with 1 tablespoon of the rosemary. Divide the pepper and salt evenly among the bowls and toss to coat the nuts.

3. Line four small baking sheets with parchment paper and spread the nuts on them (if you have only two baking sheets, bake the nuts in batches). Bake the nuts two sheets per rack, shaking the pans from time to time and rotating from top to bottom and from front to back halfway through, for 15 to 20 minutes, until they are golden brown and sizzling. Remove from the oven and allow to cool. If not using the nuts within 2 days, store airtight in the freezer.

REAL DOGGY TREATS

■ ■ ■

Nowadays many hotels allow dogs, but back then, Campton Place Hotel was one of the only hotels in San Francisco (or anywhere) to do so. I created this recipe for dog biscuits, which we would leave in the rooms of guests such as Joan Rivers and Helen Gurley Brown, who arrived with their dogs. Our housemen would leave a plate of cookies labeled "People Treats" and a silver platter of these "Doggy Treats."

2 large eggs
1 tablespoon vegetable oil
1 tablespoon honey
3/4 cup chicken stock
3 cups whole wheat flour
1/2 cup cornmeal
   All-purpose flour for dusting
1 egg beaten with 1 egg yolk, for egg wash (optional)

1. Whisk together the eggs, vegetable oil, honey, and chicken stock. Whisk in 1 1/2 cups of the whole wheat flour. Using a large wooden spoon, or in the bowl of a stand mixer fitted with the paddle attachment, fold in the remaining 1 1/2 cups flour and the cornmeal. Knead the mixture into a stiff dough, wrap in plastic wrap, and refrigerate for 1 hour.

2. Place a rack in the lowest position of the oven and preheat the oven to 350°F. Line two baking sheets with parchment paper.

3. Lightly flour your work surface and roll out the dough to a thickness of 1/2 inch. Cut into the desired shapes and place on the baking sheets. Press together the scraps, reroll, and cut out more treats until all of the dough is used. Brush with egg wash if desired.

4. Bake, one sheet at a time, for 12 minutes, rotate the baking sheet from front to back, and bake for another 5 to 8 minutes, until the treats are nicely browned. Remove from the oven and allow to cool. Serve with a big bowl of Fiji Water. If you are not planning to use the treats within 2 days, store airtight in the refrigerator or freezer.

APPLE-BUTTERSCOTCH GRUNT

SERVES 6

■ ■ ■

A grunt is an old-fashioned American dessert. The name suggests the noise one makes after eating an entire dessert, which you might be tempted to do here. You'll see when you make it that *grunt* is another word for a crumble or crisp. I like to use Black Jonathan apples for this; I get them at the farmers' market. Other apples that work well are Granny Smiths and Pink Ladies.

1. **MAKE THE CRUMBLE TOPPING:** Place a rack in the middle of the oven and preheat the oven to 350°F. Line a baking sheet with parchment paper.

2. In a food processor fitted with the steel blade, or in the bowl of a stand mixer fitted with the paddle attachment, combine all of the topping ingredients and pulse or beat until the mixture is crumbly. Sprinkle onto the parchment-lined baking sheet in an even layer.

3. Place in the oven and bake for 10 minutes. Rotate the pan from front to back, stir the crumble topping, and bake for another 3 to 4 minutes, until the mixture is nicely browned. Remove from the oven and allow to cool. (You can keep this in an airtight

FOR THE CRUMBLE TOPPING
- 1 cup all-purpose flour
- 3/4 cup almond flour (available at whole foods stores, or see Sources)
- 2/3 cup confectioners' sugar
- 2 tablespoons light brown sugar
- 1/4 teaspoon ground cinnamon
- 1/4 teaspoon salt
- 4 ounces (1 stick) unsalted butter, softened
- 1 1/2 teaspoons blackstrap molasses

FOR THE FILLING
- 2 ounces (1/2 stick) unsalted butter
- 1 vanilla bean, split, seeds scraped out and reserved
- 1/2 cup sugar
- 1/4 cup packed light brown sugar
- 1 tablespoon blackstrap molasses
- 1 1/2 pounds apples, such as Black Jonathan, Granny Smith, or Pink Lady, peeled, cored, and cut into eighths
- 1/4 cup Calvados (apple brandy)
- 1/2 cup apple juice
- 1/4 cup fresh lemon juice (from 1–2 lemons)
- 1/2 cup heavy cream

Calvados Ice Cream (page 148) or Seven-Bean Vanilla Ice Cream (page 340)

container in the freezer for several weeks. Warm briefly in a 350°F oven before topping the apple filling.)

4. **MAKE THE FILLING:** Melt the butter in a large heavy skillet over medium heat. Cook until the milk solids separate out and you begin to see them browning and the butter is a golden brown. Add the vanilla seeds. Stir in the sugar, brown sugar, and molasses. Stir until the sugar melts, then add the apples. Cook, stirring, until the apples have caramelized, about 10 minutes. Remove the pan from the heat, add the Calvados, and stir together. Add the apple juice and lemon juice, return to the heat, and bring to a boil. Cook for 2 minutes and add the heavy cream. Cook for 1 minute and remove from the heat.

5. Place the warm filling in bowls and cover with the topping. Serve with the ice cream.

CALVADOS ICE CREAM

SERVES 6

■ ■ ■

I've put some apple into vanilla ice cream by fortifying the ice cream with Calvados, the apple brandy made in Normandy. What better accompaniment for an apple dessert, especially apple pie à la mode?

2 cups heavy cream
¾ cup milk
2 vanilla beans, split, seeds scraped out; seeds and beans reserved
6 large egg yolks
⅔ cup sugar
3 tablespoons Calvados (apple brandy)

1. Place a 1-quart freezer container in the freezer.

2. In a medium nonreactive saucepan, combine the cream, 6 tablespoons of the milk, and the vanilla seeds and beans. Place the pan over medium heat and bring to a simmer. Turn off the heat, cover tightly with plastic wrap, and allow the cream mixture to infuse for 30 minutes.

3. Prepare an ice bath: fill a large bowl halfway with ice, add a small amount of water, and nestle a medium bowl in it. Combine the egg yolks and sugar in a medium bowl and whisk them together.

4. Remove the plastic wrap from the infused cream mixture, return to the heat, and bring back to a simmer. Remove from the heat and slowly whisk ½ cup into the eggs. Once the cream is incorporated into the eggs, whisk the eggs back into the cream. Be sure to scrape all the eggs into the pan with a rubber spatula.

5. Place the pan over low heat and immediately begin to stir the custard with a heat-resistant spatula. Stir in figure eights, around the edge of the pan and into the center. After about 2 minutes, the custard will begin to thicken. Keep stirring until the consistency is like thick cream. The custard is done when the temperature reaches 180°F on an instant-read thermometer. Test for readiness with your spatula: Dip it into the custard, pull it out, and run your finger across the back of the spatula. Your finger should leave a clear trail, and the rest of the

spatula should remain coated with custard. If the custard does not run into the finger trail, it is thick enough and can be taken off the heat. If it does run, cook it for another minute, or until the consistency is right.

6. Immediately remove the pan from the heat and pour the mixture through a fine-mesh strainer into the medium bowl in the ice bath. Stir in the remaining 6 tablespoons milk and stir the mixture occasionally until the mixture is cold. Stir in the Calvados. If possible, chill for an hour or two in the refrigerator before freezing.

7. Transfer the mixture to an ice cream maker and freeze according to the manufacturer's directions. Transfer the ice cream to the freezer container and place in the freezer for at least 2 hours to firm.

MANGO UPSIDE-DOWN CAKE
WITH BLUEBERRIES

■ ■ ■

The top of this cake looks like a big sunflower. It was inspired by the sunflowers that I saw everywhere in the wine country.

FOR THE TOPPING

- 3 ounces (¾ stick) unsalted butter
- 1 cup packed light brown sugar
- 2 tablespoons dark rum
- 2 mangoes, peeled and cut into very thin slices
- 1 cup blueberries

FOR THE CAKE

- 1½ cups all-purpose flour
- 1½ teaspoons baking powder
- ½ teaspoon salt
- 4 ounces (1 stick) unsalted butter, softened
- 1 cup sugar
- 3 large eggs, at room temperature
- 1 teaspoon vanilla extract
- 1 teaspoon dark rum
- ¾ cup milk

1. Place a rack in the middle of the oven and preheat the oven to 350°F. Spray a 9-inch round cake pan with pan spray and line with parchment paper. Spray the parchment.

2. **MAKE THE TOPPING:** Melt the butter and mix with the brown sugar and rum. Spread over the parchment in the cake pan in an even layer. Fan the mango slices over the butter mixture, leaving a space in the center. Place ½ cup of the blueberries around the edge and the remaining ½ cup blueberries in the center and set aside.

3. **MAKE THE CAKE:** Sift together the flour, baking powder, and salt two times. Set aside.

4. In the bowl of a stand mixer fitted with the paddle attachment, or in a large bowl with a hand mixer, cream the butter and sugar on medium speed until light and fluffy, about 2 minutes. Add the eggs one at a time, scraping down the bowl after each addition. Add the vanilla and rum.

5. At low speed, add the milk and the flour mixture, alternating wet and dry ingredients.

6. Pour the batter over the mangoes and blueberries. Bake for 20 minutes. Rotate the pan from front to back and bake for an additional 15 to 20 minutes, until a

tester inserted in the center comes out clean. Remove from the oven and let rest for 15 minutes in the pan, then run a knife around the inside of the pan. Flip onto a serving platter and serve while still warm.

Sherry's Secrets

PEELING AND SLICING MANGOES

I like to use a Swiss peeler (also called a Y-peeler) to peel mangoes. Cut off the ends of the fruit and then peel straight down the sides to remove all the skin. Stand the mango up on a flat end and slice straight down on either side of the pit to remove the flesh in two large pieces. Lay the pieces down on the flat side and slice on an angle using a serrated knife. Cut off the flesh from the two narrow edges of the pit and slice it.

BUTTERMILK PIE

■ ■ ■

This rich double-crusted pie is almost like a cake with a buttermilk filling. Jared Doumani, who worked at Catahoula (and whose father, Carl, owned the nearby Stags' Leap Winery in Napa and now owns Quixote), loved this dessert. He would come into work just as the pies were coming out of the oven. As they cooled down next to the hot line where he worked, he'd step off the line and sneak small slices. If I didn't keep my eye on him, he'd eat half a pie before the dessert rush.

I like to serve this with a rhubarb and strawberry compote. Note that the dough is very moist and requires several hours in the refrigerator before you can roll it out and line the pie dish.

FOR THE DOUGH

- 4 cups all-purpose flour
- 2 teaspoons baking powder
- 1/2 teaspoon salt
- 8 ounces (2 sticks) unsalted butter, softened
- 1 cup sugar
- 2 large eggs
- 2 tablespoons milk
- 2 teaspoons vanilla extract

- 1 egg beaten with 1 egg yolk, for egg wash
- 3 tablespoons sugar for sprinkling

FOR THE FILLING

- 2/3 cup sugar
- 5 tablespoons all-purpose flour
- 1/2 teaspoon salt
- 1 teaspoon grated lemon zest
- 1/4 teaspoon ground cinnamon

- 1 tablespoon plus 1 teaspoon butter
- 2 1/2 cups buttermilk
- 2 large eggs
- 1/4 cup fresh lemon juice (from 1–2 lemons)
- 2 teaspoons vanilla extract
- 1 teaspoon Ginger Juice (page 364)

FOR THE RHUBARB AND STRAWBERRY COMPOTE

- 1 cup verjus (available at gourmet markets and whole foods stores, or see Sources)
- 1/2 cup fresh orange juice (from 1 large orange)
- 1/2 vanilla bean, split, seeds scraped out and reserved
- 1/2 cup sugar
- 2 cups 1/2-inch pieces peeled rhubarb
- 2 cups halved fresh strawberries

1. **MAKE THE DOUGH**: Sift together the flour, baking powder, and salt and set aside.

2. In the bowl of a stand mixer fitted with the paddle attachment, or in a large bowl with a hand mixer, cream the butter and sugar on medium speed 2 to 3 minutes. Add the eggs one at a time, scraping down the bowl and paddle or beaters after each addition.

3. Combine the milk and vanilla, and with the mixer at low speed, add in 2 or 3 additions, alternating with the sifted dry ingredients. The dough will be extremely sticky. Scrape out onto a piece of lightly floured plastic wrap, cover, and refrigerate for at least 2 hours.

4. Divide the dough into 2 pieces. Roll out to 12-inch circles. Since the dough will be very wet, the best way to do this is to generously dust sheets of parchment with flour, dust the dough with flour, and roll out between the sheets. Pull the parchment up and lightly dust the dough on both sides each time you roll. Place the rolled-out dough on two baking sheets and refrigerate for 30 minutes to 1 hour, until slightly firm.

5. Place a rack in the middle of the oven and preheat the oven to 350°F. Spray with pan spray or butter a 10-inch Pyrex pie dish.

6. Remove one piece of rolled-out dough from the refrigerator and line the pie dish, gently easing the dough up the sides of the dish. Keep in the refrigerator while you make the filling.

7. **MAKE THE FILLING**: Place the sugar, flour, salt, lemon zest, cinnamon, and butter in a medium bowl and work together with your fingers or by rubbing between your palms until there is no sign of butter. Slowly whisk in the buttermilk. Whisk in the eggs one at a time, then whisk in the remaining filling ingredients.

8. Pour into the lined pie dish. Remove the other piece of dough from the refrigerator. Peel off the top piece of parchment, dust the dough lightly with flour, then cover again. Flip the dough over and peel off the bottom piece of parchment. Invert the dough over the filling, peel off the top piece of parchment, and trim off the excess dough with scissors. Pinch together the bottom and top edges and mark with a fork. Dip the point of a paring knife into some flour and pierce the top crust in the middle. Brush with the egg wash and sprinkle on the sugar in an even layer.

9. Place the pie on a baking sheet. Bake for 1 hour and 10 minutes, or until nicely browned and there is only a slight jiggle when you move it. Remove from the oven and allow to cool on a rack for at least 2 hours before serving.

10. MAKE THE COMPOTE: Combine the verjus, orange juice, vanilla seeds, and sugar in a medium saucepan and bring to a boil. Cook for 2 to 3 minutes, until the sugar is dissolved. Add the rhubarb and cook for 2 to 3 minutes, until the sauce is slightly thickened and the rhubarb is tender. (The sauce can be made up to 2 days ahead and refrigerated.)

11. Just before serving, reheat the sauce and add the strawberries. Toss with the sauce for 30 seconds, or until the strawberries are coated but not cooked.

12. Cut the pie into wedges and serve with the compote on the side.

Spago Hollywood

ONE SUNDAY IN OCTOBER, I CAME HOME AFTER A long day at Catahoula and checked my answering machine. There was a message from Mom; and one from Stephanie, a friend I'd known since working at McDonald's as a teenager; and then one from a strange voice, saying, "Hi, dis is Wolfgang. Call me back at 310 . . . " "Wow," I thought, "my friend Bob back in New York has gotten really good with his impressions" (the last time he'd called, he'd left me a Spam recipe in a foreign accent). I called Bob, forgetting it was 1 a.m. in New York, and woke him up.

"I didn't call you, you loser! Stop drinking and dialing!"

Puzzled, I played back the message and took down the number. Then I dialed. A voice on the other end picked up: "Good evening, Spago." Double yikes! I hung up. It had been Wolfgang Puck, not a prank caller! Why was he calling me? My mind raced. It was late, so I decided to phone back in the morning. Of course, I couldn't sleep.

I waited until 9:30 A.M. and called the number again. This time I asked for Wolfgang. We spoke briefly. He told me he was looking for a pastry chef for Spago and asked when my day off was. I told him the next day. He said, "Okay, den I see you tomorrow." I thought to myself, "Tomorrow! I have no résumé, no plane ticket . . . ," but before I could answer, he said, "Hold on," and Patty, his assistant, picked up the phone. "If you live in Napa, it would be best for you to fly out of Oakland Airport. We'll get you on the nine A.M. flight. Just go to the counter and you can pick up your ticket. Now, how do you spell your name?"

I was late for work and had no time to think about anything except the fact that I didn't have a résumé. I ran to Catahoula, did my shift, and gathered up a collection of laminated recipe cards that I'd put together over the years, illustrations of my dessert creations that I'd drawn and colored.

The next morning, dressed in a black business suit and high heels and carrying a duffel bag filled with pastry tools and chef's garb, I boarded the plane to my next adventure.

I entered Spago through the back kitchen entrance. I walked down a ramp, then deeper down a flight of stairs, and into the kitchen. It looked like the inside of a submarine! And it scared me. When I walked into the dining room, there was Wolfgang Puck sitting by a window overlooking Sunset Boulevard, with Los Angeles extending to the Pacific Ocean. He sat there, a bottle of Evian and two glasses on the table, and my jitters dissipated. Looking back on it, I think I knew that I was meeting a kindred spirit.

We talked about our love for the guest and about the environment Wolf creates in the kitchen, which is one of family, love, and passion. We chatted about our favorite foods, about his love of ginger and other spices. I told him of my passion for working with the farmers of California, and he told me stories of Provence and L'Oustau de Baumanière, the restaurant in Les Baux where he had once worked. It was a match right down to the menus. All I had to show him were those laminated recipe cards. Wolf glanced at the stack, then jumped up from the table and ran over to the bar and back. He held a menu to his chest and explained that years ago when he opened Spago, designers wanted to charge him an arm and a leg to create a cover for his menus. He went on, "I told them that I could do it ten times better, and it vouldn't cost so much!" He flipped over the menu to reveal a hand-drawn illustration, then placed one of my cards directly next to it. It was an identical pear tart!

"Vhen can you start?" he said.

When I came back to Napa later that day, I knew that in January I would be moving to Los Angeles, where the job of Spago pastry chef awaited me.

*T*HE WINTER OF 1994 was the rainiest one L.A. had seen in half a century. For two weeks, it poured nonstop torrential rain, and I wondered if sunny southern California was just a myth. When the Northridge earthquake struck on Martin Luther King Day, I doubted I would last a year in this city.

The restaurant was as challenging as the weather. On the day I arrived, wheeling in my red Sears toolbox, I was sent off to my station in the kitchen with hardly a welcome, quite a shock after the open arms with which I had been received in San Francisco. Starting at Spago was like trying to jump on a train that was moving fast down the track—it was going with or without me, and my only choice was to run as fast as I could and jump on.

Some of the best restaurant advice I had ever gotten was to be the first person in the restaurant and the last one out, so that you learn what everybody does and can begin your shift organized and in a clean kitchen. I decided to arrive every morning at 6 A.M., and for weeks I would arrive before everybody and leave last, with the night dishwasher. My apartment was only a few blocks away, and I loved walking to work along Sunset Boulevard in the quiet predawn.

I scanned the reservation book every day to get to know our guests' names. Our maître d', Michael Dargin, was a gracious man and a dessert lover, and he helped me understand this unique establishment. Perched on a hillside curve above Sunset Boulevard, the original Spago was in an unprepossessing building that Barbara and Wolf had transformed into a restaurant that buzzed. Huge picture windows revealed the lights of the City of Angels spreading out below as far as the eye could see. In the other direction was the open kitchen, located right in the dining room area, where all of the guests could watch Wolfgang and his chefs turn out his signature cuisine, including the California pizzas that had made him famous.

$\mathcal{G}$OING TO SPAGO was like attending a social event. It was a neighborhood restaurant with regular guests, but those regulars happened to be the Hollywood elite—not just movie stars, but also the powerful agents, studio executives, producers, and entertainment lawyers who were "the players" in this town. Our waiters and cooks catered to their every whim. I learned who the guests were, where they should sit, what they liked and didn't like. To this day, I have a book with pages devoted to return guests and their families, with birthdays, favorite desserts, allergies, likes and dislikes. There are hundreds of entries, and you would recognize many of the names.

In the decade that Spago had been open, few changes had been made to the dessert menu. When I got there, it was a bit like taking up residence in someone else's furnished house. Wolfgang wanted me to make changes, and

I was happy to, right away. There were far too many items on the menu (sixteen), so I trimmed it down. Why have four different chocolate cakes when one great one would suffice? The cookies were American confections, and I replaced them with more refined European-style cookies that I had learned to make at the Rainbow Room. Why not offer a dessert soufflé? Wolf said it would be too difficult to run soufflés all the way out to the front of the house from the pastry station, which piggybacked onto the kitchen. I knew that with organization it could be done. After all, we had managed soufflés at the Rainbow Room, where the kitchen was one floor down from the dining room. I put them on the menu, and they were a hit.

*W*OLFGANG SOMETIMES RESISTED the changes he had asked me to make, claiming that customers were attached to the old desserts, like the crème brûlée that I thought was horrible and took off the menu. So although I worked very hard at re-creating the dessert menu, I always made a few of those crème brûlées and had them tucked away for those die-hard guests who absolutely insisted on them. It was a challenging time, but I navigated my way through. I lived and breathed Spago, 24/7.

Most important, I made sure that the customers were happy. Nothing was too much to ask of me, and that, I could see, was the key to success in Hollywood. From my dessert station perched above two coveted tables, I had the perfect spot for looking out on the dining room, and night after night, I watched it fill with luminaries ranging from Madonna to Frank Sinatra to Milton Berle. One night Steven Bochco, creator of many popular television series, came in with his son and his son's friend Leonardo DiCaprio, who couldn't have been more than fourteen years old. Now when Leonardo comes into Spago, all I can think of is watching him sneaking cookies between courses when he was a young teenager.

Wolf soon changed his tone, especially after the actress Suzanne Pleshette, a regular guest, asked him to call me out to the table one night. She picked up a cookie and said to Wolfgang, "Finally, you've got it right!" Then she turned to me and said, "I got one thing to say to you: Bitch, you're gonna make me fat!" And I knew, from that moment on, that no matter how difficult this job was, I was going to be okay.

CAFÉ GLACÉ

■ ■ ■

When Wolfgang's son Byron was little, he would request only one dessert: coffee ice cream. We changed the menu at Spago often, and sometimes coffee ice cream wasn't on it. On one such day, Byron was in for lunch, and I came up with this solution to the problem: I mixed decaf espresso into my vanilla ice cream. Wolfgang, watching me do this, was reminded of a Viennese favorite and asked if he could have some "Viennese café glacé" as well. Voilà! A great lunch dessert special, served complete with whipped cream, chocolate-dipped tuile cookies, and chocolate shavings, was born.

1 pint Seven-Bean Vanilla Ice Cream (page 340) or store-bought vanilla ice cream, slightly softened
½ cup cold brewed espresso
¾ cup heavy cream, whipped to medium-stiff peaks
1 tablespoon finely shaved chocolate or thin chocolate curls
Chocolate-Dipped Tuiles (page 162)

1. Place the bowl of a stand mixer, or a large bowl and the beaters of a hand mixer, and six 4-ounce cups or glasses (or four 6-ounce cups or glasses) in the freezer for 30 minutes.

HOW TO MAKE CURLED CHOCOLATE SHAVINGS

Place an 8-ounce block of chocolate on a microwave-safe plate or a sheet of parchment. Microwave at 50 percent power for 10 seconds, just to warm it very slightly. Remove from the microwave and place on a sheet of parchment paper on your work surface. Place a chef's knife across the chocolate, parallel to the edge of your work surface, with the blade angled away from you at a 45-degree angle. With one hand on the handle and the other holding the tip end, pull the knife toward you, scraping off long curled shavings of chocolate as you go.

Sherry's Secrets

2. Spoon the ice cream into the ice-cold bowl and add the espresso. Using a stand mixer fitted with the paddle attachment or a hand mixer, blend at low speed until smooth. Spoon into the frozen cups or glasses, top with the whipped cream, and sprinkle on the chocolate shavings or curls. Serve immediately, with the cookies, or place in the freezer for up to 4 hours.

CHOCOLATE-DIPPED TUILES

MAKES 36 COOKIES

■ ■ ■

I make these ganache-dipped Viennese cookies to accompany Café Glacé (page 160). You've probably seen packaged versions, but these are the real thing.

FOR THE TUILES
- 2 ounces (1/2 stick) unsalted butter, softened
- 1/2 cup confectioners' sugar
- 1/3 cup plus 1 tablespoon all-purpose flour
- 2 large egg whites, at room temperature

FOR THE GANACHE
- 2 ounces bittersweet chocolate, finely chopped
- 1 tablespoon unsalted butter
- 1/3 cup heavy cream

1. **MAKE THE TUILES:** Place a rack in the middle of the oven and preheat the oven to 325°F. Line a 12-x-17-inch half sheet pan with a silicone baking mat.

2. In the bowl of a stand mixer fitted with the paddle attachment, or in a large bowl with a hand mixer, cream together the butter and confectioners' sugar on medium speed until combined, about 1 minute. Don't overbeat, because tuile batter shouldn't be too aerated. Scrape down the bowl and paddle. Add the flour and mix at medium speed for 30 seconds. Scrape down the bowl and paddle and mix for an additional 15 seconds. Add the egg whites one at a time, scraping down the bowl after each egg white is incorporated. Beat on low speed until the batter is smooth.

3. To form the paper-thin cookies, place three or four 1-tablespoon mounds of batter 3 inches apart on the silicone-lined baking sheet. Using a metal spatula, preferably offset, smear each mound in a 180-degree semicircle, like a windshield wiper. Rotate the baking sheet 180 degrees and smear the other side of the rounds 180 degrees using the same motion, to complete the circle, making 3-inch rounds.

4. Place in the oven and bake for 5 minutes. Rotate the baking sheet from front to back and bake for another 3 to 4 minutes, until the cookies are golden brown. (Be careful not to bake the cookies too long or they will become dark and be

difficult to shape.) Open the oven and place the cookie sheet on the oven door. Using an offset spatula, loosen all of the cookies from the silicone mat, then one by one, lift off the cookies with the spatula and roll up around the handle of a wooden spoon. If the cookies stiffen, return them to the oven for a minute to soften. If this is too difficult (the cookies are hot!), you can either leave them as they are or drape them over a rolling pin. Slide the cookies off the spoon handle. Repeat with the remaining batter. Allow the cookies to cool completely on racks.

5. **MAKE THE GANACHE:** Melt the chocolate and butter in a microwave-safe bowl at 50 percent power for 2 to 3 minutes or in a heatproof bowl set over a saucepan of simmering water, stirring occasionally. Stir until well combined. Pour in the cream and whisk together quickly.

6. Dip the cookies into the ganache, covering them halfway, or fill using a piping bag. Place on racks until the chocolate stiffens, at least 1 hour, then serve. (The cookies will keep for up to 3 days, stored airtight.)

Sherry's Secrets

When you make tuiles, it's important not to overbeat the batter, or the cookies will have too many air bubbles. The key is to add the egg whites last.

CHOCOLATE-COVERED
CHOCOLATE-MINT COOKIES

MAKES 72 COOKIES

■ ■ ■

When I was a Girl Scout, I sold more cookies than anyone in my troop. I knew that Friday, payday, was the day to sell in my neighborhood. I would make my rounds on Friday nights and nab dads with fresh cash in their pockets. Now I buy the cookies by the case every year and give them out to the gang in the kitchen. I developed my own versions of Girl Scout cookies for the launch party of a book that the Girl Scouts produced about inspiring women; Barbara Lazaroff, co-owner of Spago, was featured in the book. The chocolate-covered chocolate-mint cookies were always my favorite. Freeze them in the summer.

1¹/₂ cups all-purpose flour
¹/₂ cup unsweetened cocoa powder
1¹/₄ cups sugar
¹/₂ teaspoon baking powder
¹/₄ teaspoon baking soda
¹/₄ teaspoon salt
6 ounces (1¹/₂ sticks) cold unsalted butter, cut into ¹/₂-inch pieces
2 large egg yolks
1¹/₂ teaspoons peppermint oil (see Sources)
¹/₄ teaspoon vanilla extract
1¹/₂ pounds bittersweet chocolate

1. Place the flour, cocoa, sugar, baking powder, baking soda, and salt in a food processor fitted with the steel blade and pulse a few times to combine the ingredients. Add the butter and pulse to cut the butter into the dry ingredients. Add the egg yolks, peppermint oil, and vanilla and pulse until a dough forms on the blades of the food processor.

2. Remove the dough from the food processor and shape into a 2-inch-thick log. Wrap in plastic wrap or parchment paper and refrigerate for at least 2 hours, or overnight.

3. Place racks in the middle and lower third of the oven and preheat the oven to 350°F. Line baking sheets with parchment paper.

4. Remove the dough from the refrigerator. Cut into ¹/₄-inch-thick disks and arrange ¹/₂ inch apart on the baking sheets. Bake for 10 minutes. Switch the

baking sheets from top to bottom and rotate from front to back and continue to bake for another 3 to 4 minutes, until the cookies are light brown. Remove from the oven and allow to cool on racks. Make sure to let the baking sheets cool between batches. Do not handle the cookies until they are cool, or they'll break; they're very delicate.

5. Melt and temper the bittersweet chocolate following the directions on page 379. Keep the chocolate warm while you dip the cookies.

6. Place a sheet pan upside down on your work surface, next to the melted chocolate. Cover with parchment paper. Dip the cookies one by one in the chocolate, using a fork to turn them over and then lift them out of the chocolate. It helps to tilt the bowl forward by leaning it on a folded kitchen towel.

7. Set the dipped cookies on the parchment, beginning at the far end so you don't drip chocolate on other cookies when you set them down. Allow to cool completely, then store in an airtight container. (The cookies will keep for 3 to 5 days in the refrigerator or freeze for 2 weeks.)

CHOCOLATE-CARAMEL TART

■ ■ ■

This tart is my incarnation of a tart developed by Claudia Fleming, one of the country's premier pastry chefs. It was on the menu at Spago when Hugh Grant came into the restaurant. When the waiter came to take his dessert order, he said, "May I have a yard of sherry?" The waiter answered, "I'm sorry, sir, that is our pastry chef!" "Well, then," said Hugh Grant, "I'll have chocolate-caramel tart instead."

1 cup Creamy Caramel Sauce (page 354)
1 9-inch tart shell made with Pâte Sucrée (page 373) or Chocolate Pâte Sucrée (page 375), prebaked
1/4 teaspoon fleur de sel (see Sources; optional)
8 ounces bittersweet chocolate, finely chopped
3/4 cup heavy cream
1/4 cup milk
2 tablespoons sugar
1 large egg, at room temperature

1. Place a rack in the middle of the oven and preheat the oven to 300°F.

2. Pour the caramel sauce into the bottom of the prebaked tart shell and spread in an even layer. Sprinkle with the fleur de sel, if using. Place in the freezer while you prepare the chocolate filling.

3. Place the chopped chocolate in a heatproof bowl. Combine the cream, milk, and sugar in a heavy saucepan and bring it to a boil over medium heat. Pour over the chopped chocolate. Tap the bowl on the work surface to settle the chocolate into the liquid, then let the mixture sit for 1 minute. Using a rubber spatula, slowly stir in a circular motion, starting from the center of the bowl and working out to the sides. Stir until all the chocolate has melted, about 2 minutes. Beat the egg vigorously in a medium bowl and whisk in the chocolate mixture.

4. Remove the tart shell from the freezer and pour in the chocolate mixture. Bake until just set, 25 to 30 minutes. Remove from the oven and allow to cool on a rack. Refrigerate for 2 hours before serving.

VARIATION

Omit the optional salt and top the caramel with 2 tablespoons chopped dried cherries or Fat Raisins (page 364) before pouring in the chocolate.

RASPBERRY SOUFFLÉS

SERVES 8

■ ■ ■

Before I became the pastry chef at Spago, Wolfgang had resisted having dessert soufflés on the menu, because of the logistics of the pastry kitchen. But we managed them, and the guests loved our soufflés, especially this beautiful, intense raspberry version.

1 pint raspberries, plus more for garnish

3/4 cup sugar, plus 2 tablespoons for dusting the ramekins

2 tablespoons Chambord

1 tablespoon fresh lemon juice

1/2 teaspoon balsamic vinegar

2 tablespoons unsalted butter, softened, for the ramekins

8 large egg whites
Pinch of cream of tartar

1. Combine 1 1/2 cups of the raspberries, 1/4 cup of the sugar, the Chambord, lemon juice, and balsamic vinegar in a medium saucepan and bring to a boil over medium heat. Cook for 4 to 5 minutes, until the liquid is reduced and the raspberries have cooked down to a jam-like consistency. Allow to cool to room temperature.

2. Measure out 1 cup of the sauce and transfer to a large bowl. Reserve the rest in the pan.

3. Place a rack in the lowest position of the oven and preheat the oven to 425°F. Generously butter eight 8-ounce ramekins with the softened butter and dust with the 2 tablespoons sugar, dividing it evenly among the ramekins.

4. Divide the remaining 1/2 cup raspberries among the ramekins. Top the raspberries with the raspberry sauce in the pan.

5. In the bowl of a stand mixer fitted with the whisk attachment, or in a large bowl with a hand mixer, beat the egg whites on low speed for 1 minute, or until they foam. Add the cream of tartar and continue to beat on low speed for 1 minute. Turn the speed to medium and slowly stream in the remaining 1/2 cup sugar while you continue to beat to firm peaks, about 7 minutes. Fold one third of the beaten whites into the reserved 1 cup raspberry sauce to lighten it. Fold in the remaining egg whites. Spoon into the ramekins, mounding the soufflé mixture over the top like cotton candy.

6. Place the ramekins on a baking sheet and bake for 15 to 20 minutes, until the soufflés are puffed and dark golden; they should remain pudding-like on the inside. Serve immediately, garnished with raspberries.

NOTE: You can also make the soufflé in a 2-quart soufflé dish. Bake for 10 minutes at 425°F, then reduce the heat to 350°F and continue to bake for 25 to 30 minutes.

UPSIDE-DOWN CHEESECAKE FLAN

MAKES ONE 9-INCH FLAN

■ ■ ■

Great desserts have a way of becoming fashionable and moving from restaurant to restaurant. In the 1980s it was Crème Brûlée (page 359). In the 1990s it was warm Chocolate Truffle Cakes (page 80). Michel Richard, who I believe is the greatest pastry chef working in America today, invented this simple, yet sophisticated upside-down cheesecake. It's made like a flan, with a dark caramel coating the pan, but instead of a custard, it's a cheesecake. You can make the caramel the day before you prepare the cheesecake, and the cheesecake is best made 1 day before you serve it, so it can chill overnight and so the caramel can melt into a sauce (just as it does with flan).

FOR THE CARAMEL

- ½ cup water
- 1½ cups sugar
- 1 tablespoon fresh lemon juice

FOR THE CHEESECAKE

- 1½ pounds cream cheese, at room temperature
- 1 cup sugar
- 1 vanilla bean, split, seeds scraped out and reserved
- ½ teaspoon vanilla extract
- 1 tablespoon fresh lemon juice
- ½ teaspoon grated orange zest
- 4 large eggs, at room temperature
- 1 cup heavy cream

Fresh berries for serving (optional)

1. **MAKE THE CARAMEL:** In a medium saucepan, combine the water, sugar, and lemon juice. Stir the ingredients together with your fingers, making sure no lumps of dry sugar remain. Brush down the inside of the pan with a little water, using your hand to feel for stray granules of sugar. Cover the saucepan and place it over medium heat for 4 minutes. After 4 minutes, remove the lid, increase the heat, and bring to a boil. Do not stir from this point on. If stray sugar crystals appear on the sides of the pan, brush them down with a wet pastry brush. Insert a candy thermometer. When the temperature reaches 300°F, lower the heat to medium to slow the cooking. Continue to cook the sugar until it reaches 340°F, 10 to 12 minutes more. Immediately remove the pan from the heat and let sit for 2 minutes, or until the bubbles subside.

2. Carefully pour and scrape the caramel into a 9-x-2-inch round cake pan, scraping all of it from the saucepan (take care not to let the caramel touch your fingers—it will be hot!). Let sit for 1 minute. Then, wearing oven mitts, tilt the cake pan so that the bottom and sides are coated. (The caramel can be left at room temperature for as long as overnight.)

3. MAKE THE CHEESECAKE: Place a rack in the middle of the oven and preheat the oven to 325°F.

4. In the bowl of a stand mixer fitted with the paddle attachment, or in a large bowl with a hand mixer, blend the cream cheese and sugar together on low speed for 1 minute, until smooth. Add the vanilla seeds, vanilla extract, lemon juice, and orange zest. Scrape down the sides of the bowl and continue to blend for 2 minutes. Add the eggs one at a time, scraping down the bowl after each addition. While still on low speed, stream in the heavy cream. Pour into the caramel-coated cake pan.

5. Place the cake pan in a roasting pan and place in the oven. Fill the roasting pan with enough hot water to come halfway up the sides of the cake pan. Bake for 1 hour and 30 minutes. Turn the oven off—do not open the oven door—and leave the cheesecake in the oven for another hour. Remove from the oven and allow to cool to room temperature, then cover with plastic wrap and refrigerate overnight. (The cake can be refrigerated for up to 2 days.)

6. To serve, remove from the refrigerator and place a 12-inch (or larger) rimmed plate over the top of the cake pan. Holding the plate down firmly, with your other hand on the bottom of the pan, flip the pan over. Set the plate down, with the cake pan still inverted on it, and wait for a few seconds. Carefully lift off the pan. Serve at room temperature and, if you like, with fresh berries.

CHOCOLATE PURSES

SERVES 8

■ ■ ■

These crispy purses are made with *feuilles de brick,* phyllo-like pastry rounds used in North African cuisine. I fill them with what is actually cold chocolate truffle cake batter (page 80), tie them up with butcher's twine, and bake them. *Feuille de brick* is slightly thicker and more moist than phyllo dough, which can't be substituted here because it is too dry. I made these purses for a dinner that Wolfgang catered for the Democratic National Committee when they came to Los Angeles to decide whether or not to choose the city for the 2000 Democratic National Convention. After dinner the chairperson said, "If we choose Los Angeles, it will be because we want to come back for this dessert." And they did. I served this with Rainier cherries.

8 ounces bittersweet chocolate, finely chopped
8 ounces (2 sticks) unsalted butter, cut into 1-inch pieces
6 large eggs, at room temperature
3/4 cup sugar
1/4 cup all-purpose flour, sifted
8 feuilles de brick (or brik) (available through Amazon.com, or see Sources)

8 10-inch lengths butcher's twine

1. Place the chocolate in a medium heatproof bowl. Place the butter in a saucepan over medium heat. Place the bowl with the chocolate over the saucepan to warm the chocolate as the butter melts.

2. When all of the butter has melted, pour it over the chocolate. Stir until the chocolate has melted and has reached 100°F. Set aside on top of a hot oven or in another warm place to keep the mixture hot.

3. In the bowl of a stand mixer fitted with the whisk attachment, or in a large bowl with a hand mixer, combine the eggs and sugar and beat on medium speed until just lemony yellow, about 3 minutes.

4. Whisk the flour into the chocolate mixture. Turn the mixer to low speed and add the chocolate mixture to the eggs all at once. Scrape down the bowl and continue to mix for 30 seconds, until well combined. Scrape down the bowl. Cover tightly with plastic wrap and refrigerate for at least 4 hours, or overnight.

5. Place a rack in the lowest position of the oven and preheat the oven to 400°F.

6. Lay a *feuille de brick* on your work surface and top with ½ cup of the chilled filling. Pull up the edges of the pastry, creating a little purse around the batter and a flower top. Tie with butcher's twine just above the filling. Repeat with the remaining pastry. (You can do this a day in advance. Cover with plastic wrap and refrigerate.) Place on a 12-x-17-inch half sheet pan and bake for 10 minutes. Rotate the sheet pan from front to back and bake for another 2 to 3 minutes, until the edges of the purses are golden. Remove from the oven and cut the twine off with kitchen scissors. Serve hot.

   NOTE: The purses can be baked in advance and reheated for 4 minutes at 400°F.

COFFEE STRACCIATELLA ICE CREAM

■ ■ ■

*S*tracciatella means "little rags" in Italian, and here it refers to the chocolate flecks in this luxurious coffee ice cream. They're achieved by streaming melted high-quality bittersweet chocolate into the ice cream just before removing the ice cream from the ice cream maker. It's important to add the melted chocolate in a very thin stream, or the ice cream will be more like coffee chocolate clump than chip. I find the easiest way to do this is to lift the chocolate above the bowl with a spatula and let it drizzle off the spatula into the ice cream maker. The chocolate stays in your mouth after the ice cream melts and adds a nice little crunch.

$2^{1}/_{3}$ cups milk
1 cup heavy cream
$^{2}/_{3}$ cup strong brewed espresso (regular or decaf)
1 cup sugar
5 large egg yolks
1 tablespoon Tia Maria or other coffee liqueur
1 teaspoon fresh lemon juice
Pinch of salt
4 ounces bittersweet chocolate, finely chopped

1. Place a 1-quart freezer container in the freezer. Prepare an ice bath for quickly cooling the finished ice cream base: fill a large bowl halfway with ice, add a small amount of water, and nestle a medium bowl inside the ice.

2. In a medium nonreactive saucepan, combine the milk, cream, espresso, and $^{1}/_{2}$ cup of the sugar. Place the pan over medium heat and bring to a simmer. Meanwhile, quickly whisk together the egg yolks and the remaining $^{1}/_{2}$ cup sugar in a medium bowl. When the milk mixture comes to a simmer, remove the pan from the heat and ladle out $^{1}/_{2}$ cup of the hot milk mixture. Drizzle it slowly into the eggs, whisking. Once the $^{1}/_{2}$ cup of milk is incorporated into the eggs and the eggs are warmed, pour the mixture back into the hot milk, whisking constantly. Be sure to scrape all the eggs into the pan with a rubber spatula.

3. Place the pan over low heat. Immediately stir the custard, using a heat-resistant rubber spatula. Stir in figure eights around the edge of the pan and into the center. Keep stirring until the consistency is like thick cream. The custard is done when the temperature reaches 180°F on an instant-read thermometer. Test for readiness with your spatula: dip it into the custard, pull it out, and run your finger across the back of the spatula. Your finger should leave a clear trail and the rest of the spatula should remain coated with custard. If the custard does not run into the finger trail, it is thick enough and can be taken off the heat. If it does run, cook the custard for another minute, or until the consistency is right.

4. Remove the pan from the heat and immediately pour the mixture through a fine-mesh strainer into the medium bowl in the ice bath. To cool evenly, stir the custard constantly for 5 minutes, or until the temperature drops to 40°F and the custard is cold. The custard will become thicker as it cools. Stir in the liqueur, lemon juice, and salt. Chill for several hours in the refrigerator.

5. Transfer the custard to an ice cream maker and freeze according to the manufacturer's directions. While the machine is running, melt the chocolate in a microwave-safe bowl at 50 percent power for 2 to 3 minutes or in a heatproof bowl set over a saucepan of simmering water. Allow to cool to 100°F, or tepid. Just before removing the ice cream from the machine, with the machine running, drizzle the melted chocolate into the ice cream in a fine stream. Scrape the ice cream into the freezer container and freeze for 2 hours to firm before serving. Or for soft-serve ice cream, serve at once.

CRISPY HERBED FLATBREAD

MAKES EIGHTEEN 3-X-6-INCH TRIANGLES

■ ■ ■

Spago has always served this signature flatbread, which they refer to as their matzo. The crisp savory triangles disappear from their baskets as quickly as the waiters can replenish them. I make this dough in a food processor. It comes together like pasta dough and has just the right texture for rolling out with a pasta machine. We bake the flatbread in the wood-burning pizza oven at Spago; it will work great at home as long as you have a pizza stone for your oven and a pasta machine for rolling out the dough.

FOR THE FLATBREAD DOUGH

- 3/4 cup plus 2 tablespoons cool water (60°F)
- 1 tablespoon honey
- 2 cups bread flour
- 1 cup whole wheat flour
- 1 1/2 teaspoons sugar
- 1 1/2 teaspoons salt
  All-purpose flour for dusting

- 1/2 cup olive oil
- 1/4 cup minced shallots
- 3 tablespoons kosher salt
- 1/2 cup freshly grated Parmesan
- 3 tablespoons chopped fresh thyme

1. **MAKE THE FLATBREAD DOUGH:** Mix together the water and honey in a small bowl.

2. Place the flours, sugar, and salt in the bowl of a food processor fitted with the steel blade. Pulse a few times to combine well. Turn on the processor and slowly stream in the water mixture. This should take about 30 seconds. Continue to mix for 1 1/2 minutes, until the dough comes together. It should be dense, stiff, and just a little tacky, like pasta dough. Wrap airtight in plastic wrap and let rest for 4 hours, or refrigerate overnight.

3. Set up a pasta roller on your work surface. Using a rolling pin, pound the dough into a 1-inch-thick rectangle, the width of your pasta roller. Dust with all-purpose flour as necessary. Roll out the dough, cutting it into pieces to make it easier to handle as you move through increasingly narrow settings, until it is 1/8 inch thick. Lightly dust with flour each time you roll it through. Place on lightly dusted pieces of parchment paper, stack the parchment, wrap in plastic, and refrigerate for at least 4 hours, or overnight.

4. Place a rack in the lowest position of the oven and preheat the oven to 450°F, with a pizza stone in it.

5. Working with one sheet at a time, lay the dough out on your lightly dusted work surface. Brush evenly with a light coating of olive oil and sprinkle on a light coating of shallots. Mix together the salt, Parmesan, and thyme and sprinkle over the dough. Cut the sheet crosswise on the diagonal to make 18 triangles 3 inches across at the bottom. Place 4 or 5 triangles at a time on the hot baking stone and bake for 5 to 7 minutes, until blistered and browned. Remove from the stone and allow to cool on a rack before serving.

FINAL BAOS

■ ■ ■

A *bao* (pronounced "bow," as in "final") is a Japanese bun. These are like miniature chocolate-filled doughnuts. They're made with sweet dough, filled with chocolate ganache, and fried like beignets. Capitalizing on the pun, I created them for Spago Hollywood's star-studded last-night gala, to represent all of the sweet memories I had for that famous hillside restaurant. All of the chefs who had ever worked at Spago—Nancy Silverton and Mark Peel (the first chefs), Lee Hefter and Hiro Sone, Lissa Doumani, Joseph Manzare and Kazuto Matsusaka, Annie and David Gingrass, Mary Bergin, Makoto Tanaka and François Kwaku-Dongo, and Matt Nichols and Jennifer Jasinski—came back to cook that night. Most had already moved on to open their own restaurants; Lee Hefter and I were about to move on to a grander Spago in Beverly Hills.

FOR THE GANACHE

- 6 ounces bittersweet chocolate, finely chopped
- 3/4 cup heavy cream
- 2 tablespoons light corn syrup

FOR THE DOUGH

- 1 cup cake flour
- 1 1/4 cups all-purpose flour
- 3 tablespoons sugar
- 1 teaspoon baking powder
- 1/2 teaspoon baking soda
- 1/4 teaspoon salt
- 2 large eggs
- 4 ounces (1 stick) unsalted butter, melted and still hot
- 1/4 cup milk

Vegetable oil for deep-frying
Confectioners' sugar or Vanilla Sugar (page 349) for dusting

1. **MAKE THE GANACHE:** Place the chopped chocolate in a bowl. Bring the cream and corn syrup to a boil in a saucepan or in a microwave-safe bowl for about 1 minute. Pour over the chocolate and tap the bowl against your work surface to settle the chocolate into the cream. Let sit for 1 minute, then stir with a rubber spatula or a whisk until the chocolate is melted and the mixture is smooth. Allow to cool in a cool spot for about 1 hour, to 70°F; it should have the consistency of peanut butter.

2. Line a baking sheet with parchment paper. Fit a piping bag with a #6 plain tip. Fill the pastry bag with the ganache. Pipe 35 large-marble-sized kisses of the ganache (about the diameter of a quarter) onto the parchment, lifting up the piping bag as you pipe. Transfer to the freezer. Freeze for 1 hour (or for up to 1 week).

3. MAKE THE DOUGH: Sift together the flours, sugar, baking powder, baking soda, and salt into a large bowl. (Or sift into the bowl of a stand mixer fitted with the paddle attachment.)

4. In a medium bowl, whisk the eggs. Stream in the hot butter, whisking. Whisk in the milk. Scrape down the bowl.

5. Make a well in the center of the dry ingredients and pour in the wet ingredients. Stir (or beat on medium speed) until the dough comes together, about 2 minutes. Scrape out onto a lightly floured work surface and knead for 2 minutes, until the dough is homogeneous. Wrap in plastic wrap and refrigerate for at least 1 hour.

6. ASSEMBLE THE *BAOS*: Lightly dust your work surface with flour. Roll out the dough to a 10-x-14-inch rectangle, about ⅛ inch thick. Cut into thirty-five 2-inch squares. Place a frozen chocolate kiss in the center of each square. Pull up the edges of the dough and pinch together so that you have a tightly sealed bundle. Transfer to a parchment-lined baking sheet, cover with plastic, and allow to rest for 15 to 20 minutes in the refrigerator.

7. In a wide deep saucepan or a deep fryer, heat 3 inches of oil over medium heat to 350°F on a deep-fry thermometer. One at a time, place 4 *baos* on a large slotted spoon and carefully dip and release into the oil. Fry for 1½ minutes, turning constantly. Remove from the oil with a slotted spoon, drain on paper towels or on a rack, and allow to cool slightly. Repeat with the remaining *baos*. Dust with confectioners' sugar or roll in vanilla sugar and serve.

Farmers' Market Inspirations

WHEN SPRING ARRIVED, I DISCOVERED THE SANTA Monica Farmers' Market, where every Wednesday since July 1981, just blocks from the Pacific Ocean, more than 100 farmers set up their wares.

In my former jobs, I had always done the food purchasing through kitchen managers and in-house purchasers, but I had never experienced the thrill of buying fruit directly from farmers. In a short time, the Spago dessert menu evolved from classic to fruit-driven.

Wolfgang loved what I was doing, and he encouraged me as I foraged for the restaurant. He wanted me to hunt down the best ingredients and to buy in bulk. "Vy do you alvays buy so little?" he would say. "Buy more!" I rose to the challenge with a checkbook full of blank checks, a driver named Marvin, and a van for hauling the precious cargo back to Spago. I bought raspberries, strawberries, and boysenberries by the flat and made them into berry jams and preserves. Since Blenheim apricots have a very short season in June, I purchased sixty cases and preserved them in jars to use as a filling for Austrian crepes in the middle of winter. Once I had my fill of Concord grape tarts and soufflés, I cooked, cooled, and froze the juice from the grapes in the fall for the jelly candy I sent out with confections. I did the same with huckleberries and blackberries, making them into sauce as well as jelly candy. When I bought boxes of Meyer lemons for tarts, I froze the zest or candied the peels for use in other desserts. These rituals have become part of the daily routine in my bakeshop. Nothing goes to waste.

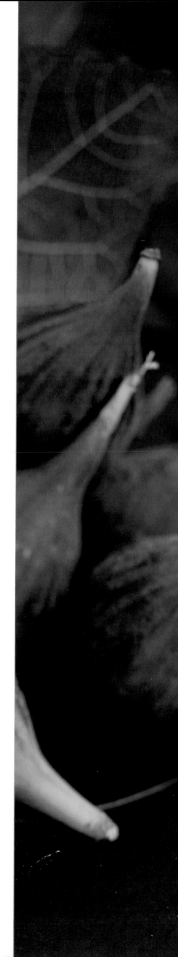

AQUA D-KULA
Lemon-Mint Tea

SERVES 4

■ ■ ■

In the South Pacific, the word *Kula* means "well-being." Aqua d-Kula is a magic formula, and at Spago, we all drink it to keep ourselves healthy. It beats all the cold remedies I've ever known, hands down. It was given to me by Ricky Flores, a "runner" at Spago (who brings the food from the kitchen out to the guests). He got it from his mother, who is from the South Pacific. Serve it hot, or freeze it in an ice cream maker for a great sorbet, or use it to make granita.

2 lemons, thinly sliced, seeds removed
3/4 cup honey, such as orange blossom
32 1-inch fresh mint leaves
1 4-inch piece fresh ginger, peeled and thinly sliced
4 cups boiling water

1. Reserve 4 lemon slices for garnish. Place the honey, mint leaves, ginger, and the remaining lemon slices in a large mortar and pound to a paste with the pestle. Transfer to a saucepan with a lid or to a teapot, add the boiling water, and allow to steep for 10 to 15 minutes.

2. Reheat if necessary and serve hot, floating a lemon slice in each cup.

3. Or, for sorbet, allow to cool and freeze in an ice cream maker following the manufacturer's directions, or make granita, following the directions on page 377.

NECTARINE COBBLER

■ ■ ■

This is everybody's favorite cobbler. The secret ingredients in the filling are nutmeg, honey, and champagne; you could substitute Prosecco or another dry sparkler.

My nectarines are grown by Arthur Lange, a retired professor of horticulture from UC Davis, now a farmer in Reedley, California. Art grows amazing nectarines at his Honey Crisp Farms. His Snow Queen nectarines are so delicious that I don't even cook with them; I save them for eating.

Dough for Campton Shortcuts (page 124; omit the crystallized ginger)

2 tablespoons unsalted butter, softened

2 tablespoons sugar for dusting

FOR THE FILLING

1/4 cup all-purpose flour

3/4–1 cup sugar, depending on the acidity of the fruit

1/4 teaspoon freshly grated nutmeg

1/8 teaspoon grated orange zest

1/8 teaspoon grated lemon zest

1 1/2 cups champagne

1/4 cup honey

2 tablespoons fresh lemon juice

6 nectarines, pitted and cut into eighths

1 egg beaten with 1 egg yolk, for egg wash

About 1/4 cup sugar for dusting

1. Place the dough for the biscuit topping in the freezer while you prepare the filling.

2. Place a rack in the lowest position of the oven and preheat the oven to 375°F. Brush a 12-inch square baking dish with the 2 tablespoons butter and dust with the 2 tablespoons sugar.

3. **MAKE THE FILLING:** In a medium bowl, combine the flour, sugar, nutmeg, orange zest, and lemon zest. Whisk in the champagne. Heat the honey in a microwave-safe bowl at 50 percent power to just warm and stir into the flour mixture. Add the lemon juice and stir together. Add the nectarines and toss everything together, then scrape into the prepared pan.

4. Remove the biscuit topping from the freezer and cut into diamond shapes. Place over the nectarines. Brush with the egg wash and coat the tops of the biscuits with a generous dusting of the sugar. Immediately place in the oven and bake for 35 to 40 minutes, until the biscuits are golden brown and the filling is bubbling.

RHUBARB, APPLE, AND FENNEL CRUMBLE

SERVES 6

■ ■ ■

Mike Cirone, of See Canyon Fruit Ranch in the San Luis Obispo Valley, sells Jonagold apples as well as Braeburns, Fujis, Granny Smiths, and Pink Ladies at the Beverly Hills Farmers' Market, and I use them for everything from crumbles to pies and tarte Tatins. I love to combine fresh fennel with apples. The fennel contributes crunch, spice, and a licorice flavor to the crumble, and grating the two on a box grater makes for a tender, melt-in-your-mouth texture.

At the restaurant, we always bake our crumble toppings separately, then bake the filling, sprinkle the crumble over the top, and heat through just before serving; see Sherry's Secrets.

1. **MAKE THE FILLING:** In a large skillet over medium heat, combine the sugar, brown sugar, flour, vanilla seeds (if using), star anise, and salt and stir together. Add the remaining ingredients and cook, stirring occasionally, until the rhubarb is tender and the mixture is bubbling and slightly thickened, about 10 minutes. Remove from the heat.

2. **MAKE THE TOPPING:** Combine the confectioners' sugar, brown sugar, salt, nutmeg, flour, and oatmeal in a food

FOR THE FILLING

- 1/3 cup sugar
- 1/4 cup packed light brown sugar
- 3 tablespoons all-purpose flour
- 1/2 vanilla bean, split, seeds scraped out and reserved (optional)
- 1/4 teaspoon ground star anise
- 1/8 teaspoon salt
- 3/4 pound rhubarb, peeled and cut into 1/2-inch-thick slices (3 cups sliced)
- 1 1/2 pounds Braeburn or Fuji apples, peeled, cored, and grated on the large holes of a box grater
- 1 8-ounce fennel bulb, quartered, cored, and grated on the large holes of a box grater
- 1/2 cup apple juice

FOR THE CRUMBLE TOPPING

- 3/4 cup confectioners' sugar
- 1/4 cup packed light brown sugar
- 1/8 teaspoon salt
- 1/4 teaspoon freshly grated nutmeg
- 3/4 cup all-purpose flour
- 1/2 cup instant oatmeal
- 4 ounces (1 stick) cold unsalted butter, cut into 1/2-inch cubes

- 1 tablespoon unsalted butter for the pan
- 1 tablespoon sugar for the pan
  Vanilla ice cream or crème fraîche for serving

processor fitted with the steel blade or in a medium bowl and pulse or whisk together. Add the butter and pulse until the mixture is crumbly, or rub between your thumbs and fingers until the mixture is crumbly, pressing any larger clumps between your thumbs and forefingers. Refrigerate until ready to use.

3. Place a rack in the middle of the oven and preheat the oven to 350°F. Butter a 10-inch ceramic pie dish or a 2-quart baking dish and sprinkle with sugar.

4. Fill with the rhubarb-apple-fennel mixture. Top with the crumble topping. Bake, rotating the dish from front to back halfway through, for 35 to 45 minutes, until the crumble is browned and bubbling. Serve hot, with vanilla ice cream or crème fraîche.

Sherry's Secrets

Bake the topping and filling separately— that way, the topping will always be crisp.

Follow Steps 1 and 2 as directed and preheat the oven to 350°F. Place the crumble topping on a sheet pan and bake for 30 minutes, or until browned and crisp. Remove from the oven and allow to cool. Store in the freezer if not using right away.

Fill the buttered and sugared baking dish with the rhubarb-apple-fennel mixture. Place in the oven and bake until bubbling, 30 to 40 minutes. Top with the baked topping and heat through, or run it very quickly under the broiler.

RING OF SATURN PEACH "DOUGHNUTS"

SERVES 12

■ ■ ■

A Ring of Saturn (or Saturn) peach is a squat peach that looks like a doughnut—but in flavor it's very much a peach! It's about 3 inches wide and 1 inch tall, with white creamy flesh and a tiny pit. Fitz Kelly from Aerie Farms, who is known for his Irish charm and for his creative naming of fruit (Carmen Miranda and Leather and Lace peaches, the Lady in Red peach), brought them to the market for the first time in the mid-1990s. He brought only three flats, and the minute I laid eyes on them, I envisioned this recipe: I knew I would marinate them in a verbena syrup, dip them into crushed anise-scented biscotti, and bake them, so they looked like doughnuts. I'd dust them with powdered sugar and serve them with ice cream. I told Fitz I wanted all three flats. "I can't sell you all of them," he said, "I have to let some of the other chefs have some." "Okay," I replied, "I'll make a deal with you. I'll tell you what I'm going to do with them—and you have to promise not to tell anybody. Ask everyone who wants them what they're planning on doing. If they say pie, crumble, sorbet, or ice cream, they're out. If they have a better idea than mine, they can have them all. I'll come back in one hour." In an hour, I came back, and Fitz handed me my three cases.

The recipe uses half of the anise biscotti. Save the rest for another use (see Note). If you can't find doughnut peaches, you can use regular peaches cut into 1-inch-thick slices.

FOR THE ANISE BISCOTTI

- 1⅓ cups plus 1 tablespoon all-purpose flour
- ¾ teaspoon baking powder
- 2 tablespoons unsalted butter, softened
- ½ cup plus 1 tablespoon sugar
- 1½ teaspoons crushed aniseed
- 1 large egg
- 1 tablespoon fresh lemon juice
- 1½ teaspoons dark rum
- 2 tablespoons dry white wine
- ¼ cup pistachios, coarsely chopped

FOR THE MACERATED PEACHES

- 1 cup sugar
- 1 cup water
- 4 whole lemon verbena leaves or 1 tablespoon grated lemon zest
- 12 doughnut peaches (see headnote)

- 1 cup all-purpose flour
- 2 large eggs
  About ¼ cup confectioners' sugar
  Vanilla ice cream for serving

1. **MAKE THE BISCOTTI CRUMBS:** Place a rack in the middle of the oven and preheat the oven to 350°F. Line a cookie sheet with parchment paper.

2. Sift together the flour and baking powder and set aside.

3. In the bowl of a stand mixer fitted with the paddle attachment, or in a large bowl with a hand mixer, cream together the butter, sugar, and crushed aniseed for 2 minutes on medium speed. Scrape down the bowl and blend for another 2 minutes. Add the egg and beat for 1 minute. Scrape down the sides of the bowl. Add the lemon juice and rum and blend until incorporated.

4. Mix in one quarter of the flour mixture, then 1 tablespoon of the white wine, then another one quarter of the flour mixture and the remaining 1 tablespoon wine. Blend in the remaining flour mixture. Add the pistachios and mix until just incorporated. The dough will be very tacky.

5. Dust your work surface and hands generously with flour. Form the dough into a 3-x-8-inch log. Place the log on the parchment-lined cookie sheet. Bake for 20 minutes. Rotate the pan from front to back and continue to bake for 10 to 12 minutes, until a tester inserted in the center comes out clean.

6. Remove the biscotti log from the oven and allow to cool. Cut the log in half. Reserve half for another use (see Note). Break the remaining half into pieces and place in the bowl of a food processor fitted with the steel blade. Pulse the biscotti until you have coarse crumbs. You will have about 2 cups of crumbs. Place the biscotti crumbs in a bowl and set aside.

7. **MACERATE THE PEACHES:** Place the sugar, water, and lemon verbena leaves or lemon zest in a small saucepan and bring to a boil. When the sugar has dissolved, remove the mixture from the heat. Pour the syrup into a small bowl and place the small bowl in a larger bowl filled with ice and water to cool down the syrup quickly. Set aside.

8. Skin the peaches. Or to loosen the skins and make peeling easier, plunge the peaches into a pot of boiling water for 30 seconds and then into a bowl of ice water. Carefully poke out the pits, leaving a hole in the center.

9. Place the peeled peaches in the cooled verbena syrup to macerate for at least 30 minutes, or up to 4 hours.

10. **COAT AND BAKE THE PEACHES:** Place a rack in the middle of the oven and preheat the oven to 350°F. Line a baking sheet with parchment paper.

11. Place the flour in a small bowl. In another small bowl, whisk the eggs to break them up. Place the biscotti crumbs in a shallow baking dish. Arrange the bowls of flour and eggs and the dish of crumbs side by side. Remove a peach from the syrup and let it drain slightly, then dip it in the flour to lightly coat. Shake off the excess, then dip it in the eggs to coat. Shake off any excess, then roll in the biscotti crumbs. Press the crumbs to pack them. Place the crumb-covered peach on the parchment-lined baking sheet. Continue the dipping and crumb-coating process with the remaining peaches. (The crumb-coated peaches can be refrigerated for up to 4 hours before baking.)

12. Bake for 15 minutes. Rotate the pan from front to back and continue to bake for an additional 5 to 10 minutes, until golden on the outside and the peaches are tender when pierced with a tester. Remove from the oven and dust the "doughnuts" with the confectioners' sugar. Serve with vanilla ice cream.

NOTE: To make biscotti with the remaining half of the biscotti log, place a rack in the middle of the oven and preheat the oven to 350°F. Cut the log on the diagonal into 1-inch-thick slices. Place the slices on a parchment-lined baking sheet and bake for 10 minutes. Rotate the baking sheet from front to back and bake for another 5 minutes, until the biscotti are hard. Remove from the oven and allow to cool on a rack. (The log can be wrapped airtight and stored for 2 days in the refrigerator. The biscotti will keep for 2 weeks in an airtight container.)

FIG BARS

■ ■ ■

Betty and Truman Kennedy always have the best dried fruit at the market, even during the summer, when there's lots of fresh fruit available. These are unlike any fig bars you've ever tasted. A great short cookie dough and dried Black Mission figs are all you need. (It's best to make the filling a day ahead.)

FOR THE FIG FILLING

- 1 cup finely chopped dried Black Mission figs
- 1½ cups water
- 1 cup apple juice
- ¼ cup sugar
- ⅛ teaspoon grated orange zest

FOR THE COOKIE DOUGH

- 4 ounces (1 stick) unsalted butter, softened
- ½ cup Vanilla Sugar (page 349)
- ½ teaspoon grated orange zest
- 1 large egg white
- ½ teaspoon vanilla extract
- 1½ cups all-purpose flour

1. **MAKE THE FILLING:** Combine the chopped figs, water, apple juice, and sugar in a medium saucepan and bring to a boil. Reduce the heat to low and cook at a bare simmer for 1 to 2 hours, until the figs are so soft that they're spreadable.

2. Transfer to a food processor fitted with the steel blade, add the orange zest, and process until smooth. Remove from the food processor and allow to cool.

3. **MAKE THE DOUGH:** Cream together the butter, vanilla sugar, and orange zest in the bowl of a stand mixer fitted with the paddle attachment, or in a large bowl with a hand mixer, for 2 to 3 minutes on medium speed. Scrape down the bowl and paddle or beaters. Add the egg white and vanilla and beat in. Scrape down the sides of the bowl and the paddle. Add the flour and beat on low speed until the dough comes together. Wrap in plastic wrap and refrigerate for 2 hours.

4. Place racks in the middle and lower third of the oven and preheat the oven to 350°F. Line baking sheets with parchment paper.

5. On a floured surface, roll the dough out to a 12-x-16-inch rectangle. Cut into 4 equal strips, each 12 x 4 inches. Spoon a line of filling down the center of each

strip. Fold the dough over the filling and pinch the edges together. Place on the parchment-lined baking sheets, seam side down. (At this point the fig bars can be frozen for up to 2 weeks, wrapped airtight.)

6. Using a serrated knife, slice each log on the diagonal into ten cookies. Bake, rotating the baking sheets from top to bottom and from front to back halfway through, for 12 to 15 minutes, until golden. Remove from the oven and allow to cool on a rack. (The bars will keep, stored airtight, for 2 days.)

DEVILISH ANGEL FOOD CAKE WITH BERRIES OR CITRUS

SERVES 10

■ ■ ■

When I started going to the farmers' market, I couldn't get exotic European berries like red currants and *fraises des bois* (wild strawberries). I convinced one of the farmers, PY and Randy Pudwill, to grow these berries just for me, and they were immediately popular. Now if I don't get to the Wednesday market by eight or eight-thirty, he's already sold out! My angel food cake is just a little devilish, because I enrich the delicate batter with butter, but it's still light as a feather. In summer, it's meant to be eaten with an assortment of berries—boysenberries, blueberries, strawberries, and *fraises des bois,* if you can get them—or a mix of golden and red raspberries. In winter, serve it with a mélange of blood oranges, kumquats, and mandarins.

FOR THE CAKE

- 1 cup plus 2 tablespoons cake flour
- 1 cup plus 2 tablespoons sugar
  Scant $\frac{1}{2}$ teaspoon baking powder
- 9 large egg whites
- $\frac{1}{4}$ teaspoon cream of tartar
- 1 vanilla bean, split, seeds scraped out and reserved
- 4 ounces (1 stick) unsalted butter, melted and still hot

FOR THE FRUIT (WINTER)

- 1 cup Simple Syrup (page 350)
- 4 kumquats, sliced into rounds
- 1 blood orange, peeled and divided into suprêmes (see Sherry's Secrets, page 201)
- 2 mandarins, peeled and divided into segments

FOR THE CREAMY MASCARPONE

- 1 cup mascarpone
- 2 tablespoons heavy cream
- 2 tablespoons Marsala
- 2 tablespoons sugar

FOR THE FRUIT (SUMMER)

- $1\frac{1}{2}$ cups mixed berries (see headnote)

1. **MAKE THE CAKE:** Place a rack in the middle of the oven and preheat the oven to 350°F. Line the bottom of a tube pan with a ring of parchment paper; *do not* grease the pan.

2. Sift together the flour, $\frac{1}{2}$ cup plus 1 tablespoon of the sugar, and the baking powder 2 times and set aside.

3. In the bowl of a stand mixer fitted with the whisk attachment, or in a large bowl with a hand mixer, beat the egg whites on low speed until they begin to foam. Add the cream of tartar and 1 tablespoon of the sugar, then continue to beat while gradually adding the remaining ½ cup sugar a tablespoon at a time. Beat until the whites form medium-firm peaks. Stop the mixer. Add the vanilla seeds and continue beating while you quickly stream in the hot butter. Remove from the mixer and gently fold in the dry ingredients.

4. Spoon the batter into the cake pan, spreading it evenly, and place in the oven. Bake for 30 minutes, rotate the pan from front to back, and bake for 10 to 15 additional minutes, until the cake is firm to the touch and a tester inserted in the center comes out clean.

5. Remove from the oven and flip the cake pan upside down on a rack. Let sit for 1 hour, then run a knife around the edge of the pan and invert the cake onto a serving platter. Remove the parchment from the cake.

6. MEANWHILE, PREPARE THE WINTER FRUIT IF USING: Bring the syrup to a boil, remove from the heat, and add the sliced kumquats. Allow to cool to room temperature, then add the blood orange suprêmes and the mandarin segments. Remove the fruit from the syrup before serving.

7. MAKE THE MASCARPONE: With a hand mixer, beat the mascarpone and heavy cream together to soft peaks. Beat in the Marsala and sugar.

8. To serve, cut the cake into thick slices. Place the slices on plates. Garnish with the berries or citrus. Place a dollop of the creamy mascarpone on each plate, next to the cake.

PERFECT CITRUS SUPRÊMES

A serrated paring knife is perfect for segmenting citrus fruit and removing it from its tough membranes to make tender suprêmes. Place the fruit on a cutting board and slice off the top and bottom of the fruit. Stand the fruit on one end, and using a sawing motion from top to bottom, cut away strips of peel and pith, running the knife along the curve of the fruit inside of the skin, until the fruit is completely peeled, with no white pith remaining. The strips should be no more than an inch wide. Now hold the fruit in the palm of one hand above a bowl (to catch the juice) and saw along the inside of one of the segment membranes toward the center of the fruit. When you get to the center, angle the knife to release the segment from the center, then cut the membrane on the other side away from the suprême. This produces very clean suprêmes. Continue with the remaining segments.

PERFECT MANDARIN SEGMENTS

Dip the separated segments in cold water and gently scrape off the white pith and strings with the back of a knife.

PASSION FRUIT CHEESECAKE

■ ■ ■

What else would a man named Romeo sell but passion fruit? Romeo Coleman and his dad, Bill, of Coleman Family Farm, are the only passion fruit producers at the Santa Monica Farmers' Market. This tangy cheesecake has a surprising perfume of jasmine. Look for wrinkled fruit if you're making your own puree, or, if you don't want to bother, buy the puree frozen (see Sherry's Secrets). I don't think this cheesecake needs a crust, but if you want to use one, a thin round of white cake works.

Butter for the pan

1 9-inch round cut from one 1/2-inch-thick layer white cake, such as White Chocolate–Buttermilk Cake (page 267), or your favorite cheesecake crust (optional)

1 1/2 cups passion fruit puree, preferably fresh (passed through a fine-mesh strainer if fresh; see Sherry's Secrets, page 204)

8 ounces cream cheese, at room temperature

1 cup sugar

4 large eggs plus 2 large egg yolks, at room temperature

3/4 cup sour cream, at room temperature

1. Place a rack in the middle of the oven and preheat the oven to 325°F. Butter a 9-inch springform pan and line the outside tightly with aluminum foil so that no water can seep through the cracks. Line the bottom with a parchment-paper circle and place the cake round or crust on top if using.

2. Place 1 cup of the passion fruit puree in a saucepan and bring to a boil. Reduce to 1/2 cup and remove from the heat. Stir in the remaining 1/2 cup puree to make 1 cup of intensely flavored puree and allow to cool to room temperature.

3. In the bowl of a stand mixer fitted with the paddle attachment, or in a large bowl with a hand mixer, blend together the cream cheese and sugar on low speed until the sugar has dissolved. Do not overbeat; you should not have any air bubbles. Add the eggs and egg yolks one at a time, scraping down the bowl after each addition. This should take about 5 minutes. Add the sour cream and beat in. Scrape down the bowl. Still beating on low speed, add the passion fruit puree in a slow stream.

4. Pour the batter into the prepared pan. Place the pan in a large baking dish or roasting pan and add enough hot water to come halfway up the sides of the springform pan. Bake for 1 hour, or until the cheesecake does not jiggle at all when you move it. Remove from the oven and the hot water bath and place on a rack. Allow to cool to room temperature, then cover with plastic wrap and chill. Remove the ring and parchment circle before serving.

PASSION FRUIT PUREE

It takes about 30 passion fruits to yield a cup of puree, but that puree has an intense exotic, floral flavor. For the best results, buy the most wrinkled fruit. Cut the fruit in half and scoop out the pulp. Puree with a handheld blender or in a food processor fitted with the steel blade, then strain. When I'm working with lots of passion fruit, I squeeze it on a citrus juicer, then blend the pulp and pass through a fine-mesh strainer. Press hard against the strainer to extract all of the juice. I save the seeds and infuse them in champagne vinegar to use for salads. If you can't get fresh passion fruit or don't want to go through the trouble of making the puree, you can find high-quality frozen passion fruit puree at gourmet food markets or through the Internet (see Sources).

GINGER CREAM TARTLETS WITH POACHED FIGS AND PERSIAN MULBERRIES

■ ■ ■

Persian mulberries are unique, heaven-on-earth, intensely juicy berries with a growing season that comes and goes in the blink of an eye. At the Santa Monica Farmers' Market, they have a cult following. Word goes out when the season begins, and people line up well before the market opens at the Circle "C" Ranch stand. A group of us have been named the Purple People because of the stains we are willing to sustain from this delicate, incredibly sweet purple fruit. There are never enough to go around during their one-month stint at the market. The first time I met Kim Blaine, proprietor of Circle "C," I stood in line for thirty minutes. She asked me, "How much?" and, naively, I answered, "Five pounds." "No. Go away," she said and sold me one box. I came

FOR THE GINGER CREAM
- 2 cups heavy cream
- 1/4 cup plus 3 tablespoons sugar
- 2 tablespoons fresh ginger, peeled and thinly sliced
- 4 large egg yolks

FOR THE FIGS AND BERRIES
- 9 fresh figs
  Blackberry Merlot Sauce (page 361)
- 2 cups Persian mulberries (see Note)

- 6 4-inch tartlet shells made with Pâte Sucrée (page 373), prebaked

back the next week with the desserts I had made, and that won her over. "How much?" she said. "Whatever you want to sell me," I replied. "How about five pounds?" That was the jackpot. From then on, Kim ("Mama") was part of my extended family. She recently passed away, and I dedicate this recipe to her.

1. **MAKE THE GINGER CREAM:** Bring the cream, sugar, and ginger to a simmer in a large saucepan over medium heat. Remove from the heat, cover the pan with plastic wrap, and let steep for 15 to 30 minutes.

2. Place a rack in the middle of the oven and preheat the oven to 300°F. Place a 1-quart soufflé dish or baking dish in a larger baking pan.

3. Gently whisk the egg yolks in a large bowl. Gently whisk in the cream mixture. Pour through a fine-mesh strainer into the soufflé dish or baking dish. Fill the baking pan with enough hot water to come two thirds of the way up the sides of the dish. Cover loosely with aluminum foil and bake for 40 to 45 minutes. The custard is done when it is set but has a uniform jiggle; it should not brown or rise. Remove from the oven, cover with plastic, and chill for at least 2 hours, or until firm. (The ginger cream will keep for up to 2 days in the refrigerator.)

4. **PREPARE THE FIGS AND BERRIES:** Peel 6 of the figs. Cut the other 3 figs into wedges and reserve for garnish. Bring the blackberry merlot sauce to a

boil in a small saucepan and reduce by one third, until it is thick but still runny. Add the peeled figs and remove from the heat. Allow the figs to infuse for 1 hour.

5. Transfer the ginger cream to a piping bag fitted with a #6 plain tip and fill the pastry shells three-quarters full. Or spoon the cream into the shells. Smooth the tops.

6. Return the peeled figs to the heat and bring the sauce back to a simmer. Baste the figs with the hot liquid, then remove with a slotted spoon and place one in the middle of each tart shell, on top of the ginger cream. With scissors, snip the figs across the top like a cross, then gently pull apart the four pieces to reveal the pink, juicy centers.

7. Bring the sauce back to a simmer and add the mulberries. Stir for 15 to 30 seconds, until heated through. Remove the berries with a slotted spoon and divide among the tart shells. Garnish each shell with a few of the reserved fig wedges and serve with the remaining sauce.

NOTE: If you want to make this and can't get Persian mulberries, substitute boysenberries for the mulberries.

Sherry's Secrets

WHEN YOUR HEART IS IN YOUR WORK

One year I made this dish for a James Beard event. I ordered the figs two weeks in advance from my favorite fig producer, Frank Tenerelli, who brought the seeds from Italy more than sixty years ago. Four days before I was scheduled to leave, I got a phone call from Frank's wife, Ann. He had had a heart attack and was in a coma. Frank came out of the coma a couple of days later. The first thing he said was, "I have to get Sherry her figs!" Ann, not knowing whether she wanted to kill me or kiss me, realized that Frank would be all right. And I proudly brought the 200 figs to New York.

CONCORD GRAPE POACHED PEARS

■ ■ ■

Concord grapes are the grapes used in the grape jelly and grape juice we all grew up on. They have a familiar flavor that can be made extraordinary. Nobody grows better Concord grapes than the Chino gang down at Chino Farms in Del Mar, San Diego County. In this dish, I cook the grapes and puree them, then use the puree as a poaching medium for pears. The color of the pears is spectacular— deep purple on the outside and pink underneath—and the flavor out of this world. Ripe pears are a must. Serve them with Pain Perdu (page 210) or with Meyer Lemon Gelato (page 214).

FOR THE PEARS
- 1 cup water
- 1 pound Concord grapes, stemmed
- 2 cups dry white wine
- 1 cup sugar
- 1 teaspoon black peppercorns, crushed
- 2 ripe but firm Bartlett, Anjou, or French Butter pears, peeled

FOR THE SAUCE
- 1 tablespoon cornstarch
- 1 tablespoon cold water
- 1 tablespoon sugar

1. **PREPARE THE PEARS:** Combine all of the ingredients except the pears in a medium saucepan and bring to a boil. Reduce the heat and simmer for 5 minutes. Remove from the heat, cover tightly with plastic wrap, and allow the grapes to macerate for 1 hour.

2. Press the mixture through a fine-mesh strainer into a bowl. Return to the saucepan. Add the pears to the pan and bring to a simmer over low heat. Poach the pears for 12 to 15 minutes. They should be tender but intact. Remove from the heat. To stop the cooking process more quickly and prevent the pears from becoming mushy, remove the pears from the pan using a slotted spoon and place on a plate. Pour the liquid from the pan into a bowl and set the bowl in a larger bowl full of ice. Allow the liquid to cool in the ice bath, then return the fruit to the cold liquid. Cover with plastic wrap until ready to serve. (The pears can be held for up to 4 hours.) Remove the pears from the liquid, cut them in half lengthwise, and remove the cores. Slice on the bias and fan out on plates.

3. **MAKE THE SAUCE:** Place the poaching liquid in a saucepan and bring to a simmer. Dissolve the cornstarch in the cold water in a small bowl. Add the sugar and stir together. Add to the poaching liquid, bring to a simmer over low heat, and whisk for 2 minutes, or until slightly thickened. Spoon the sauce over the pears and serve.

Sherry's Secrets

To make your pears perfectly smooth and shiny, use a brand-new scrubby. Once the pear is peeled, gently rub the surface with the scrubby to sculpt it.

PAIN PERDU
WITH CONCORD GRAPE POACHED PEARS

SERVES 4

■ ■ ■

Pain perdu—French toast—is one of my favorite desserts. I serve this fluffy, custardy version with a salty soft cheese like Camembert on the side, Concord Grape Poached Pears, and a drizzle of honey.

2 large eggs
2 cups whole milk
1/4 cup heavy cream
1/2 vanilla bean, split, seeds scraped out and reserved
1/8 teaspoon grated orange zest (optional)
1 tablespoon sugar (optional)
2 ounces (1/2 stick) unsalted butter
4 1-inch-thick slices brioche or good-quality white bread
Concord Grape Poached Pears (page 208), with sauce
4 ounces Camembert or Humboldt Fog cheese, cut into 4 slices
1/4 cup honey, preferably orange blossom or clover, warmed

1. Beat together the eggs, milk, cream, vanilla seeds, the orange zest (if using), and, if desired, the 1 tablespoon sugar in a wide bowl. Set aside.

2. Heat a large skillet over medium-high heat and add half the butter. When it stops foaming, dip 2 slices of the bread into the egg mixture, turning to coat, and add to the pan. Cook until golden, then flip and cook on the other side until golden. Transfer to a plate and keep warm in a low oven while you repeat with the remaining butter and the remaining bread.

3. Spoon 3 tablespoons of the sauce from the pears onto each plate. Cut the French toast in half on the diagonal. Place 2 halves on each plate, with a slice of cheese on the side. Drizzle the warm honey over the toast. Fan the poached pears over the plate on the side and serve.

CONCORD GRAPE SOUFFLÉS

SERVES 4

■ ■ ■

These airy soufflés melt in your mouth, leaving behind the intense, jammy flavor of Concord grapes. I developed the recipe in late summer, when we were beginning to get Concord grapes from Chino Farms, for a wine-tasting dinner, one of the many that we do regularly at Spago. If I'm not serving the soufflés with wine (such as Brachetto d'Acqui, an Italian red dessert wine), I serve them with Meyer Lemon Gelato (page 214).

1½ pounds Concord grapes, stemmed
½ cup water
2 tablespoons butter, softened, for the ramekins
¼ cup plus 3 tablespoons sugar, plus 2 tablespoons for the ramekins
2 teaspoons tapioca flour (available at whole foods stores, or see Sources) or cornstarch (I prefer tapioca flour)
2 large egg yolks
2 teaspoons fresh lemon juice
4 large egg whites
⅛ teaspoon cream of tartar

1. Combine the grapes and water in a wide medium saucepan and bring to a simmer over medium heat. Simmer for 15 minutes, or until the grapes have softened and burst. Using the back of a spoon, smash the grapes against the sides and bottom of the pan. Then pour into a food mill fitted with the medium blade or into the bowl of a food processor fitted with the steel blade, and press through or process. If using a food processor, pass through a fine-mesh strainer after pureeing the grapes. You should have 1½ cups puree. Return to the pan and reduce to ¾ cup over low heat, stirring often. Set aside to cool.

2. Place a rack in the lowest position of the oven and preheat the oven to 400°F. Butter and sugar four 8-ounce ramekins.

3. In a medium bowl, whisk together the 3 tablespoons sugar and the tapioca flour or cornstarch. Whisk in the egg yolks, grape puree, and lemon juice and set aside.

4. In the bowl of a stand mixer fitted with the whisk attachment, or in a large bowl with a hand mixer, beat the egg whites on low speed until they begin to foam. Add the cream of tartar and continue to beat on low speed for 1 minute. Increase the speed to medium and continue to beat while you slowly stream in the remaining ¼ cup sugar. Continue to beat until the egg whites form medium-stiff peaks.

5. Fold half the egg whites into the grape-yolk mixture. Fold in the remaining egg whites. Spoon into the prepared ramekins. Place the dishes on a baking sheet and bake for 15 to 18 minutes, until puffed and golden on the outside. They should remain pudding-like on the inside. Serve immediately.

MEYER LEMON GELATO

■ ■ ■

Meyer lemons are a California lemon with a soft, thin skin and an amazing sweet floral flavor and aroma. They are a cross between a lemon and a tangerine. If you can't find Meyer lemons, make this gelato with regular lemons.

Mary and Bob Polito of Polito Family Farms, a third-generation San Diego farmer specializing in citrus, raises everything from Valencia and navel oranges to juicy Bearss limes to incredibly sweet Oroblanco and Ruby Red grapefruits. He always has Meyer lemons, mandarins, and Tom's Terrific mandarins during their season, and I use them for all of my citrus desserts.

5 large egg yolks
2 tablespoons water
1 tablespoon grated lemon zest
1 cup fresh Meyer lemon juice
   (from about 6 lemons)
   or regular fresh lemon juice, or
   more to taste
1 cup sugar
1 cup heavy cream
1 cup milk
2 tablespoons light corn syrup
1/4 teaspoon vanilla extract
   Pinch of salt

1. Place a 1-quart freezer container in the freezer. Fill a large bowl with ice and water and set aside. Fill a medium saucepan halfway with water and bring to a simmer.

2. In a medium stainless-steel bowl, beat the egg yolks, water, and lemon juice. Gradually whisk in 1/2 cup of the sugar. Add the lemon zest.

3. Place the bowl over the saucepan of water, making sure that it isn't touching the simmering water, and using a whisk, preferably a balloon whisk, whisk the egg yolk mixture continuously and vigorously in a circular motion until you have a thick foam, 3 to 4 minutes. Remove from the heat, nestle the bowl in the ice bath, and continue to whisk for another minute to cool.

4. Drain the water from the saucepan, wipe the pan dry, and add the heavy cream, milk, corn syrup, and the remaining ½ cup sugar. Place over medium-high heat and bring to a boil. Remove from the heat. Slowly whisk into the egg mixture. Return to the ice bath. Add the vanilla and salt. Taste, and if desired, add a touch more lemon juice. Allow to cool in the ice bath, stirring often.

5. Freeze the gelato in an ice cream maker following the manufacturer's directions. Transfer to the freezer container and freeze for at least 2 hours to firm.

Vienna Interlude

I HAD ALWAYS DREAMED OF TRAVELING TO VIENNA, especially after a few years at Spago. Wolfgang was constantly talking about his mom and the Austrian desserts of his childhood. Finally, after a few years of his saying, "You should go to Austria!" I called his travel agent and booked a ticket. The art of pastry is a continuing education, and I wanted to learn from the masters.

I was already a fan of Austrian pastries. Austria is a melting pot of cultures at the crossroads of central Europe. Because of this, you find influences in its cuisine from France, Hungary, Turkey, Russia, Poland, and Italy. The Austrians cook the way they dance and make music—enthusiastically and with a light heart. I loved their use of fruits and spices. I was especially drawn to Austrian "hot desserts," which have both hot and cold elements, like warm *apfelstrudel* served with cold *schlag* (whipped cream). They're homey, yet their flavors are sophisticated. A luscious plate of *kaiserschmarren,* souffléed pancakes with strawberry sauce, is less studied and precise than a French napoleon, yet more welcome on a plate after a big meal. It's a light dish—like so many Austrian desserts, there isn't a lot of flour involved.

Before I left for Vienna, I called a friend and asked her to get me a room in the hotel she managed on Stephansplatz, one of the city's most beautiful squares. I was enthralled from the moment I arrived. I toured every bakeshop in the city. As I walked down Stephansplatz past the majestic Gothic St. Stephen's Cathedral, with its tiled roof that looks just like a knitted blanket, I marveled at the Viennese architecture and its history. My first stop was Demel Konditorei (pastry shop). From the sidewalk, I looked into the massive windows filled with lavish displays of pastries. Then I opened the door to the gilded room, its antique cabinets overflowing with confections, cakes, cookies, and chocolates. The air was so sweet with sugar, almonds, and spices that I could almost taste it.

My head was spinning. My eyes bounced back and forth, then up to the golden ceiling. It was so grand! Like no pastry shop I had ever seen before— or since. The array of cake slices (*schnitten*) alone was overwhelming. How could I choose? I ordered and grabbed a seat in the dining hall. When the waitress came, the group of men at the next table stopped reading their giant newspapers, and gossiping ladies on the other side rubbernecked at the sight of one girl with six pieces of cake.

My idea of a perfect day in Austria was to sit in a *kaffeehaus* morning, afternoon, and evening, sipping tea and enjoying cake. I ate my way through Vienna and I was in heaven.

As planned, I learned from the masters. (Luckily, most of them spoke English.) I spent time in one of the oldest bakeries in Vienna, K.U.K. Hofzuckerbäcker L. Heiner, a 200-year-old bakery housed in a four-story building. Each floor was devoted to a different type of production—one for chocolate, one for marzipan, one for cakes, and one for *viennoiserie* "rich pastries," like croissants. The breads were baked on two underground floors. Some of the equipment was over a hundred years old.

*A*T KURKONDITOREI OBERLAA, the bakers made strudels by the yard and vats of their own jams and marmalades. Rolling racks were filled with sheet trays of strudels elbow to elbow. An entire 100-square-foot walk-in refrigerator was filled with finished cakes ready to be shipped. At the Hotel Sacher, I watched bakers pull strudel at an immense table. Two men pulled the largest gossamer sheets of dough imaginable, stretching them thinner and thinner over tables at least 6 feet long. This was a huge inspiration to me, and I owe the quality of my own *apfelstrudel* to those bakers.

My friend Gerte was the pastry chef for the Café Gloriette at the huge Schönbrunn Palace, summer residence of the Habsburgs. Schönbrunn is surrounded by magnificent gardens and even has a zoo. I worked in Gerte's production kitchen creating layered cakes that tourists would eat while gazing at the palace and its glorious fountains.

I traveled by train to Salzburg, and from there to a small village called Werfen. As I walked the ten minutes from the rail station down the only main street, I was transported back in time. Nestled in the Salzach Valley, the thousand-year-old village of Werfen is known for three things: the Burg Hohenwerfen, a castle that crowns the hill overlooking the town below; the Eisriesenwelt, the world's largest ice caves; and my destination, the Michelin two-star Restaurant Obauer. Brothers Karl and Rudolf Obauer have owned their restaurant since 1979. It's an intimate establishment that is recognized worldwide for its regional Austrian cooking infused with foreign flavors.

THE CENTURIES-OLD FACADE of Obauer was in direct contrast to the modern decor of the dining room. The food was all about detail. I worked with the pastry chef, Maria, and made jams, jellies, and confits. I got to work with chocolate and made *à la minute* preparations for both lunch and dinner services. Chef Karl let me make the *amuse-bouche* (little appetizer) each night, so I made little knishes and pizzas, and the guests adored them. I also made "family meal" for the staff. It was a real family affair—the brothers' cousin across the street was their butcher, and their uncle owned the bakery. Rudi taught me how important it is for a restaurant to evolve. Each year, he and Karl make improvements, always striving toward perfection.

I returned to California floating on air. I couldn't wait to get back into my kitchen, particularly because the fruit we have in California is the same fruit we used in Austrian desserts—apricots, plums, apples, and quinces. My interpretations of the Austrian desserts went onto the new Spago Beverly Hills menu in a category called "Austrian Imports." Some of them, like the souffléd pancakes *Kaiserschmarren*, have never come off. It's the most popular dessert we make.

LINZER COOKIES

▦ ▦ ▦

Here's a signature Austrian cookie, one of the prettiest cookies we make in the bakeshop. I use the same sweet, nutty linzer dough that I use for some of my tarts and fill the melt-in-your-mouth cookies with raspberry jam.

1 recipe Linzer Dough (page 368), chilled
About 1 cup raspberry jam
Confectioners' sugar for dusting

1. Remove the dough from the refrigerator and divide it into quarters. Place one quarter between two pieces of lightly floured parchment paper and roll out to an even ⅛-inch thickness. Place on a baking sheet with the parchment. Repeat with the other pieces of dough, rolling them out between parchment paper and stacking them, still on the parchment, on the baking sheet. Place in the freezer for at least 15 minutes.

2. Place racks in the middle and lower third of the oven and preheat the oven to 350°F. Line two baking sheets with parchment paper.

3. Remove the dough from the freezer, one sheet at a time. Carefully peel the top piece of parchment off the dough. Lay the parchment on a work surface and lightly dust it with flour. Lightly dust the dough with flour, flip it over onto the dusted paper, and carefully peel off the bottom piece of parchment. Using a 2-inch fluted or straight-edged round cookie cutter, cut out circles of dough. With a ½-inch-diameter circular cookie cutter, cut out holes from the centers of half of the circles, giving the circles shapes resembling rings (the holes can be baked, too, for nice mini cookies).

4. Carefully transfer the cookies to the baking sheets, about ½ inch apart. If the dough is too soft to transfer easily, return it to the freezer for 15 to 30 minutes, until firm. Bake the cookies until golden, 10 to 14 minutes, rotating the baking sheets from top to bottom and from front to back halfway through. Slide the parchment onto cooling racks and wait for 10 minutes, then carefully transfer

the cookies to the racks to cool completely. Make sure to let the baking sheets cool between batches. (At this point the cookies can be stored airtight for up to 5 days.)

5. Lay the cookies out on your work surface. Place a scant teaspoon of jam on the cookies without the holes and spread in an even layer. Generously dust the cookies with the holes with confectioners' sugar, either from a sugar sifter or from a fine-mesh strainer held over the cookies and tapped with your hand. Carefully place them on top of the jam-topped cookies so that the jam pokes out the center. Once filled, the cookies should be served within a day.

VARIATIONS

VIENNESE CRESCENTS: Omit the jam. Instead of rolling out the dough, pull off pieces of dough and shape into 1-inch balls. Roll the balls into small sausages, taper the ends, and shape into pointed crescents. Place on parchment-lined baking sheets ½ inch apart and bake until golden. Remove from the oven and immediately coat generously with confectioners' sugar.

LINZER THUMBPRINTS: Pull off pieces of dough and shape into 1-inch balls. Place on parchment-lined baking sheets ½ inch apart and press your thumb into the centers. Bake until golden. Remove from the oven and immediately dust generously with confectioners' sugar. Fill the centers with raspberry jam.

KAISERSCHMARREN
Souffléed Crème Fraîche Pancakes with Strawberry Sauce

SERVES 6 TO 8

■ ■ ■

Kaiserschmarren is a large souffléed pancake. The name means, literally, "the Emperor's little nothing." This is one of those Austrian dessert items that will forever be on the Spago menu. Traditionally it's a more savory affair, served to children on Sunday afternoons. We bake the pancakes in buttered and sugared baking dishes and serve them with a strawberry sauce, and we love to watch people's eyes widen with pleasure and surprise when they taste them for the first time.

FOR THE STRAWBERRY SAUCE
- 2 pounds 2 ounces strawberries, hulled and quartered
- ³/₄ cup plus 2 tablespoons sugar
- ¹/₄ cup water
- ³/₄ cup fresh orange juice (from 3 medium oranges)
- 1 star anise, lightly toasted (see page 378)
- 1 tablespoon Grand Marnier

FOR THE PANCAKES
- Softened butter for the pans
- 9 tablespoons sugar, plus more for dusting the pans
- 4 large egg yolks, at room temperature
- ¹/₄ cup fromage blanc (available at gourmet markets)
- ³/₄ cup crème fraîche
- 2 tablespoons dark rum
- ¹/₄ cup all-purpose flour
- 2 tablespoons Fat Raisins (page 364)
- 8 large egg whites
- ¹/₂ teaspoon cream of tartar

- ¹/₄ cup confectioners' sugar for dusting

1. **MAKE THE STRAWBERRY SAUCE:** Set aside 2 cups of the strawberries and the 2 tablespoons sugar. In a heavy saucepan, combine the remaining strawberries, the water, the ³/₄ cup sugar, the orange juice, star anise, and Grand Marnier. Bring to a boil over medium heat. Stir occasionally to prevent scorching. Reduce the heat and simmer for 10 minutes.

2. Remove from the heat and cover with plastic wrap. Allow to infuse for 10 minutes, then remove the plastic and discard the star anise. Cover with plastic again and allow to sit for 2 hours.

3. Pass the sauce through a fine-mesh strainer and set aside, or refrigerate if not using right away.

4. **MAKE THE PANCAKES:** Place a rack in the middle of the oven and preheat the oven to 400°F. Generously butter two 9- or 10-inch 2-inch-deep (I recommend Pyrex) pie pans or round cake pans. Add a heaping tablespoon of sugar to each pan and tap and turn the pans to dust evenly. Tap out any excess sugar.

5. In a medium bowl with a hand mixer, beat the egg yolks with 2 tablespoons of the sugar until the mixture is light and lemony yellow. Beat in the fromage blanc and scrape down the bowl and beaters. Beat in the crème fraîche and rum and scrape down the bowl and beaters. Beat in the flour and raisins. Set aside.

6. In the bowl of a stand mixer fitted with the whisk attachment, or in a large bowl with the hand mixer, beat the egg whites on medium-low speed until they foam, then add the cream of tartar. Turn the speed up to medium and continue to beat while streaming in the remaining 7 tablespoons sugar, a tablespoon at a time. Beat the whites to medium-stiff peaks.

7. Whisk half the egg whites into the crème fraîche base. Gently fold in the remaining egg whites. Divide the batter between the two pans. Bake for 15 minutes. Turn the pans 180 degrees and bake for another 5 to 8 minutes, until puffed and brown. The center should be pudding-like.

8. **FINISH THE SAUCE:** Meanwhile, in a large skillet, bring the strawberry sauce to a boil over high heat. Add the reserved 2 tablespoons sugar and stir until the sugar has dissolved. Add the reserved 2 cups strawberries and heat through, then divide among the serving plates.

9. When the pancakes are done, remove from the oven and, using a serving spoon, divide each one into 6 or 8 portions. Place 2 portions on each plate and dust with confectioners' sugar. You can also arrange all the portions on a platter, with the sauce, and serve family style. Serve immediately.

PALATSCHINKEN
Dessert Crepes with Poached Apricot Filling

SERVES 6

■ ■ ■

These velvety crepes are one of Wolfgang's favorite childhood food memories. His mother would make them for supper, filling them with farmer's cheese and dusting them with powdered sugar. At the restaurant, I serve them with this apricot filling, which I have on hand throughout the year, having preserved the summer's bounty in jars.

FOR THE CREPES

- ¾ cup plus 2 tablespoons all-purpose flour
- Pinch of salt
- 1 tablespoon sugar
- 2 large eggs, at room temperature
- 1 tablespoon unsalted butter, melted and still hot, plus more for cooking the crepes
- 1⅓ cups milk, at room temperature
- ¼ cup plus 3 tablespoons heavy cream

FOR THE APRICOT FILLING

- ½ cup sugar
- 2 cups fresh orange juice (from 4 large oranges)
- 1 vanilla bean, split, seeds scraped out and reserved
- 9 ripe apricots, halved and pitted
- 1 tablespoon fresh lemon juice

Confectioners' sugar for dusting

1. **MAKE THE CREPES:** Sift together the flour, salt, and sugar and set aside.

2. In a medium bowl, whisk the eggs until broken up. Add the hot butter in a stream, then whisk in the milk, being careful not to incorporate too much air. Whisk in the flour mixture and then the cream until smooth. (You can also mix this in a blender: Place the eggs, hot butter, and milk in the blender. With the machine running, add the flour mixture, then the cream. Blend for about a minute.) Set the batter aside, covered, to rest for 30 minutes to an hour.

3. Heat an 8-inch crepe pan or omelet pan over medium-high heat until it feels hot when you hold your hand above it. Brush lightly with melted butter. Ladle in about 3 tablespoons of batter (or use a scant ¼-cup measure) and tilt or swirl the pan to spread the batter evenly. Cook until the surface of the crepe is covered with bubbles and the edges can easily be lifted away from the pan, so that

you can see if the underside is golden, about 2 minutes. When the underside is golden, flip the crepe, using a thin spatula or, very carefully, your fingertips. Cook the other side for 30 seconds, then transfer to a plate. Top with a piece of parchment paper. Repeat with the remaining batter, stacking the crepes between pieces of parchment as you go along. You should have 12 crepes. (Stacked between the parchment paper and wrapped airtight, the crepes can be refrigerated for up to 2 days or frozen for up to 2 weeks. Defrost at room temperature and warm in a dry skillet.)

4. **MAKE THE APRICOT FILLING:** In a medium saucepan, combine the sugar, orange juice, and the vanilla seeds and bring to a boil. Boil to reduce the mixture by a third. Add the apricots, turn the heat down to medium, and cook until softened, 4 to 5 minutes. Stir in the lemon juice. Set aside. (The filling can be refrigerated, covered, for up to 1 week.)

5. **ASSEMBLE THE CREPES:** Place 2 crepes on each plate. Place 3 apricot halves with their syrup on top of each crepe. Roll up, dust with confectioners' sugar, and serve.

VARIATION

BAKED CREPES WITH CUSTARD GLAZE: Place a rack in the middle of the oven and preheat the oven to 350°F. In a medium bowl, beat together 1 large egg, 2 tablespoons sugar, 3/4 cup heavy cream, and 2 teaspoons fresh lemon juice. Fill the crepes as above and place, seam side down, in a buttered baking dish. Spoon the custard over the crepes. Place the crepes in the oven and bake for 30 minutes, or until nicely browned. Serve hot, sprinkling each serving with confectioners' sugar.

Sherry's Secrets

For lacy crepes, add
2 to 3 tablespoons
brandy to the batter.

TOPFENKNÖDEL
Tender Farmer's Cheese Dumplings with Apricot Sauce

SERVES 6

■ ■ ■

Please take the time to make these! Austrians are known for their dumplings, even their dessert dumplings. These are made with a combination of farmer's cheese, goat cheese, and fromage blanc. They're substantial but not heavy, great for a Sunday brunch. The dumplings are poached, then rolled in a mixture of browned bread crumbs, sugar, and cinnamon and served with apricot jam. They're soft and pillowy on the inside, crunchy on the outside. I especially love the variation (page 231), with its magical layers of flavor and texture. It has an apricot hidden in the middle and a lump of brown sugar inside the apricot, like a little edible surprise. Make sure to use small sugar cubes.

FOR THE DUMPLING DOUGH
- 2 tablespoons unsalted butter, softened
- 3 tablespoons sugar
- 1 vanilla bean, split, seeds scraped out and reserved
- Grated zest and juice of 1/2 lemon
- 1 teaspoon grated orange zest
- 6 ounces farmer's cheese
- 3 ounces soft fresh goat cheese
- 3 ounces fromage blanc (available at gourmet markets)
- 1 large egg, plus 2 large egg yolks
- 2 tablespoons all-purpose flour
- 1 tablespoon dark rum
- 4 ounces sliced white bread, crusts removed, cut into 1/4-inch cubes (about 5 cups)

FOR THE BREAD CRUMB MIXTURE
- 2 ounces (1/2 stick) unsalted butter
- 1/3 cup sugar
- 1 1/2 cups dried homemade bread crumbs
- 1/2 teaspoon ground cinnamon

FOR THE POACHING LIQUID
- 2–3 quarts water
- 1 cup dry white wine
- Zest of 1 orange removed in wide strips with a vegetable peeler
- 1 cup sugar
- 1 cinnamon stick, lightly toasted (see page 378)

Confectioners' sugar for dusting
Apricot Schmutz (page 367) or apricot jam for serving

1. **MAKE THE DUMPLING DOUGH**: In the bowl of a stand mixer fitted with the paddle attachment, or in a large bowl with a hand mixer, cream together the butter, sugar, vanilla seeds, and the lemon and orange zests for 2 minutes, or until fluffy. Scrape down the sides of the bowl. Add the farmer's cheese, goat cheese, and fromage blanc and beat on medium speed for 4 to 5 minutes. Add the egg and the yolks one at a time, scraping down the sides of the bowl after each addition. Beating at low speed, add the flour, then add the lemon juice and rum. On low speed, add the bread cubes. Blend for 30 seconds. Cover the bowl tightly with plastic wrap and refrigerate for 2 hours.

2. To shape each dumpling, moisten your hands and scoop out ¼ cup of the dough. Gently shape it into a ball. (You should have 12 balls.) Set the dumplings on a piece of lightly floured parchment paper.

3. **MAKE THE BREAD CRUMB MIXTURE:** In a medium skillet, melt the butter over medium heat and cook until light brown. Mix together the sugar, bread crumbs, and cinnamon and stir into the butter. Turn the heat to medium-low and cook, stirring continuously, until the crumbs are lightly browned and crispy, 4 to 5 minutes. Transfer to a bowl or a plate. Keep warm in a low oven.

4. **POACH THE DUMPLINGS:** Combine the water, white wine, orange zest, sugar, and cinnamon stick in a large wide saucepan—make sure the poaching liquid is deep enough to cover the dumplings—and bring to a simmer. Carefully place the dumplings on a large slotted spoon and tip into the simmering liquid. Simmer for 12 minutes.

5. Using a slotted spoon, carefully remove the dumplings from the pan and roll in the warm bread crumb mixture. Dust generously with confectioners' sugar and serve 2 on a plate with apricot schmutz or jam.

VARIATION

APRICOT-FILLED TOPFENKNÖDEL: For the filling, you will need 6 small apricots, slit on one side and pitted, 6 small brown sugar cubes, and dark rum. Make the dough as directed. Dip a sugar cube in the rum, then insert into the middle of a pitted apricot. To shape each dumpling, moisten your hands and scoop out a scant ½ cup of dough. Hold it in your hand, and with your other hand, use your fingers to hollow out the middle. Place the apricot in the hollow. Work the dough back over the apricot. Patch with more dough if necessary, and pat the dough firmly around the apricot to make a round ball. Set the dumpling on a piece of lightly floured parchment paper and make 5 more dumplings in the same way. Continue as directed in the above recipe, making the bread crumbs and poaching the dumplings for about 12 minutes. Serve 1 per plate.

Apfelstrudel
Apple Strudel

MAKES 1 BIG STRUDEL, ABOUT 20 SERVINGS

■ ■ ■

This is the quintessential Austrian apple strudel, the one that Wolfgang grew up eating. Wolfgang insisted that only Austrians could make really good strudel dough, but when I made this, he said, "You deserve an Austrian passport!" I made it for his family when they came to Spago, and his sisters, Maria and Christina, said that mine was the best they'd ever tasted. Wolf and his brother, Klaus, predictably, stuck by their mom's as the best in the world.

I like doing this dough by hand. The whole process of making strudel is a tactile one, from the mixing of the dough through the pulling and shaping of the strudel. At Hotel Sacher in Vienna, a city where you can buy strudel dough in every supermarket, the dough is always made from scratch and pulled by hand.

FOR THE FILLING

- 8 firm apples, preferably 4 Granny Smiths and 4 Braeburns or Fujis, peeled, cored, and sliced feather-thin
- 1/2 cup fresh lemon juice (from 2 large lemons)
- 1/2 cup sugar
- 1/2 teaspoon ground cinnamon
- 1 cup Fat Raisins (page 364)

- 8 ounces (2 sticks) unsalted butter, melted, for brushing
- 1 cup dried homemade bread crumbs
- 1 cup applesauce
- 1/2 cup Vanilla Sugar (page 349)

FOR THE DOUGH

- 1 1/2 cups bread flour
- 1 cup all-purpose flour
- 1/4 teaspoon salt
- 1 large egg
- 2 tablespoons vegetable oil, plus more for coating
- 3/4 cup warm (90°F) water

1. **MAKE THE FILLING:** In a large bowl, toss together the apples, lemon juice, sugar, and cinnamon. Stir in the raisins. Set aside. (Allowing the apples to sit with the lemon juice and sugar will tenderize them so that the filling will be nice and soft when the strudel is done.)

2. **MAKE THE DOUGH:** Sift together the bread flour, all-purpose flour, and salt into a medium bowl. In a small bowl, using a fork, beat together the egg, the 2 tablespoons vegetable oil, and the warm water. Create a well in the center

of the dry ingredients and pour in the liquid ingredients. Using the fork, work the flour mixture into the egg mixture, scraping it in from the sides of the well into the center and turning the bowl as you do so. At first the mixture will be like paste, but as you work in the flour, it will become a dough.

3. Once the fork is no longer useful for incorporating the flour, use your hands to work the rest of the flour into the dough, and turn out onto a lightly floured work surface. Knead the dough for 10 minutes (it will be sticky at first, but resist the urge to add flour to it or to the work surface; just keep rubbing the dough off your hands and kneading, and it will soon stop sticking). Knead by folding the dough toward you and then pressing down and toward the folded edge, leaning in with all of your weight, from your shoulders, through your arms, and to the heels of your hands. Think of the dough as a clock—from 12 o'clock, you fold the dough over to within a couple of inches of the bottom edge (6 o'clock) and lean in along the seam, pressing until there is no more line. Turn the dough

a quarter turn, to 3 o'clock, fold over, and knead again. Continue in this rhythm, moving the dough from 3 to 6 to 9 to 12 and around again, until it is satiny. When the dough is ready, round it out with both hands, shaping it into a ball and leaving no seam on the bottom. Coat the dough with a thin film of vegetable oil and wrap it airtight and wrinkle-free with plastic wrap. Let rest in a warm spot for 30 minutes to 2 hours. The dough should be soft.

4. Place a rack in the middle of the oven and preheat the oven to 375°F. For easy cleanup, line the bottom and edges of a 12-x-17-inch half sheet pan with aluminum foil and line the bottom of the foil with parchment paper.

5. PULL THE DOUGH AND ASSEMBLE THE STRUDEL: This has to be done fairly quickly so the dough doesn't dry out, but you will find it easy and pleasurable. Cover a table that is at least 4 feet long and 3 feet wide with a tablecloth and dust the tablecloth with a thin layer of flour. Take off any rings with sharp edges. Carefully remove the plastic from the dough and dust the dough with flour. With a lightly dusted rolling pin, roll the dough into a 12-inch square. Dip your hands in flour. As you pull the dough, you will be working it out toward the ends of the table. It's important not to let it fold over itself and not to tear it—although if this does happen, you can bring the edges of the tear together and pinch a small fold to mend it.

6. Place the square of dough in front of you on the table. Make your hands into loose fists and slip them under the dough with your knuckles up, then pull the dough back with your knuckles, as if you (girls) were putting on panty hose. Begin to pull the dough, pressing the backs of your hands into it as you pull. The object is to stretch out the dough into a rectangle that overhangs the edges of the table. As you work, look for the parts of the dough that are less transparent and pull there to obtain a large, silky, billowy sheet. When you reach a corner at one end of the table, pull the dough over the edge and lock it underneath the corner. Pull the dough out to the other corner at the same end of the table and lock it underneath. Continue pulling and stretching the dough, moving like a dancer from one end of the table to the other, and lock the dough over the two remaining corners. When you have finished pulling the dough, lift the edges here and there to make it billow and relax, being careful not to allow it to fold over itself. With kitchen scissors or a paring knife, trim the thicker bottom of the edges that overhang the table so that the entire sheet is gossamer (be careful not to cut your tablecloth!).

7. Working quickly, brush the dough all over with some of the melted butter. Sprinkle on ½ cup of the bread crumbs. Stand at one end of the sheet of dough. Using ¼ cup of the remaining bread crumbs, make a line 4 inches from the end of the dough, leaving a 2-inch border on each side. Top this line with ½ cup of the applesauce. Drain all of the liquid from the sliced apples and spread half of the apples over the applesauce. Top with the remaining ½ cup applesauce. Make another layer with the remaining apples. Sprinkle on the vanilla sugar and the remaining ¼ cup bread crumbs and drizzle on ¼ cup melted butter.

8. Now roll up the strudel. Fold the two 2-inch corners of the dough in toward the center over the filling, then fold the bottom edge of the dough up over the filling. Now, using the tablecloth to lift it, roll the dough over once so that the filling is completely enclosed. Stop and use your hands to make a snug log after the first half-turn, and continue to roll up. Every time you roll the strudel over, gently tuck the log so that it's nice and tight. When you finish rolling, you'll have a strudel that is almost as long as your table is wide. If any filling has seeped out, gently push it in at the ends. Cut off all but 1 inch of the overhanging dough at the ends, press together to seal, and fold it into itself.

9. To get your long strudel onto the prepared baking sheet, place the prepared pan next to the strudel. Lift up one half of the strudel, cradling the end like the head of a newborn baby, and gently place on the baking sheet. Now lift up the other half in the same way and swing it around so that the strudel forms a U on the baking sheet. Brush generously with melted butter. Keep the remaining butter warm.

10. Place the strudel in the oven and bake for 20 minutes. Remove from the oven, brush again with butter, rotate the pan from front to back, and return to the oven. Bake for another 20 to 30 minutes, until golden brown. Brush again with butter and allow to cool completely. Reheat gently before serving. To reheat, preheat the oven to 350°F. Heat the entire strudel for 15 to 20 minutes, until crisp on the outside and warm inside, or individual pieces for 10 minutes.

    NOTE: Once cooled, the strudel can be wrapped airtight and frozen for 2 weeks. Thaw, still wrapped, in the refrigerator, then unwrap, place on a baking sheet, and crisp in a 350°F oven for about 20 minutes.

BANANA SALZBURGER NOCKERLN
Banana–Chocolate Chip Soufflé Mountains

■ ■ ■

A spectacular way to present a soufflé, my version of the Austrian *nockerln* omits the layer of marzipan and jam and adds bananas and chocolate chips. Like the traditional soufflé, it is formed into three mounds to represent the three mountains surrounding Salzburg and dusted with "snowy" confectioners' sugar. It's baked in a gratin dish and served with chocolate sauce.

FOR THE BANANAS

- 1 cup fresh orange juice (from 2 large oranges)
- 1 tablespoon fresh lemon juice
- 2 tablespoons sugar
- 2 tablespoons light brown sugar
- 1 vanilla bean, split, seeds scraped out and reserved
- 2 tablespoons Tia Maria or other coffee liqueur
- 3 ripe but firm bananas

FOR THE SOUFFLÉ

- Softened butter for the gratin dish
- 3/4 cup sugar, plus more for dusting the gratin dish
- 8 large egg whites
- 1/4 teaspoon cream of tartar
- 1 cup Banana Schmutz (page 366)
- 3/4 cup chocolate chips

Confectioners' sugar for dusting
"Ten-Year" Chocolate Sauce (page 345)

1. **PREPARE THE BANANAS:** Combine the orange juice, lemon juice, sugar, brown sugar, vanilla seeds, and the liqueur in a medium bowl. Slice the bananas and toss with the mixture. Let macerate for 30 minutes.

2. **MAKE THE SOUFFLÉ:** Place a rack in the lower third of the oven and preheat the oven to 375°F. Butter a 2-quart gratin or baking dish and dust lightly with sugar.

3. Drain the bananas and spread in one layer over the bottom of the gratin dish.

4. In the bowl of a stand mixer fitted with the whisk attachment, or in a large bowl with a hand mixer, beat the egg whites on medium speed for 30 seconds, or until foamy. Add the cream of tartar. Continue to beat on medium speed as you slowly sprinkle in the 3/4 cup sugar. Beat the whites to stiff peaks, 1 to 2 minutes more.

5. Combine the banana schmutz and chocolate chips in a medium bowl. Using a rubber spatula, fold one third of the egg whites into the banana mixture. Carefully fold in the remaining egg whites to avoid deflating the mixture.

6. Mound the soufflé mixture into the gratin dish, making 3 side-by-side mountains on top of the bananas. Bake for 20 to 30 minutes, until puffed and golden brown but still creamy in the center. Remove from the oven and dust generously with confectioners' sugar (the "snow"). Serve immediately, with the chocolate sauce.

MALAKOFFTORTE
Mocha Cream Semifreddo

MAKES ONE 10-INCH TORTE

■ ■ ■

The traditional *malakofftorte* is a torte made of whipped cream and ladyfingers that have been soaked in a rum syrup. It's one of Wolfgang's favorite desserts, so he asked me to develop one for Spago. My version is more like a mocha semifreddo. When critics ask why I call mine a *malakofftorte,* I reply, "It's a ladyfinger's prerogative."

FOR THE MOCHA SEMIFREDDO
- 2¼ teaspoons (1 package) powdered gelatin
- ¼ cup plus 2 tablespoons water
- 1½ ounces bittersweet chocolate, finely chopped
- 1 cup brewed espresso
- ½ cup milk
- 1 vanilla bean, split, seeds scraped out and reserved
- 4 large eggs
- ¾ cup sugar
- 2 cups heavy cream

FOR THE COFFEE SYRUP
- 1⅔ cups sugar
- 1⅓ cups water
- ½ cup brewed espresso
- ¼ cup dark rum

- 32 ladyfingers, homemade (page 35) or store-bought

1. **MAKE THE SEMIFREDDO:** Line the bottom of a 10-inch springform pan with parchment paper. Place the gelatin in a small bowl and pour in ¼ cup of the water. Let bloom (soften) for 5 to 10 minutes.

2. Place the chocolate in a large heatproof bowl. Pour the espresso into a saucepan and bring to a boil over medium heat, stirring constantly. Reduce to ¼ cup, being careful not to burn the espresso. Add the milk and vanilla seeds and bring back to a boil, then pour over the chocolate. Tap the bowl gently against your work surface to settle the chocolate into the milk, and let stand for 1 to 2 minutes. Then, using a whisk, stir gently until the chocolate has completely dissolved and the mixture is smooth. Add the gelatin and stir until dissolved. Set aside.

3. In the bowl of a stand mixer fitted with the whisk attachment, or in a large bowl with a hand mixer, begin beating the eggs at medium speed. Meanwhile, combine the sugar and the remaining 2 tablespoons water in a saucepan and cook,

stirring, over medium heat until the sugar has dissolved. Turn up the heat to medium-high and bring to a boil. Insert a candy thermometer and continue to cook until the syrup reaches 235°F. Remove from the heat.

4. With the mixer running, carefully stream the hot syrup into the eggs, pouring it down the side of the bowl, not over the whisk or beaters. Turn the speed to high and beat until the eggs have tripled in volume, about 4 minutes. Beat for 1 additional minute at medium-low speed to stabilize the eggs. Scrape one third of the egg mixture into the bowl with the mocha mixture and whisk together. Using the whisk, fold in the remaining egg mixture.

5. Using a hand mixer, beat the cream until not quite stiff. Fold into the mocha mixture until well incorporated.

6. MAKE THE SYRUP: In a medium saucepan, combine the sugar, water, espresso, and dark rum and bring to a simmer. Simmer, stirring, until all of the sugar has dissolved, then remove from the heat and pour into a wide bowl.

7. ASSEMBLE THE SEMIFREDDO: Soak the ladyfingers 8 at a time in the syrup until they are about to fall apart but can still be lifted intact from the bowl.

8. Layer 8 ladyfingers in the bottom of the springform pan. Pour 1½ cups of the semifreddo mixture over the ladyfingers and spread to the edges of the pan with a rubber spatula or a baby offset spatula. Make another layer of ladyfingers and another layer of mocha semifreddo. Repeat two more times, so that you have 4 layers each of ladyfingers and semifreddo. Smooth the top and place a sheet of plastic wrap directly against it. Wrap tightly and place in the freezer for at least 4 hours, or up to 1 week.

9. To serve, wrap a hot moist kitchen towel around the outside of the springform pan to release the semifreddo. Carefully run a knife between the sides of the torte and the pan and remove the ring. Place the malakofftorte on a serving plate and serve.

TWELVE-LAYER
FLOURLESS CHOCOLATE DOBOS TORTE

SERVES 12

■ ■ ■

A traditional Dobos torte consists of thin layers of white cake layered with chocolate cream and finished with a crisp caramel topping. The Spago version, which I developed with Suzanne Griswold, who was the pastry chef at Spago for several years and worked with me, consists of chocolate cake brushed with coffee syrup and layered with chocolate praline cream. There are twelve feather-light, ultra-thin layers of cake and chocolate praline cream, all the same thickness, with the top dusted with croquante (pulverized almond brittle). We bake the cake in sheet pans and cut the torte into long triangular pieces or into slices. For the Governors Ball in 2004, we made enough Dobos torte to feed 1,700 people. We cut it into 4-inch circles, dusted them with the croquante, and placed them in blue cake boxes of pulled sugar whose tuile-shaped lids contained perfect round balls of coffee ice cream (see page 132).

1. MAKE THE CAKE LAYERS: Place racks in the middle and upper third of the oven. If you have three racks, space them evenly. Preheat the oven to 375°F. Spray three 12-x-17-inch half sheet pans with pan spray and line each with parchment paper. Spray the parchment.

FOR THE CAKE

- 2 ounces bittersweet chocolate, finely chopped
- 2 cups sugar
- 1/2 cup unsweetened cocoa powder, preferably Valrhona (see Sources)
- 8 large eggs, separated, plus 4 large egg whites

FOR THE COFFEE SYRUP

- 1/2 cup water
- 3/4 cup sugar
- 1/2 cup brewed espresso

FOR THE CHOCOLATE PRALINE FILLING

- 3 ounces bittersweet chocolate, finely chopped
- 2 ounces milk chocolate, preferably Valrhona Jivara Lactée (see Sources), finely chopped
- 2 ounces praline paste, homemade (page 357) or store-bought (see Sources), at room temperature
- 3/4 cup sugar
- 1/4 cup water
- 3 large eggs
- 1 1/2 cups heavy cream

FOR GARNISH

- 1/2 cup Croquante (page 355), pulverized

2. Melt the chocolate in a microwave-safe bowl at 50 percent power for about 2 minutes or in a heatproof bowl set over a saucepan of simmering water. Stir until completely melted and keep warm in a double boiler. Sift together 1/2 cup of the sugar and the cocoa powder and set aside.

3. In a small bowl, lightly beat the egg yolks. Set aside. In a stand mixer fitted with the whisk attachment, or in a large bowl with a hand mixer, beat the egg whites on low speed for 1 minute, or until they begin to foam. Continue to beat on low speed for 12 to 15 minutes (yes, it will take that long) while you very gradually add the remaining 1 1/2 cups sugar. Toward the end of the 12 to 15 minutes, turn the speed up to medium. The whites should become satiny and very fluffy.

4. When the egg whites reach medium-stiff peaks, turn the speed to low. Quickly stream the egg yolks into the whites. Add the warm chocolate and beat just until combined. Gradually beat in the sugar-cocoa mixture.

5. Divide the batter evenly among the three pans, about 3 cups per pan. Smear in an even layer with a spatula, preferably offset (see page 17 for smearing tips). Run your finger along the inside edge of each pan to remove the excess batter. Place the first two pans in the oven and bake for 7 minutes. Switch the pans from top to bottom and rotate from front to back and bake for another 3 to 5 minutes, until the cake has a matte finish and does not collapse when gently pressed. Bake the third cake on the middle rack for 10 to 12 minutes, rotating from front to back after 7 minutes. Allow the cakes to cool in the pans.

6. MAKE THE COFFEE SYRUP: Combine the water and sugar in a small saucepan and bring to a simmer. Simmer, stirring, until the sugar has dissolved and remove from the heat. Stir in the espresso and set aside.

7. MAKE THE CHOCOLATE PRALINE FILLING: Melt the bittersweet chocolate and milk chocolate in a microwave-safe bowl at 50 percent power for about 2 minutes or in a heatproof bowl set over a saucepan of simmering water. Stir with a rubber spatula until smooth. Stir in the praline paste. Keep warm in a double boiler.

8. Combine the sugar and water in a small saucepan and bring to a boil. Stir to dissolve the sugar. Insert a candy thermometer and bring the syrup to 235°F.

9. Meanwhile, beat the eggs on high speed in the bowl of a stand mixer fitted with the whisk attachment, or in a large bowl with a hand mixer, until light and

fluffy, about 5 minutes. Stream in the hot sugar syrup and continue to beat on high speed until the eggs have tripled in volume, about 5 minutes. Scrape down the sides of the bowl and the whisk or beaters.

10. Stir one third of the egg mixture into the chocolate to lighten it, then using a rubber spatula, fold the chocolate into the eggs, turning the bowl and scraping the bottom with your spatula to incorporate all the chocolate.

11. Beat the cream with a hand mixer or a balloon whisk to super-soft peaks: it should form a thick coating on the beaters but should not stand up. Fold into the chocolate mixture.

12. ASSEMBLE THE DOBOS TORTE: Place a baking sheet upside down on your work surface, spray lightly with pan spray, and cover with a sheet of parchment. Clear a space in your freezer for the baking sheet.

13. Run a knife around the edges of one of the cake layers and pull the cake from the pan by lifting up the parchment. Flip upside down onto the upside-down baking sheet. Place a hot moist kitchen towel on the parchment on the bottom of the cake, wait for 1 minute, remove the towel, and then peel and tear the parchment off in pieces. If the parchment sticks in places, place the hot damp towel on top for a minute. Brush the layer generously with $1/2$ cup of the coffee syrup. Spread one third of the chocolate filling over the cake in an even layer, using an offset spatula. Repeat with the next two cake layers, stacking them on the first layer, and the remaining filling. Place in the freezer for at least 4 hours to set the chocolate praline cream.

14. Cut the cake lengthwise in half, then again crosswise. Transfer one quarter to a serving platter. Stack the remaining quarters on top, to get 12 layers of cake and 12 layers of chocolate praline cream. Sprinkle the top with the croquante. Refrigerate or freeze until ready to serve. The cake can be frozen, wrapped airtight, for several weeks. Thaw in the refrigerator.

Sherry's Secrets

To loosen parchment paper from cake if it sticks, place a hot moist kitchen towel on top of the parchment for 1 minute. Remove the towel and gently peel back the parchment.

SACHER TORTE

■ ■ ■

Between you and me, I always felt that what the Hotel Sacher does best is its *apfelstrudel,* not its Sacher torte. I would go to the Café Demel for Sacher and to Sacher for strudel. In any case, because of the many myths and stories associated with the cake, Sacher won't reveal the recipe. The famous chocolate cake, created there in 1832, has an apricot filling and a shiny chocolate glaze. It's dense, almost like a brownie, and should always be served with whipped cream. For ten years, Wolfgang insisted that Sacher torte was a waste of time, that it was nothing but a dry chocolate cake. He changed his tune when I perfected this recipe.

FOR THE CAKE

- ⅔ cup all-purpose flour
- ½ teaspoon salt
- 6 ounces (1½ sticks) unsalted butter
- 12 ounces bittersweet chocolate, finely chopped
- 8 large eggs, separated, plus 2 large egg whites
- 1 cup plus 2 tablespoons sugar

FOR THE APRICOT FILLING

- 1½ cups apricot jam
- 1 tablespoon apricot brandy

FOR THE CHOCOLATE GLAZE

- 6 ounces bittersweet chocolate, finely chopped
- 2 tablespoons unsalted butter, softened
- ⅓ cup heavy cream
- 2 tablespoons light corn syrup

  Whipped cream for serving

1. **MAKE THE CAKE:** Place a rack in the middle of the oven and preheat the oven to 350°F. Spray two 9-inch round cake pans with pan spray and line the bottoms with parchment paper. Spray the parchment.

2. Sift together the flour and salt and set aside.

3. Melt the butter and chocolate in a microwave-safe bowl at 50 percent power for about 2 minutes or in a heatproof bowl set over a saucepan of simmering water. Stir until well combined and smooth, about 1 minute.

4. Place the egg yolks and the 2 tablespoons sugar in the bowl of a stand mixer fitted with the whisk attachment, or use a large bowl and a hand mixer, and beat

on medium-high speed until thick and lemon-colored and the mixture forms a ribbon when lifted with a spatula, about 3 minutes. Beat in the chocolate mixture.

5. In a large bowl, using a hand mixer on medium speed or a whisk, preferably a balloon whisk, beat the egg whites until they form soft peaks. Continue to beat while you gradually add the 1 cup sugar, a tablespoon at a time. The egg whites should hold stiff, shiny peaks. Stir one quarter of the egg whites into the chocolate mixture. Gently fold the chocolate mixture and the flour into the egg whites in 3 additions of each, alternating the two.

6. Carefully divide the batter between the prepared pans. Place in the oven and bake for 25 minutes. Turn the pans 180 degrees and bake the cakes for another 15 to 20 minutes, until the tops are firm when gently pressed with your finger and a tester inserted in the center comes out just about clean, with a few moist crumbs. Remove from the oven and allow to cool for 10 minutes in the pans on a rack. Then carefully run a knife along the inside of the pans, invert onto cake rounds, remove the pans, peel off the parchment, and slide the cakes onto the racks. Allow to cool completely.

7. MAKE THE APRICOT FILLING: Puree the jam in a food processor fitted with the steel blade or press through a fine-mesh strainer. Transfer to a saucepan, stir in the apricot brandy, and warm slightly so that you can spread it easily over the cake.

8. If the cakes are domed, trim the tops to create an even layer. Spread the bottom cake layer with two thirds of the apricot filling. Top with the upside-down second layer and spread the top evenly with the remaining filling. Chill for 30 minutes.

9. MAKE THE CHOCOLATE GLAZE: Place the chocolate and butter in a heatproof bowl. Bring the cream to a boil and pour over the mixture. Tap the bowl against your work surface to settle the chocolate into the cream, then stir until the chocolate and butter have melted. Add the corn syrup and stir until smooth. Allow to cool slightly (the glaze should be at 90° to 95°F).

10. Place the cake on a rack above a sheet of parchment or a newspaper. Pour the glaze over the top all at once. Turn the cake and spread the glaze over the sides. Allow to set for 5 minutes, then transfer the cake to a cake plate and refrigerate for at least 15 minutes, or up to 1 day. Serve with whipped cream.

Sherry's Secrets

FREEZING CAKE LAYERS

You can freeze most plain layers of cake before you ice or glaze them. They will not dry out if you brush them lightly with Simple Syrup (page 350), then double-wrap them in plastic wrap and seal in a freezer bag. With Sacher torte, you can freeze the double-layered cake, or if you don't have room for the double layer, you can top the individual layers with the filling and freeze them separately.

THE ORIGINS OF A CAKE

Stories about the Sacher torte's origins conflict, and the House of Demel and the House of Sacher have a long-running feud about who actually invented the cake. The Sachers claim that the cake was created by Franz Sacher while he was still a chef for Prince von Metternich. The Demels claim that the cake is theirs. The Demel version does not include the apricot glaze. In any case, the Sachers got the name and, at least in most versions, the glaze.

Spago
Beverly Hills

WITHIN THREE YEARS OF MY JOINING THE SPAGO family, Barbara Lazaroff and Wolfgang, with their partner Tom Kaplan, had found a new home for the restaurant in Beverly Hills. It was to be a larger, more ambitious establishment. The place on Sunset Boulevard needed a lot of work, and they had known for some time that they were either going to have to do a major makeover or find a new location. When they found out that a large, popular restaurant called Bistro Garden on Canon Drive in downtown Beverly Hills was about to close, they grabbed the space.

The new Spago had an altogether more serious feel. Barbara brilliantly divided the rooms into open spaces that give onto a beautiful, large courtyard dining patio that is warmer in winter with outdoor space heaters. There isn't a table in the restaurant from which the garden cannot be seen. From the main dining room, you can see the chefs on the front line through a tall window that rises like a fishbowl above the banquettes. Barbara commissioned work from more than 100 artists and also hung cherished pieces from her and Wolfgang's own private collection.

Our move to Beverly Hills required hiring new staff, which entailed interviews, tryouts, and orientation. And it took a day just to open all of the boxes filled with equipment, pots, and pans, clean everything, and organize it efficiently in its new home. All of the departments, from dishwashing to accounting, hit the ground running. The move would have been hectic under normal circumstances, but it was particularly difficult because the first parties, before the official opening in April, were scheduled for just days after the Oscars. We always cater the Academy of Motion Picture Arts and Sciences Governors Ball event, a sit-down dinner after the Oscars for 1,700 people and our most important catering event of the year. Orchestrating the Governors Ball and the move to Beverly Hills was quite a feat. To make things even more complicated, we were informed just as we were packing up that we were contractually obligated to keep Spago Hollywood open—so I was running two pastry shops.

The word *spago* refers to a circular spaghetti strand that has no end and no beginning. Spago Beverly Hills truly lives up to its name. Whereas Spago Hollywood was open only for dinner, Spago Beverly Hills is open for dinner every night and does a brisk lunch business Monday through Saturday. It seats 160 people in the formal dining areas and 90 in the private dining room. We're busy all the time, serving hundreds of people day and night.

I DESIGNED MY NEW BAKESHOP to be very accommodating, occupying one end of the kitchen. Our tasks include making specialty breads, buns, and brioche; daily desserts; and cookies and confections, in addition to filling orders for special events in the restaurant and special-occasion cakes for birthdays, graduations, and weddings.

We work in harmony with the front of the house, responding to the desires of our guests, and we receive last-minute requests on a daily basis. On many a night, I've had to think on my feet to pull a birthday cake out of a hat that wasn't ordered ahead. On one occasion, Wolfgang ran into the kitchen exclaiming, "Ve need a vedding cake!" While he was making his rounds, two guests had told him they'd just returned from Vegas, where they had decided to get married. Normally, in this situation, a chef would respond, "What date?" but at Spago, it's "What course are they on?" This has led me to my mission statement for Spago: "Difficult? Immediately. Impossible? Give me a minute."

PRESIDENT CLINTON'S OATMEAL COOKIES

MAKES 48 SMALL COOKIES OR 24 LARGE COOKIES

■ ■ ■

Former president Bill Clinton is a loyal Spago guest, and he loves these cookies. The first time I made them for him, we were catering a private party in Beverly Hills, and I'd been told that he was allergic to chocolate but was crazy about cookies. I filled the trunk of my turquoise Thunderbird with boxes of oatmeal cookies and some other desserts and took off for the party. I had just gotten my dog, Chunk, and there were some goodies for him in the car as well. When I got to the party, the security detail had me pop the trunk, as they always do, but this time I wasn't waved through. Their dogs went crazy, and suddenly I was being ordered to get out of the car and lie on the ground with my hands up. I lay there, terrified, until the guards realized what the problem was: their dogs had discovered Chunk's pepperoni sticks!

1½ cups all-purpose flour
1 teaspoon baking soda
7 ounces (1¾ sticks) unsalted butter, softened
1 cup sugar
1 cup packed light brown sugar
1½ teaspoons freshly grated nutmeg
¾ teaspoon ground cinnamon
2 large eggs, at room temperature
3 cups rolled oats
1½ cups Fat Raisins (page 364)

1. Sift together the flour and baking soda and set aside.

2. In the bowl of a stand mixer fitted with the paddle attachment, or in a large bowl with a hand mixer, cream the butter on high speed until lemony yellow, about 2 minutes. Scrape down the sides of the bowl and the paddle or beaters. Add the sugar, brown sugar, nutmeg, and cinnamon. Continue creaming the mixture on high speed until it is smooth and lump-free, about 2 minutes. Stop the mixer and scrape down the sides of the bowl and the paddle.

3. Add the eggs one at a time, scraping down the bowl and paddle after each addition. Beat on low speed for 15 to 30 seconds, until the eggs are fully incorporated. Scrape down the sides of the bowl and the paddle.

4. On low speed, add the sifted flour mixture, beating until all of the flour is incorporated. Scrape down the sides of the bowl. On low speed, mix in the oats and raisins.

5. With a rubber spatula, scoop out the dough and divide it in half. Center one half along the bottom of a sheet of parchment paper and roll it up in the paper, creating a log about 2 inches wide and 12 inches long. Repeat with the second piece of dough. Fold over the parchment, creating a sausage. Twist the ends over and wrap in plastic. Chill the dough logs for a minimum of 1 hour. (At this point the dough will keep nicely, wrapped well, in the refrigerator for up to 3 days, or up to 1 month in the freezer.) You can also simply spoon the dough onto parchment-covered baking sheets and bake at once (see Note).

6. Place racks in the middle and lower third of the oven and preheat the oven to 350°F. Line baking sheets with parchment paper. When the dough is chilled, re-move it from the parchment paper. Using a chef's knife or an offset serrated knife, slice 1/2-inch rounds off the log. Place the cookies on the prepared baking sheets, spaced 2 inches apart. Bake for 12 minutes. Rotate the baking sheets from top to bottom and from front to back, and bake for another 5 to 8 minutes, until nicely browned. Remove the cookies from the oven and carefully slide the parchment off the sheets and directly onto your work surface. Cool the baking sheets between batches. Wait a minimum of 5 minutes before eating, or allow to cool completely before storing the cookies in an airtight container. (The cookies will keep for up to 3 days at room temperature.)

NOTE: Instead of forming the logs and chilling, you can also scoop spoonfuls of dough onto the parchment-lined sheets. Spoon teaspoons for small cookies, tablespoons for large.

Making Light Oatmeal Cookies

One thing that is tricky about oatmeal cookies is that with most recipes, if you don't bake them straightaway after mixing the dough, the cookies will be hard and dense. That's because the oat-meal will continue to absorb liquid as the dough sits. I've taken that into consideration with my recipe, providing enough butter and sugar so that the dough can be stored for 3 days in the re-frigerator or in the freezer for a month, with no danger to the cookies.

JAM-FILLED PEANUT BUTTER COOKIES

MAKES 18 COOKIES

■ ■ ■

One afternoon between our lunch and dinner service, I noticed Barbara and Wolf's son, Cameron, then ten, in the dining room. He was sitting at a table talking to a gentleman I didn't know. I grabbed a plate of his favorite cookies, a sort of cookie version of a peanut butter and jelly sandwich, and a glass of milk and went out to give them to him. As I approached the table, I heard Cameron ask the man: "So what was it like on the moon?" The man was astronaut Buzz Aldrin, and Cameron was interviewing him for a report. Only at Spago!

1 cup all-purpose flour
1/2 teaspoon baking soda
1/4 teaspoon salt
4 ounces (1 stick) unsalted butter, softened
1/2 cup sugar
1/2 cup packed light brown sugar
1 cup smooth peanut butter, at room temperature
1 large egg, at room temperature (optional; the cookies will be more cakey with the egg)
1 teaspoon vanilla extract
1/2 cup grape jelly

1. Sift together the flour, baking soda, and salt. Set aside.

2. In the bowl of a stand mixer fitted with the paddle attachment, or in a large bowl with a hand mixer, cream together the butter, sugar, and brown sugar until smooth and fluffy, about 2 minutes. Scrape down the bowl. Beat in the peanut butter. Scrape down the bowl. Add the egg if using, and beat in. Beat in the vanilla. Scrape down the bowl. Gradually add the flour mixture. Wrap the dough in plastic wrap. Refrigerate for at least 4 hours. (The dough can be frozen for up to 1 month.)

3. Dust an approximately 12-x-17-inch sheet of parchment paper with flour, place the dough on it, and dust the top of the dough. Top with another sheet of parchment and roll out to about 1/4 inch thickness. Place with the parchment on a baking sheet and freeze for 30 minutes.

4. Place racks in the middle and upper third of the oven and preheat the oven to 350°F. Line two half sheet pans with parchment paper.

5. Remove the top sheet of parchment from the dough, and using a 3-inch round cookie cutter, cut 3-inch circles of dough. Top 1 circle with 1 teaspoon of the jelly and cover with another circle. Pinch the edges together and place on one of the baking sheets. Repeat with the remaining circles, placing the cookies 1 inch apart.

6. Bake for 10 minutes. Rotate the baking sheets from top to bottom and from front to back, and bake for another 3 to 4 minutes, until the cookies are nicely browned. Remove the cookies from the oven and allow to cool on the baking sheets, on racks. Do not handle the cookies until cool—they're very crumbly and could easily fall apart. (The cookies can be stored airtight for 2 days.)

Sherry's Secrets

Most rolled cookies can also be made into thumbprints. Pull off pieces of dough and shape into 1-inch balls. Place 1 inch apart on parchment-lined baking sheets and press your thumb into the center. Bake until golden. Cool on racks and fill with the jelly.

QUINTESSENTIAL
CHOCOLATE CHIP COOKIES

MAKES 48 COOKIES

■ ■ ■

One day Thomas Boyce, who was then a line cook at Spago and is now the chef de cuisine, grabbed one of my chocolate chip cookies, looked intently at it, and said, "The best chocolate chip cookie should have a reflective aspect to it, like this." What he meant was that the chips should be large and shiny. To achieve this, you have to use high-quality chocolate. I use bulk chocolate (you can find this in restaurant supply stores) with 64 percent cocoa content and good fluidity. A good brand is Callebaut. I cut the chocolate into 1-inch pieces so that my cookies have substantial chunks, which do shine and certainly melt in your mouth.

I prefer to shape the dough into logs and chill before baking. If you need to bake right away, spoon heaping tablespoons 2 inches apart on the prepared baking sheets.

1½ cups all-purpose flour
½ teaspoon baking soda
4 ounces (1 stick) unsalted butter, softened
½ cup sugar
½ cup packed light brown sugar
¼ teaspoon salt
1 large egg
1 teaspoon vanilla extract
12 ounces bittersweet chocolate, cut into 1-inch pieces

1. Place racks in the middle and lower third of the oven and preheat the oven to 350°F. Line baking sheets with parchment paper.

2. Sift together the flour and baking soda and set aside.

3. In the bowl of a stand mixer fitted with the paddle attachment, or in a large bowl with a hand mixer, cream the butter on medium speed until lemony yellow, about 2 minutes.

Sherry's Secrets

CUTTING CHOCOLATE INTO EVEN PIECES

If you soften the chocolate briefly in the microwave, you will be able to cut it up without the chocolate breaking into little shards. Place on a plate or small cutting board in the microwave and zap three times for 5 seconds each.

Scrape down the sides of the bowl. Add the sugar, brown sugar, and salt. Continue creaming the mixture on medium speed until it is smooth and lump-free, about 1 minute. Stop the mixer and scrape down the sides of the bowl and the paddle.

4. Add the egg and vanilla and beat on low speed for 15 seconds, or until the egg is fully incorporated. Do not overbeat. Scrape down the sides of the bowl.

5. On low speed, add the sifted flour mixture. Beat slowly until all of the flour is incorporated. Scrape down the sides of the bowl. Add the chocolate chunks and mix in.

6. Remove small handfuls or spoonfuls of one half of the dough from the bowl and center them along the bottom of a sheet of parchment or waxed paper, creating a log about 1½ inches wide and 12 inches long. Fold the parchment over, creating a sausage. Twist the ends over and wrap in plastic. Repeat with the remaining dough. Chill for at least 1 hour, preferably overnight. (The dough can also be frozen, well wrapped, for up to 2 weeks.) When the dough has chilled, remove it from the paper, and using a serrated knife, slice ⅓-inch-thick rounds off the log. Place the cookies 2 inches apart on the prepared baking sheets. (To bake the dough without chilling, see headnote.)

7. Bake, rotating the sheets from top to bottom and from front to back halfway through the baking, for 12 to 15 minutes, until lightly browned. Remove from the oven and slide the parchment off the baking sheets onto a work surface. Cool the baking sheets between batches. Allow the cookies to cool for at least 5 minutes before serving, or allow to cool completely before storing in an airtight container. (They will keep for up to 3 days at room temperature.)

Sherry's Secrets

If you want your cookies to be flat and crispy, when you go to turn the baking sheets from front to back halfway through the baking, tap them down on the inside of the oven door before sliding them back in. This will cause the rising cookies to fall.

CHOCOLATE MACARONS WITH BLACK CURRANT TEA ICE CREAM AND RASPBERRIES

SERVES 8

■ ■ ■

This dramatic assembly brings together chocolate and berries, always a good marriage. Since the macarons and ice cream are made well ahead, all you need to do before serving is to put the gorgeous sandwiches together and sauce the plates.

Make the ice cream preferably 3 days before making the macarons. Once you separate the yolks for the ice cream, reserve 3 egg whites for the macarons and place in the refrigerator for at least 3 days. Otherwise the macarons will crack and puff up too much. Also, in order for the macarons to develop their characteristic smooth surface, or "skin," the piped batter must sit out at room temperature long enough to dry out a bit before baking.

1. **MAKE THE ICE CREAM:** Place a 1-quart freezer container in the freezer. Prepare an ice bath: fill a large bowl with ice and nestle a medium bowl in the ice.

2. In a medium nonreactive saucepan, combine the cream, milk, and ⅓ cup of the sugar. Place the pan over medium heat and bring the mixture to a boil. Add the tea bags and turn off the heat. Cover tightly with plastic wrap and allow to infuse for 20 minutes.

FOR THE ICE CREAM
- 1 cup heavy cream
- 1½ cups milk
- ⅔ cup sugar
- 2 black currant tea bags (available at most supermarkets and whole foods stores)
- 8 large egg yolks (reserve 3 whites for the macarons)
- 1 tablespoon crème de cassis
- 2 teaspoons fresh lemon juice
  Pinch of salt

FOR THE MACARONS
- 1 cup almond flour (available at whole foods stores, or see Sources)
- 2 cups confectioners' sugar
- 3 tablespoons unsweetened cocoa powder
- 3 large egg whites, covered and refrigerated for 3 days, then brought to room temperature (see headnote)
- ¼ teaspoon cream of tartar
- 2 tablespoons sugar
- 1 drop red food coloring (optional)

FOR THE GARNISH
- ½ cup Raspberry Sauce (page 362)
- ⅔ cup raspberries

3. Combine the egg yolks and the remaining ⅓ cup sugar in a medium bowl and whisk them together until lemony yellow.

4. After infusing the cream mixture, remove the plastic wrap and the tea bags. Return to the heat and bring to a simmer. Remove from the heat and slowly ladle ½ cup into the egg yolks while whisking. Once the cream is incorporated into the eggs, whisk the eggs back into the cream. Be sure to scrape all the eggs into the pan with a rubber spatula.

5. Place the pan over low heat and immediately begin to stir the custard. After about 2 minutes, it will begin to thicken. Keep stirring until the consistency is like thick cream. The custard is done when the temperature reaches 180°F. Test for readiness with your spatula: dip it into the custard, pull it out, and run your finger across the back of the spatula. Your finger should leave a clear trail and the rest of the spatula should remain coated with custard. If the custard does not run into the finger trail, it is thick enough and can be taken off the heat. If it does run, cook the custard for another minute, or until the consistency is right.

6. Remove the pan from the heat and immediately pour the custard through a fine-mesh strainer into the bowl in the ice bath. Stir the custard occasionally for 5 to 10 minutes, until the temperature drops to 40°F. Stir in the crème de cassis, lemon juice, and salt. Transfer to an ice cream maker and freeze according to the manufacturer's directions. Transfer to the freezer container and place in the freezer for 2 hours, or until firm.

7. MAKE THE MACARONS: In a food processor fitted with the steel blade, combine the almond flour and confectioners' sugar. Pulse a few times, then add the cocoa and pulse a few times more. Pass through a fine sifter and set aside.

8. Line two baking sheets with parchment paper. Fit a piping bag with a #6 plain tip.

9. In the bowl of a stand mixer fitted with the whisk attachment, or in a large bowl with a hand mixer, beat the egg whites on low speed until they begin to foam. Add the cream of tartar and turn the speed to medium. Slowly stream in the sugar and continue to beat to stiff peaks. If you turn the bowl upside down, the whisk should remain in place. Beat in the drop of red food coloring, if using.

10. Using a rubber spatula, fold the almond mixture into the egg whites until well combined. This will take about 40 folds and turns of the bowl; after about 20 turns, the batter will come together and deflate, and after 20 more turns, it will be slightly runny, then more runny after a few minutes.

11. Fill the piping bag two-thirds full with the macaron mixture. Pipe 3-inch disks onto the parchment-covered baking sheets, holding the piping bag straight up and piping until the batter runs out to 3 inches. Allow 2 inches of space between each macaron. You should have 16 macarons.

12. Allow the piped macarons to sit for 2 to 4 hours. They will dry out on the top and develop a skin, which is what you want.

13. Place racks in the middle and the lower third of the oven and preheat the oven to 300°F (275°F if using a convection oven).

14. Bake the cookies for 15 minutes. Rotate the baking sheets from top to bottom and from front to back and continue baking for another 5 to 10 minutes, until the macarons are no longer tacky when touched lightly. If you are using a convection oven, leave the oven door cracked after you turn the pans around (you may have to wedge the handle of a wooden spoon in it to keep it vented). Remove the cookies from the oven and allow to cool on the baking sheets. (The macarons can be stored in the freezer for 2 weeks if wrapped airtight.)

Sherry's Secrets

Some pastry chefs bake their macarons at a higher temperature for a shorter period of time. This will yield a cookie with a chewier center. I make mine crisper because I use fillings that moisten the centers of the cookies.

15. **ASSEMBLE THE DESSERT:** Place 1 chocolate macaron on each plate and top with a scoop of ice cream. Press down on the scoop to flatten slightly, and place another macaron on top. Drizzle the raspberry sauce around the macarons and garnish with the raspberries.

OUT-OF-THIS-WORLD BROWNIES

■ ■ ■

The NASA mission specialist astronaut Marsha Ivins loves these ultra-ultra-chocolate brownies. I met Marsha out on the patio at Spago. She told me that when she's not flying around in space or training to do so, she's an avid baker and that she dreamed of one day spending the day with me in the Spago bakeshop. I, in turn, told her of my dream to go up into space. "I'll make a deal with you," I said. "You take me up into space, and I'll let you spend a day with me in the kitchen." Not long afterward, she showed up at Spago with a photograph of herself in space with the visible Earth behind her, holding a sign that said, "Hi, Sherry!" and with bars of Scharffen Berger chocolate that had come back from space.

3/4 cup plus 2 tablespoons all-purpose flour

1/4 teaspoon salt

4 ounces (1 stick) unsalted butter, chopped

1 ounce unsweetened chocolate, preferably Michel Cluizel Noir Infini 99% (see Sources), finely chopped

7 ounces bittersweet chocolate, preferably Scharffen Berger (see Sources), finely chopped

2 large eggs

1 cup sugar

1. Place a rack in the middle of the oven and preheat the oven to 350°F. Line an 8-inch square baking pan with aluminum foil (for easy cleanup) and spray the foil with pan spray.

2. Sift together the flour and salt and set aside.

3. Melt the butter, unsweetened chocolate, and bittersweet chocolate in a microwave-safe bowl at 50 percent power for about 2 minutes or in a heatproof bowl set over a saucepan of simmering water. Stir with a rubber spatula until the mixture is smooth. Allow to cool to tepid (90°F).

4. In the bowl of a stand mixer, or in a bowl with a hand mixer, beat together the eggs and sugar until fluffy. Using a whisk, gently beat in the butter and chocolate. Fold in the flour.

5. Scrape the batter into the pan and place in the oven. Bake, rotating the pan

from front to back halfway through, for 25 to 30 minutes, until slightly firm to the touch and a crust has formed on top. A toothpick will not come out clean.

6. Allow to cool in the pan on a rack to room temperature. Cut into 2-inch squares.

STICKY TOFFEE PUDDING CAKE

■ ■ ■

This moist date cake is topped with a marvelous decadent toffee sauce. Two secret ingredients give it incredible depth of flavor— orange zest and coffee extract. My favorite dates to use for this are Medjool, the plump, moist, thin-skinned variety. They are chewy, with an almost chocolaty flavor.

FOR THE CAKE

- 8 ounces pitted Medjool dates, finely chopped
- 1 cup boiling water
- 1³/₄ cups all-purpose flour
- 1¹/₂ teaspoons baking powder
- ¹/₈ teaspoon salt
- 1 teaspoon baking soda
- 4 ounces (1 stick) unsalted butter, softened, plus more for pan(s)
- 1 cup packed light brown sugar
- ¹/₄ cup sugar
- ¹/₄ teaspoon grated orange zest
- 1 teaspoon Trablit coffee extract (available at pastry supply stores, or see Sources)
- 2 large eggs, at room temperature

FOR THE TOFFEE SAUCE

- 1 cup packed dark brown sugar
- 1 cup heavy cream
- 1 tablespoon unsalted butter
- ¹/₂ vanilla bean, split, seeds scraped out; seeds and bean reserved
- ¹/₄ cup milk
- 3 tablespoons light corn syrup
- 1 tablespoon water, if needed

1. **MAKE THE CAKE:** Place the dates in a bowl and pour on the boiling water. Let sit for 1 hour.

2. Place a rack in the middle of the oven and preheat the oven to 350°F. Butter a 9-inch round cake pan or eight 6-ounce ramekins.

3. Sift together the flour, baking powder, and salt and set aside. With the back of a fork, mash the dates in the bowl with the water. Stir in the baking soda. Set aside.

4. In the bowl of a stand mixer fitted with the paddle attachment, or in a large bowl with a hand mixer, cream together the butter, brown sugar, sugar, orange zest, and coffee extract on medium speed until fluffy, about 2 minutes. Scrape down the sides of the bowl and the beaters. Add the eggs one at a time, scraping down the bowl after each addition.

5. Beating on low speed, beat in half the date mixture. Still on low speed, beat in half the flour mixture. Add the remaining date mixture and the remaining flour. Pour into the prepared cake pan or ramekins and place in the oven. Bake for 25

minutes (15 minutes for ramekins). Rotate the pan or ramekins from front to back and bake for another 25 minutes (10 minutes for ramekins), or until a tester inserted in the center comes out clean.

6. **MEANWHILE, MAKE THE TOFFEE SAUCE:** Place the brown sugar, cream, butter, vanilla seeds and bean, milk, and corn syrup in a heavy saucepan and simmer over medium-high heat until the mixture thickens and coats the back of a spoon, about 10 minutes. Continue to cook until golden brown, 1 to 2 minutes more. Remove from the heat and keep warm. Remove the vanilla bean.

7. When the cake is done, remove from the oven. If the sauce is too thick to pour, add the tablespoon of water. While the cake is still hot and in the pan, poke it with a skewer in several places. Pour on the toffee sauce and serve. Or cut the cake into pieces, place in serving bowls, pour on the toffee sauce, and serve.

NOTE: I prefer to serve this in individual portions, but it is also dramatic as one cake with the sauce poured over.

STRAWBERRY AND WHITE CHOCOLATE—BUTTERMILK CAKE

SERVES 12

■ ■ ■

This strawberry-filled masterpiece was created by Sixto Pocasangre, the executive pastry chef of Wolfgang Puck Catering. Sixie, whose last name means "little blood," is an amazing production baker. With a perpetual smile on his face, he oversees the baking for ballroom banquets of more than 2,000 people while managing the pastry operations at two restaurants, not to mention the concessions for the Kodak and El Rey theatres, Griffith Observatory, Pacific Design Center, and multiple museums. Whenever I ask him what he is making, his response is always the same: "Everything!" He has kindly given me his permission to reveal one of our secret weapons. This cake is so good that it will change your cake-making life forever.

FOR THE CAKE
- 2 cups cake flour
- 1 teaspoon baking powder
- 1/2 teaspoon baking soda
- 1/8 teaspoon salt
- 3 ounces white chocolate, preferably Valrhona (see Sources)
- 6 ounces (1 1/2 sticks) unsalted butter, softened
- 1 3/4 cups sugar
- 4 large eggs, separated
- 1 teaspoon vanilla extract
- 1 cup buttermilk

FOR THE FILLING AND TOPPING
- 2 cups heavy cream
- 1 cup crème fraîche
- 1 tablespoon sugar
- 2 pints strawberries, hulled and quartered

1. **MAKE THE CAKE:** Place a rack in the middle of the oven and preheat the oven to 350°F. Spray a 12-x-17-inch half sheet pan with pan spray and line with parchment paper. Spray the parchment.

2. Sift together the flour, baking powder, baking soda, and salt and set aside.

3. Melt the white chocolate in a microwave-safe bowl at 50 percent power for about 2 minutes or in a heatproof bowl set over a saucepan of simmering water and set aside. Be careful, because white chocolate burns easily.

4. In a stand mixer fitted with the paddle attachment, or in a large bowl with a hand mixer, cream together the butter and 1 1/2 cups of the sugar on high speed

for 2 minutes. Scrape down the bowl and beaters and continue to beat for 3 more minutes, until light and creamy. Scrape down the sides of the bowl. Whisk 2 tablespoons of the whipped butter into the melted white chocolate until blended. Scrape this mixture back into the butter and beat on low speed until well blended. Add the egg yolks in 2 additions, scraping down the bowl after each addition. Beat in the vanilla.

5. On low speed, alternating the wet and dry ingredients, add the buttermilk and the flour mixture in 4 additions. Scrape down the bowl.

6. In a large bowl, beat the egg whites on medium speed with a hand mixer until they form soft peaks. Slowly add the remaining ¼ cup sugar while you continue to beat on medium speed. Beat until the egg whites form stiff, glossy peaks. Fold half the egg whites into the cake batter, then gently fold in the rest.

7. Scrape the batter into the prepared pan. Using a spatula, preferably offset, smear the batter evenly over the pan (see page 17). Bake, rotating the pan from front to back halfway through, until golden brown and firm to the touch, 25 to 30 minutes. Remove from the oven. Allow to cool in the pan. Lightly spray the back of a half sheet pan with pan spray and cover with parchment. Invert the cake onto the parchment-covered tray, remove the pan, and peel off the parchment.

8. When the cake is completely cool, cut crosswise into 3 equal pieces.

9. MAKE THE FILLING AND TOPPING: Whip the cream, crème fraîche, and sugar together to medium-stiff peaks.

10. ASSEMBLE THE CAKE: Place the first piece of cake on a serving platter. Spread 2 cups of the whipped cream evenly over the top. Lay half the strawberries in the whipped cream and spread a little of the cream over the strawberries. Lay the second cake layer on top, and repeat with 2 cups more cream and the remaining strawberries. Top with the last layer of cake and spread the remaining whipped cream over the top. Chill until ready to serve. The cake can be assembled up to 4 hours ahead.

VARIATIONS

Use two 9-x-2-inch round cake pans instead of the sheet pan. The cakes will take longer to bake—about 45 minutes—because they will be thicker. When the cakes are cool, slice them horizontally in half to make 2 layers each and make a 4-layer cake. Use 1¼ cups whipped cream and one third of the berries for each layer.

Leave the cream off the top and fill the middle layers with more cream.

LEMON TART

■ ■ ■

Johnny Romoglia has been the floor manager at Spago for more than twenty-four years. He is my official lemon taster; he knows if a lemon dish is too tart or too sweet. If the amount of lemon in a dessert passes with his approval, it goes on the menu. This is a classic French tart, inspired by Swiss chef Fredy Girardet's recipe. In California, I often use Meyer lemons, which have their own special tart, yet soft, floral flavor. If you do use Meyer lemons, use ¾ cup lemon juice and omit the lime juice.

1 10-inch tart shell made with Pâte Sucrée (page 373), prebaked
4 large eggs
1 cup sugar
1 tablespoon grated lemon zest
½ cup fresh lemon juice (from 3 lemons; see headnote)
¼ cup fresh lime juice (from 3 limes)
3 tablespoons heavy cream
1 tablespoon confectioners' sugar

1. Place a rack in the middle of the oven and preheat the oven to 350°F. Place the tart shell on a baking sheet.

2. Whisk together the eggs and sugar. Add the lemon zest, lemon juice, lime juice, and cream and whisk until blended. Pour into the tart shell. Transfer to the oven on the baking sheet and bake for 15 minutes. Turn the heat down to 325°F and bake for another 15 to 20 minutes, until just set. The tart should jiggle ever so slightly. Remove from the oven and allow to cool. Dust with the confectioners' sugar before serving.

DO-AHEAD TARTE TATIN

SERVES 8

■ ■ ■

I love this easy method for making tarte Tatin. The puff pastry is shaped into a framed square tart shell (vol-au-vent) and prebaked so that it remains crisp when the apples are placed in it. It creates a pocket for the marvelous caramel juices, and it's not awkward to unmold, the way a traditional tarte Tatin is.

1. Place a rack in the middle of the oven and preheat the oven to 425°F. Line a baking sheet with parchment paper.

2. Shape the puff pastry into a vol-au-vent (see page 271). The instructions for shaping the pastry may sound difficult, but it's actually quite easy; if you have difficulty visualizing it, make a vol-au-vent with a square sheet of paper before you cut the pastry.

3. Using a fork, prick ("dock") the center of the pastry all over. Then brush the border of the pastry shell twice with egg wash, being careful not to let the glaze drip down and glue the border to the bottom of the pastry, which would prevent it from puffing up when it bakes.

1 12-inch square all-butter puff pastry (see Sources)
1 egg beaten with 1 egg yolk, for egg wash
3 ounces (3/4 stick) unsalted butter
3/4 cup sugar
2 tablespoons light brown sugar
6 Fuji apples, peeled, cored, and cut into quarters
1/2 cup heavy cream (optional; see Note)
1 teaspoon fresh lemon juice
Whipped Caramel Crème Fraîche (page 363)

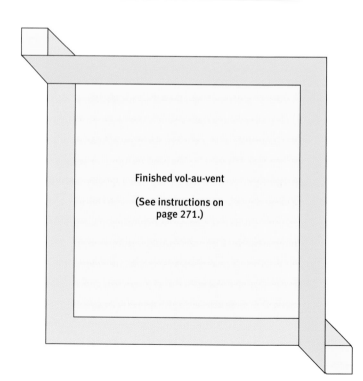

Finished vol-au-vent

(See instructions on page 271.)

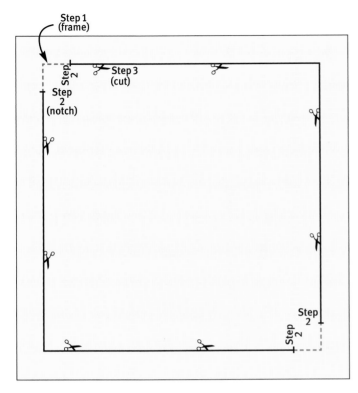

Step 1
(frame)

Step 2

Step 3
(cut)

Step 2
(notch)

Step 2

Step 2

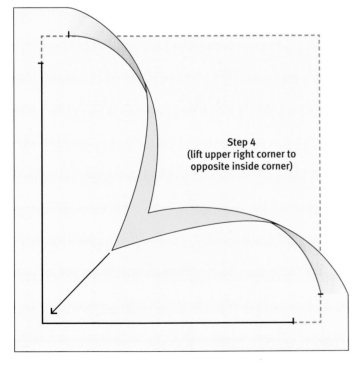

Step 4
(lift upper right corner to
opposite inside corner)

MAKING THE VOL-AU-VENT:

(1) Mark a border, or frame, about $3/4$ inch wide, inside the edge of the 12-inch-square pastry.

(2) On the inside edge of the frame, measure 1 inch from the top left corner on both sides and mark the spots with notches. Do the same thing at the diagonally opposite (bottom right) corner, and mark the spots with notches (see diagram).

(3) Using the tip of a paring knife, cut along the inside edge of the frame from the notch 1 inch below the upper left corner to the notch that you made 1 inch to the left of the lower right corner. Now cut from the notch on the right side of the upper left corner to the notch above the lower right corner. Your frame will now be attached to the square of dough at the notched corners and cut free of the dough at the other 2 corners.

(4) Lift the frame away from the dough at the upper right corner and fold it over so that the outside corner of the frame is flush with the opposite corner of the square of dough. Now repeat this step with the bottom left corner of the frame. You will end up with a framed square puff pastry shell with 2 pretty looped corners diagonally across from each other. (See the drawing on page 270.)

4. Place on the parchment-covered baking sheet and bake for 15 minutes. Reduce the heat to 350°F and continue to bake for another 20 minutes. Rotate the baking sheet from front to back and bake for another 20 to 25 minutes, until dark brown. Remove from the oven and allow to cool on a rack. Once cool, crack a hole in the center of the vol-au-vent so that you have a nest for the apples.

5. Heat a 12-inch nonstick skillet over medium heat and add the butter. Melt and allow to turn light brown, then remove from the heat and sprinkle in the sugar in an even layer. Sprinkle the brown sugar over the sugar, then arrange the apples, cut side down, in a tight circular pattern on top.

6. Return the pan to medium-high heat and cook for 12 minutes. The apples will release juice and begin to color. Turn the apples onto their other cut side, using tongs or a spatula, and continue to cook for another 12 to 15 minutes, or until the apples are a deep golden color. Remove the apples, leaving the caramel in the pan. Place rows of apples in the puff pastry. (The apples can be made up to 30 minutes ahead and refrigerated, covered. Just before serving, reheat for 10 minutes in a preheated 375°F oven, then place in the puff pastry.)

7. Add the heavy cream, if using, and lemon juice to the pan, reduce the heat to medium-low and, whisking constantly to deglaze the bottom of the pan, cook for 1 to 2 minutes, until the sauce is thickened and warm.

8. Spoon the caramel over the apples or, alternatively, cut the tart into servings, then pour the caramel over each serving. Serve at once, with the whipped crème fraîche.

   N O T E : You may omit the cream. Add the lemon juice to the pan and pour over the apples. The sauce will be clear instead of creamy.

Sherry's Secrets

Ice-cold puff pastry is always easier to work with than warm dough. Store in the freezer, then defrost slightly before cutting and shaping.

CHOCOLATE BREAD PUDDING
WITH BUTTERSCOTCH GELATO

SERVES 8

■ ■ ■

This rich, chocolaty bread pudding is like a moist chocolate cake. The baked pudding is cut into layers, which are then spread with ganache and topped with chocolate sauce, and it's served with an absolutely amazing butterscotch gelato. You can bake the bread pudding, assemble it, and freeze it or freeze the bread pudding sheets before assembling. I always have kept bread pudding in the freezer.

There are two ways to plate this: you can cut long slices of the pudding and lay them on their sides and then spread them with the ganache and top with a scoop of the gelato (see photo), or you can cut wide slices and serve like a layer cake as described in the recipe.

FOR THE BREAD PUDDING

- 1 1-pound loaf brioche
- 2 cups milk
- 2 cups heavy cream
- 1 cup sugar
- 8 ounces bittersweet chocolate, finely chopped
- 2 ounces ($\frac{1}{2}$ stick) unsalted butter
- 2 vanilla beans, split, seeds scraped out and reserved
- 3 tablespoons Tia Maria or other coffee liqueur
  Pinch of salt
- 6 large eggs

FOR THE BUTTERSCOTCH GELATO

- 3 cups milk
- $\frac{1}{4}$ cup heavy cream
- 1 cup packed light brown sugar
- 4 large egg yolks
- 2 tablespoons sugar
- 1 teaspoon fresh lemon juice

FOR THE GANACHE

- 6 ounces bittersweet chocolate, finely chopped
- 1 tablespoon unsalted butter
- $\frac{3}{4}$ cup heavy cream
- 2 tablespoons milk
- 1 tablespoon Tia Maria or other coffee liqueur

"Ten-Year" Chocolate Sauce
(page 345)

1. **MAKE THE BREAD PUDDING:** Cut the crust off the brioche, then cut the loaf lengthwise into ¹/₂-inch slices.

2. Place a rack in the middle of the oven and preheat the oven to 325°F. Spray a 12-x-17-inch half sheet pan with pan spray. Line with parchment paper and spray the parchment. Line the parchment with the bread slices, filling the pan completely.

3. Combine the milk, cream, sugar, chocolate, butter, vanilla seeds, liqueur, and salt in a saucepan. Stir over medium-low heat, without allowing the mixture to come to a boil, until the chocolate melts. Remove from the heat. Whisk the eggs in a medium bowl, then slowly whisk in the hot chocolate milk. Combine well. Pour half the custard mixture over the bread and allow it to soak in. Pour on the remaining custard mixture.

4. Place in the oven and bake for 45 to 60 minutes, until set. Remove from the oven and allow to cool to room temperature. Cover and refrigerate for at least 4 hours. (Or wrap airtight and freeze for up to 2 weeks.)

5. **MAKE THE BUTTERSCOTCH GELATO:** Place a 1-quart freezer container in the freezer. Prepare an ice bath: fill a large bowl with ice and a little water and nestle a medium bowl in the ice.

6. Combine the milk, heavy cream, and ¹/₂ cup of the brown sugar in a saucepan and bring to a simmer. Whisk the egg yolks with the remaining ¹/₂ cup brown sugar and the sugar in a bowl. When the cream and milk come to a simmer, remove from the heat and slowly ladle ¹/₂ cup into the egg yolks while whisking. Once the milk is incorporated into the eggs, whisk the eggs back into the hot milk. Be sure to scrape all the eggs into the pot with a rubber spatula.

7. Place the pan over low heat and immediately begin to stir the custard. Stir until the consistency is like thick cream. The custard is ready when the temperature reaches 180°F. Test for readiness with your spatula: dip it into the custard, pull it out, and run your finger across the back of the spatula. Your finger should leave a clear trail and the rest of the spatula should remain coated with custard. If the custard does not run into the finger trail, it is thick enough and can be taken off the heat. If it does run, cook the custard for another minute, or until the consistency is right.

8. Remove the pan from the heat and immediately pour the custard through a fine-mesh strainer into the bowl in the ice bath. Stir the custard occasionally for 5 to 10 minutes, until the temperature drops to 40°F and the custard is cold. Stir in the lemon juice. If possible, chill in the refrigerator for at least 2 hours. Transfer to an ice cream maker and freeze according to the manufacturer's directions. Transfer to the freezer container and place in the freezer for 2 hours, or until firm. (The gelato will keep for a couple of weeks in the freezer.)

9. MAKE THE GANACHE: Place the chocolate and butter in a heatproof bowl. Bring the heavy cream to a boil in a small saucepan and pour over the chocolate. Tap the bowl against your work surface to allow the chocolate to settle into the cream. Wait for 1 minute, then stir with a rubber spatula until the chocolate and butter have melted. Stir in the milk and liqueur. Allow to cool until thick enough to spread; you can speed up this process by placing the bowl in an ice bath.

10. ASSEMBLE THE DESSERT: Remove the chilled sheet of bread pudding from the refrigerator. Run a knife around the edges of the pan and invert onto your work surface. Remove the parchment paper and cut the pudding crosswise into 3 equal pieces. Using a large spatula place the first piece on a platter or on the sprayed and parchment-covered reverse side of a sheet pan. If necessary, warm the ganache. Spread half the ganache on the first piece of pudding and stack another piece on top. Spread the remaining ganache on the second layer and stack the third layer on top. (At this point you can wrap the bread pudding airtight and freeze for a couple of weeks.)

11. Cut the pudding into 8 slices and serve on large dessert plates, with the gelato and topped with the chocolate sauce.

MARSHMALLOW BONSAI TREE

■ ■ ■

One of our regular guests, Tim Gallagher, is expansive and full of joie de vivre. He throws huge parties at the restaurant and always tells me to "do whatever I want" for them. So one year, we presented bonsai trees in pots, with marshmallows at the tip of each branch. Waiters wheeled ten of them through the room and placed one in the center of each table. Guests picked the marshmallows off the branches and dipped them in "Ten-Year" Chocolate Sauce.

¼ cup cornstarch
¼ cup confectioners' sugar
1½ cups cold water
4½ teaspoons (2 packages) powdered gelatin
¼ cup light corn syrup
2 cups sugar
1 teaspoon vanilla extract
"Ten-Year" Chocolate Sauce (page 345)

1. Line a 9-x-13-inch baking pan with aluminum foil and spray the foil with pan spray. Combine the cornstarch and confectioners' sugar in a small bowl and sift half of it over the foil.

2. Pour ½ cup of the water into the bowl of a stand mixer fitted with the whisk attachment or into a large heatproof bowl. Sprinkle on the gelatin. Let stand for 5 minutes. Place the bowl over a pan of simmering water and stir for 2 to 3 minutes, until the gelatin has dissolved. Remove from the heat and place the bowl on the mixer stand or use a hand mixer.

3. Combine the remaining 1 cup water, the corn syrup, and sugar in a medium saucepan, stir together with a rubber spatula, and wash down the sides of the saucepan with a pastry brush dipped in water. Cover the saucepan and bring to a boil over medium-low heat. Uncover, insert a candy thermometer, raise the heat to high, and cook, without stirring, until the mixture reaches 240° to 245°F. Remove from the heat immediately.

4. Beat the gelatin mixture on medium speed while you slowly stream in the hot sugar syrup, drizzling it down the sides of the bowl, not over the whisk or beat-

ers. Continue beating the mixture for about 5 minutes, until thick and fluffy. Beat in the vanilla.

5. While it is still warm, pour the marshmallow mixture over the foil in the baking pan and smear it in an even layer with a spatula. Dust with the remaining cornstarch mixture. Allow to cool completely and allow to dry until it is firm enough to cut, 4 to 6 hours.

6. Using kitchen scissors dusted with cornstarch, cut into 1-inch cubes (for the little bonsai trees, I cut ½-inch cubes). Stick the marshmallows on the tips of a bare tree branch, or spear them with lollipop sticks or skewers, or simply stack them on plates, and serve with the chocolate sauce.

STRACCIATELLA GELATO

MAKES 1 QUART

■ ■ ■

This is a milky-white, fine-flecked chocolate chip ice milk. There are no eggs or cream here, which makes this a very popular dessert among the movie star crowd at Spago. One of our chefs, Ari Rosenson, sandwiches this gelato, with a schmear of peanut butter, between pieces of Chocolate Pâte Sucrée (page 375).

3 cups milk
1/2 cup sugar
1/4 cup powdered milk
1 teaspoon vanilla extract
1/4 cup light corn syrup
Pinch of salt
4 ounces bittersweet chocolate, finely chopped

1. Place a 1-quart freezer container in your freezer.

2. In a heavy saucepan, combine the milk, sugar, powdered milk, vanilla, and corn syrup and bring to a boil. Whisk until the sugar and powdered milk have dissolved. Remove from the heat, pour into a bowl, and allow to cool to room temperature, or chill in the refrigerator. Add the salt.

3. Freeze in an ice cream maker following the manufacturer's directions.

4. Meanwhile, shortly before the gelato is ready, melt the chocolate in a microwave-safe bowl at 50 percent power for about 2 minutes or in a heatproof bowl set over a saucepan of simmering water. Cool to 100°F (tepid).

5. When the gelato has reached the desired consistency, continue running the machine while you drizzle in the chocolate in a very fine stream. You can control the drizzle by lifting the melted chocolate from the bowl on a spatula and letting it drizzle from the spatula into the ice cream maker. If the stream is too thick or too fast, the chocolate will form into clumps instead of flecks.

6. Transfer the gelato to the freezer container and freeze for at least 2 hours, to firm before serving.

HONEY-GLAZED SPAGO CORN BREAD

■ ■ ■

Spago's executive chef, Lee Hefter, is known for his Southern cooking. Whenever David Robinson ("The Admiral") and the San Antonio Spurs were in town playing the Lakers, the Spurs would come to the restaurant. Lee would always make them a Southern-style meal—smothered pork chops, fried chicken with collard greens, macaroni and cheese, ribs, mashed potatoes, creamed corn, green beans, and brisket. They couldn't get enough of it, and I'd always make extra batches of corn bread for them to take home. I've never seen so many tall men at one table. They couldn't even get their knees underneath!

1 cup yellow cornmeal
1 cup all-purpose flour
1/4 cup cake flour
1 cup sugar
2 tablespoons baking powder
1 1/2 teaspoons salt
4 large eggs, at room temperature
3 ounces (3/4 stick) unsalted butter
1/3 cup vegetable oil
1 cup milk
1/2 cup buttermilk

FOR THE GLAZE
3 ounces (3/4 stick) unsalted butter
1/4 cup honey
1/3 cup water

1. Place a rack in the middle of the oven and preheat the oven to 350°F. Line a 9-x-13-inch baking pan with aluminum foil and spray the foil with pan spray.

2. Sift together the cornmeal, all-purpose flour, cake flour, sugar, baking powder, and salt 2 times. Set aside.

3. In a medium bowl, whisk together the eggs. Melt the butter and immediately whisk into the eggs in a slow stream. Whisk in the oil, milk, and buttermilk. Whisk in the dry ingredients just until combined.

4. Scrape the batter into the pan and bake for 30 minutes. Rotate the pan from front to back and continue to bake for 10 minutes, or until a tester inserted in the center comes out clean.

5. **MAKE THE GLAZE:** While the corn bread is baking, melt the butter in a medium saucepan. Add the honey and water and whisk until blended.

6. When the corn bread is done, remove from the oven and poke holes all over the bread, about ½ inch apart, with a toothpick. Brush with the glaze and allow to cool.

Chinois on Main

ALWAYS ON THE VANGUARD OF WHAT HAS BECOME California fusion cooking, Wolfgang had the ingenious concept of creating a restaurant that brought together California, Asian, and French cuisines. Wolfgang Puck and Barbara Lazaroff opened Chinois on Main in 1983, a year and a half after Spago opened in West Hollywood. Barbara designed a relaxed, brightly colored Fellini-esque space in south Santa Monica. The restaurant features an open kitchen, family-style service, and waiters dressed in black silk Chinese pajamas. From the outset, Chinois was a sensation, and it's been an institution for nearly twenty-five years.

The food is vibrant, with sweet and pungent Asian flavors, satiny textures, and lots of flair. Guests come back again and again for the same dishes—whole sizzling catfish with ginger and ponzu sauce, spicy Shanghai lobster, and Mongolian lamb chops with cilantro-shallot sauce. When I began to envision a fitting ending for such dinners, I imagined light creations with clean citrus flavors that paired well with spicy food. I thought of tropical fruits like mango, passion fruit, and cool, creamy coconut, and spices like ginger and Chinese five-spice. Traditional Asian desserts—buns filled with sweet, sticky bean paste, cloying puddings, and the like—have never appealed to the American palate (in Asia these dishes are eaten on their own, and not at the end of a meal). But a rich chocolate cake wouldn't do either. Working closely with executive chefs René Mata and Louis Diaz and pastry chef Julian Saldana, I developed desserts that reflected the Chinois Franco-Asian spirit and that could easily be baked ahead and/or served cold, in keeping with the restaurant's family-style approach.

ALMOND-GINGER FORTUNE COOKIES

MAKES 36 COOKIES

■ ■ ■

These ginger-scented fortune cookies are delicate folded wafers, an elegant far cry from standard fortune cookies. The easy batter is much like tuile batter. You spoon it onto baking sheets lined with silicone mats, bake until the wafers are just golden, then quickly shape the cookies while still hot. You can wear plastic surgical gloves to protect your fingertips from the heat.

⅔ cup sugar
½ teaspoon ground ginger
   (1 teaspoon if you like heat)
2 large eggs
⅓ cup water
⅔ cup cornstarch
¼ cup almond oil (see Sources)

Before you begin these, print out your fortunes and cut the paper into strips no more than 1½ inches long and ¼ inch wide. Have them ready to place on the wafers when you shape the cookies.

1. Place a rack in the middle of the oven and preheat the oven to 350°F. Line baking sheets with silicone mats and place in the oven to heat before spooning on each batch (see Note). Place an empty egg carton or four espresso cups by your work area. You will be placing the shaped cookies inside to prevent them from popping open before they cool.

2. Mix together the sugar and ginger in a medium bowl. Add the eggs and water and whisk for 30 seconds.

3. Place the cornstarch in a separate bowl and whisk in the egg mixture and the oil.

4. Spoon 4 cookies at a time onto each hot silicone-lined baking sheet, using 2 teaspoons of batter for each cookie and placing them 2 inches apart. Spoon the batter onto the mat, then with the back of your spoon, smear the batter into a 3-inch round.

5. Bake, one sheet at a time, for 8 to 9 minutes, until the edges of the cookies are lightly browned and the interiors are blond. Don't worry if the batter runs a bit

and the wafers lose their round shape; this won't really matter once you've shaped the fortune cookies.

6. Put on plastic gloves to protect your fingertips. Open the oven and place the baking sheet on top of the open door. Using a metal spatula, preferably offset, remove a cookie and place it on your work surface. Working quickly, place a fortune on top of the cookie and fold the cookie in half, folding away from you. Grasp the edges of the cookie, stand it up on the fold, and quickly bend it at the middle of the crease over the edge of your work surface, pressing down as you do (you'll need to do this quickly, as the cookie will be hot). Then immediately pinch the corners together, like a tortellini, and place in the egg carton or an espresso cup. Repeat with the remaining hot cookies. Once the cookies have set, transfer to a rack to cool completely. Store airtight. (The cookies will keep for 3 to 4 days.)

NOTE: Wait 10 minutes for the oven to come up to temperature before baking the next batch of cookies.

Sherry's Secrets

TUILES AND THEIR RELATIVES

When you are making pliable cookies with a wet batter, such as tuiles, you will have an easier time of it if your baking sheets are perfectly flat—that is, not warped or dented. Make sure to line the baking sheets with silicone mats and preheat them before spooning on the batter, so that the batter will spread easily.

If the cookies begin to crisp up and crack as you shape them, put them back into the oven for a minute to warm. They will become pliable again and you can reshape the cookies.

STRAWBERRY SIAM PARFAITS

SERVES 8

■ ■ ■

In 2003 Wolfgang opened Wolfgang Puck Bar and Grill in Roppongi Hills, Tokyo. Working in Tokyo taught me how spoiled we are in California. When I ordered strawberries for my Strawberry Siam Parfaits, I received a neat box of 24 strawberries—6 down, 4 across—for $20. That was a far cry from the bountiful cases that I was accustomed to buying at the Santa Monica Farmers' Market. With fruit being so dear there, I learned to make the most of small quantities.

Strawberries and coconut make a very good marriage, so I put them together here in a whipped coconut cream parfait. I like to serve it in martini glasses.

1 13.5-ounce can unsweetened coconut milk (I prefer Chaokoh brand; it comes in a brown can)
1½ pounds strawberries
¼ cup plus 1 tablespoon sugar
2 tablespoons Grand Marnier
½ teaspoon grated lemon zest
½ teaspoon grated orange zest
¼ cup fresh orange juice
1 cup heavy cream

1. In a medium saucepan, bring the coconut milk to a boil, and boil to reduce to ½ cup. Remove from the heat, transfer to a bowl, and refrigerate until cold (or chill in an ice bath).

2. Set aside 8 small berries for garnishing. Hull the remaining strawberries and cut the strawberries in half if small or into quarters if large. Toss the cut strawberries in a bowl with the ¼ cup sugar, the Grand Marnier, lemon zest, orange zest, and orange juice. Let sit for 30 minutes at room temperature. Drain off the juice and reserve it.

3. Combine the chilled coconut milk, the heavy cream, and the 1 tablespoon sugar and whip to medium peaks. Refrigerate.

4. Just before serving, distribute the reserved juice from the strawberries among eight martini glasses or serving bowls. Combine three quarters of the cut strawberries with the whipped coconut cream and fold together. Divide the mixture among the glasses or bowls, spooning it in a layer over the strawberry juice. Top with the remaining cut strawberries, then garnish each with one of the small whole strawberries. Serve at once.

MANGO PUDDING

■ ■ ■

This elegant pudding, sprinkled with crystallized ginger and topped with whipped cream, is one of the simplest desserts you can make. The key to success is finding perfect mangoes; if that's not possible, use frozen mango puree, preferably Boiron brand (see Sources). I was inspired to develop the dessert after talking to two of our regular guests, Alan and Bonnie Engel, world travelers who raved about a mango pudding they had eaten at the Mandarin Oriental Hotel in Hong Kong. I investigated and came up with this winner.

½ cup cold water
2¼ teaspoons (1 package) powdered gelatin
1 cup heavy cream
¼ cup sugar
½ cup sweetened condensed milk
2 cups mango puree (2 large mangoes, peeled, diced, and pureed; see headnote)
2 tablespoons fresh orange juice
1 tablespoon fresh lemon juice
Pinch of salt
2 tablespoons finely chopped crystallized ginger

1. Pour the cold water into a bowl and sprinkle on the gelatin. Allow to soften (bloom) for 2 minutes.

2. Combine ½ cup of the heavy cream and the sugar in a small saucepan and bring to a boil. Remove from the heat, add the gelatin mixture, and whisk together until the gelatin has completely dissolved. Whisk in the condensed milk, mango puree, orange juice, lemon juice, and salt. Strain into six 6-ounce glasses or bowls, cover, and chill in the refrigerator.

3. Using a hand mixer, whip the remaining ½ cup heavy cream to soft or medium peaks, as desired. Just before serving, sprinkle the pudding with the crystallized ginger and top with the whipped cream.

FORBIDDEN RICE PUDDING

■ ■ ■

Donald Wressell, one of the most amazing pastry chefs in the country, learned to make incredible rice pudding at the Four Seasons Sayan, nestled in the jungle in Bali. He taught me this trick of combining black rice, which is actually purple in color, with starchy white rice to get a rice pudding with some texture and a vivid purple color. The purple rice remains al dente while the white rice softens. The pudding, which is wonderful for breakfast as well as dessert, is called *bubur injin*, or black pudding, in Thailand. It can be served warm or cold.

Forbidden Rice (Chinese black rice), packaged by Lotus Foods, can be found at gourmet markets. Do not substitute any other rice.

¼ cup jasmine rice
¼ cup Forbidden Rice
   (see headnote)
1½ cups water
¼ teaspoon salt
   Seeds from 2 green cardamom
   pods
1½ cups milk
1 cup unsweetened coconut milk
¼ cup sugar
1 teaspoon vanilla extract

1. Wash the jasmine rice in several changes of cold water until the water runs clear. Combine with the black rice, water, and salt in a medium saucepan. Bring to a boil, reduce the heat, cover, and simmer until all of the water is absorbed, about 35 minutes. The rice will be very purple.

2. While the rice is cooking, lightly toast the cardamom seeds in a small skillet over medium heat until fragrant. Remove from the heat and grind the seeds with a mortar and pestle or in a spice mill. Measure out ⅛ teaspoon.

3. Add the milk, coconut milk, ground cardamom, and sugar to the rice and stir together. Bring to a boil, reduce the heat, and cook, stirring often, for 10 minutes. Stir in the vanilla and scrape into a bowl.

4. Cover and chill for at least 2 hours before serving.

CHOCOLATE RICE KRISPIES BARS TOPPED WITH OVALTINE AND MILK CHOCOLATE BAVARIAN CREAM

MAKES SIXTEEN 4-X-1-INCH BARS OR SIXTY-FOUR 1-INCH SQUARES

■ ■ ■

This silky-crunchy chocolate dessert has the added malt-chocolate flavor of Ovaltine. The bars can be cut into standard 4-x-1-inch rectangles, or into miniature 1-inch squares for petits fours. The recipe comes from my friend and fellow pastry chef Pichet Ong, owner of P*Ong in New York. Pichet is the world's expert on Asian and Asian-inspired desserts. I asked him if he would share one with me, and he graciously traded me this inventive dish for a recipe of mine.

Until I made this, I didn't know that Ovaltine comes in two versions, Thai and American. Thai Ovaltine, which comes in a glass jar, has a much richer, maltier flavor than the American variety. You can often find it in Thai markets. If you can't get it, the bars are still wonderful made with American Ovaltine.

FOR THE BARS

- 8 ounces milk chocolate, preferably Valrhona Jivara (see Sources), finely chopped
- 2 tablespoons vegetable oil
- 3/4 cup Rice Krispies
  Pinch of salt

FOR THE BAVARIAN CREAM

- 8 ounces milk chocolate, preferably Valrhona Jivara, finely chopped
- 2 cups heavy cream
- 1/2 cup Ovaltine, preferably Thai (see headnote)

1. **MAKE THE BARS:** Line an 8-inch square pan with parchment paper. Melt the chocolate in a microwave-safe bowl at 50 percent power for 2 to 3 minutes or in a heatproof bowl set over a saucepan of simmering water. With a rubber spatula, stir in the oil and mix until it is incorporated and the mixture is shiny. Fold in the Rice Krispies and salt. Spread the mixture evenly in the prepared pan. Place in the refrigerator.

2. **MAKE THE BAVARIAN CREAM:** Place the chocolate in a medium bowl. Bring 1 cup of the cream to a simmer in a medium saucepan and whisk in 1/3 cup of the Ovaltine. Whisk vigorously to break up any lumps as you bring the

mixture to a boil. Pour the mixture over the chocolate. Tap the bowl on your work surface to settle the chocolate into the cream and let sit for 1 minute, then whisk until smooth. Let cool to room temperature.

3. Whip the remaining 1 cup cream to soft peaks. Fold half of the whipped cream into the chocolate mixture to lighten it, then fold in the remaining cream. Remove the Rice Krispies base from the refrigerator and spread the Bavarian cream over it in an even layer. Tap the pan lightly against your work surface to flatten the top. Refrigerate for at least 4 hours, or overnight.

4. Just before serving, dust the top with the remaining Ovaltine. To serve, run a knife along the inside of the pan and unmold. Using a warm knife, cut into 4-x-1-inch bars or 1-inch squares.

YUZU LEMON-LIME MERINGUE PIE

SERVES 8

■ ■ ■

Yuzu, a popular Japanese citrus fruit with a highly perfumed flavor of its own, tastes like something between a Meyer lemon and a grapefruit. This is a heavenly, intensely citrusy dessert, a lemon-lime and yuzu sabayon hidden inside a little meringue mountain that sits atop a disk of short pastry. It is particularly good after a lobster dinner.

You can buy yuzu at Japanese and specialty markets. The fruit is expensive, but you can find the juice bottled, and it's more reasonably priced. However, make sure you don't buy the salty variety!

FOR THE SABAYON
- 4 cold large eggs plus 4 cold large egg yolks
- 1 cup sugar
- 1 teaspoon grated lemon zest
- 1 cup yuzu juice (see headnote or Sources)
- 2 tablespoons fresh lemon juice
- 2 tablespoons fresh lime juice
- 2 ounces ($1/2$ stick) cold unsalted butter, cut into $1/4$-inch pieces
- 1 10-inch pie shell made with Pâte Sucrée (page 373), prebaked

FOR THE MERINGUE
- $1^1/4$ cups packed dark brown sugar
- 3 tablespoons water
- 4 large egg whites
- $1/4$ teaspoon cream of tartar
- 3 tablespoons sugar

1. **MAKE THE SABAYON:** In a medium heatproof bowl, using a whisk, preferably a balloon whisk, whisk together the eggs, egg yolks, sugar, and lemon zest until pale yellow and smooth.

2. Place the bowl over a saucepan of simmering water, making sure that it is not touching the water, and whisk continuously all around the sides of the bowl for 2 minutes.

3. Very slowly stream in the yuzu juice, lemon juice, and lime juice, whisking vigorously for 3 to 5 minutes, until the mixture is pale and thick, almost pulling away from the sides of the bowl, and has the consistency of sour cream. It should hold a shape when lifted with a spoon. Remove from the heat and, one piece at a time, whisk in the cold butter, whisking each piece until melted. Pour into the prepared tart shell and set aside.

4. **MAKE THE MERINGUE:** Place a rack in the lowest position of the oven and preheat the oven to 375°F.

5. In a medium heavy saucepan, combine the brown sugar and water. Cook over high heat, stirring, until the sugar has dissolved and the mixture begins to boil. Insert a candy thermometer and cook until the mixture reaches 235°F, about 10 minutes. Remove from the heat.

Whenever I beat egg whites for an Italian meringue, which involves adding a concentrated hot syrup to the whites while beating, I set aside a small amount of the sugar. Instead of using it for the syrup, I add it slowly to the egg whites as I beat. This prevents the egg whites from drying out and separating before all of the syrup has been added. This technique also works for dessert soufflés.

6. Meanwhile, in the bowl of a stand mixer fitted with the whisk attachment, or in a large bowl with a hand mixer, beat the egg whites on medium speed until foamy. Add the cream of tartar and 1 tablespoon of the sugar and continue to beat while slowly adding the remaining 2 tablespoons sugar, until the egg whites form soft peaks. With the mixer running, carefully stream in the hot syrup, drizzling it along the sides of the bowl and not over the whisk or beaters. When all of the syrup has been added, stop the mixer and scrape down the sides of the bowl. Then turn the mixer to high speed and continue to beat until the egg whites are stiff, glossy, and cool.

7. ASSEMBLE AND BAKE THE PIE: Spoon or pipe the meringue over the yuzu filling, piling the meringue high and making sure that the edges of the pie shell are sealed with the meringue. Bake for 20 to 25 minutes, until the meringue is golden brown. Remove from the oven, slip off the ring, and serve warm.

NOTE: If you want a more caramelized meringue, use a kitchen torch after baking (see page 69).

MACADAMIA NUT BAKLAVA

■ ■ ■

This macadamia nut version of baklava is always on the menu at Chinois on Main. Working with phyllo dough can be laborious. The sheets sometimes tear, they can easily dry out once you've separated them, and I find it frustrating at best when I have to pull them all apart and then restack them to make baklava. So I've figured out an easier, more logical way to do it. Here's the trick: After unrolling the dough from the package, I fold the stack in half like a book and place it on a large sheet of parchment, with the seam in the center of the parchment. I begin to "read" the book by turning the pages, buttering each one after I turn it, and sprinkling on the nut filling at intervals.

FOR THE BAKLAVA

- 12 ounces (3 sticks) unsalted butter, melted
- 3 cups (14 ounces) finely chopped macadamia nuts (or your favorite nuts)
- 1/2 cup sugar
- 2 teaspoons ground cinnamon
- 1/8 teaspoon ground cloves
- 1 16-ounce package phyllo dough

FOR THE SYRUP

- 3 cups sugar
- 2 cups water
- 1/2 cup honey
- 2 tablespoons fresh lemon juice
- Pinch of salt

1. **MAKE THE BAKLAVA:** Place a rack in the middle of the oven and preheat the oven to 350°F. Brush a 12-x-17-inch half sheet pan with melted butter.

2. Combine the chopped nuts, sugar, cinnamon, and ground cloves. Divide into 6 equal portions.

3. **ASSEMBLE THE BAKLAVA:** Take the phyllo dough out of its package and unroll the dough on a large sheet of parchment paper so that a long side of the dough is toward you. Then fold the dough in half, folding the left side over the right, so it looks like a book, with the spine in the middle of the parchment. Starting with the top "page" of dough, turn over 7 pages, brushing each page with melted butter as you go. After brushing the seventh page, cover it with one sixth of the nut mixture. Turn 3 more pages, brushing each sheet with butter and pressing down firmly over the nut mixture. Cover the third page with an-

other sixth of the nut mixture. Turn 7 more pages of dough, brushing each sheet with butter and pressing firmly down over the nut mixture. Top with another portion of the nuts. Continue to turn pages of dough, brushing each one with butter, until the dough is opened out flat, with one side filled and the other unfilled. Brush the top left-hand sheet of dough, top this page with a portion of the nut mixture, and begin to "close the book": turn 7 more pages, brushing each page with butter, and then top with a portion of nuts. Turn 7 more pages, brushing each page with butter, press down firmly, and top with the remaining portion of nuts. Turn the remaining pages of the book, brushing each with butter, until you have finished "reading" the book and it's closed. Lift the parchment paper, with the baklava, onto the half sheet pan, and cut away any paper that hangs over the edges of the tray.

4. Starting 2 inches in from a corner, make diagonal cuts in the baklava, 2 inches apart, with a sharp knife or an offset serrated knife, making sure you cut down all the way through the bottom of the baklava. Turn the pan and make diagonal cuts in the baklava, again 2 inches apart, to make diamonds. Place in the oven and bake for 45 minutes to 1 hour, until crispy and dark golden brown.

5. MEANWHILE, MAKE THE SYRUP: In a medium saucepan, combine the sugar, water, honey, lemon juice, and salt and bring to a boil over medium heat. Reduce the heat and simmer until the syrup reaches 225°F on a candy thermometer. Remove from the heat.

6. When the baklava is ready, remove from the oven. Pour the warm syrup all over the baklava. Serve hot, warm, or at room temperature. (The baklava can be stored, airtight, at room temperature for up to 5 days.)

ALMOND ICE MILK

MAKES 1 QUART, SERVING 8

■ ■ ■

This surprising ice milk looks like vanilla but tastes like almonds. I once paired it with chocolate beignets for a tasting, and I'll never forget the excited look on Wolfgang's face when he tasted it. He thought he was putting ordinary vanilla ice cream into his mouth, then I heard him exclaim, "Vhat's *that*!" You can buy almond milk, but the flavor just isn't the same.

1½ cups blanched almonds (8 ounces)
4 cups milk or rice milk
2 cups water
½ cup sugar
1 tablespoon plus 2 teaspoons almond extract
½ teaspoon fresh lemon juice
Pinch of salt

1. Place a rack in the middle of the oven and preheat the oven to 325°F. Place a 1-quart freezer container in the freezer.

2. Place the almonds on a baking sheet and toast them lightly, 8 to 10 minutes. Remove from the oven, allow to cool, and coarsely chop them (you can do this by pulsing them in a food processor, but be careful not to pulverize them, because you don't want the almonds to release their oil).

3. Combine the milk or rice milk, water, and sugar in a medium saucepan and bring to a simmer. Add the hot nuts to the simmering liquid. Cook over low heat until the liquid is reduced by half. Pour through a cheesecloth-lined strainer into a medium bowl, pressing out every last bit of liquid; discard the nuts.

4. Fill a large bowl with ice and water and set the bowl of strained almond milk in it. Allow to cool, stirring often. Add the almond extract, lemon juice, and salt. If possible, chill in the refrigerator for 1 to 2 hours before freezing.

5. Freeze in an ice cream maker following the manufacturer's directions. Pack the ice milk in the freezer container and place in the freezer for at least 2 hours to firm before serving.

MANDARIN GRANITA

■ ■ ■

For the Chinese, mandarins signify good health. At Chinese New Year, I fill bowls with this citrus fruit and garnish them with gold leaf to represent sweet prosperity for the up-coming year. I also love to use mandarins for this clean-tasting granita.

1. Place a large flat-bottomed pan in the freezer.

2. In a heavy saucepan, combine the sugar, water, and corn syrup and stir over medium heat until the sugar has completely dissolved and the mixture comes to a boil.

3. Remove from the heat. Stir in the mandarin zest and juice, lemon juice, and salt. Allow to cool slightly, then pour into the chilled pan.

4. Freeze following the basic granita instructions on page 377. Serve right from the freezer in chilled bowls.

1/3 cup sugar
1/2 cup water, preferably sparkling water
1/4 cup light corn syrup
1 teaspoon grated mandarin (tangerine) zest
4 cups fresh mandarin (tangerine) juice
2–3 tablespoons fresh lemon juice, depending on the sweetness of the tangerine juice
Pinch of sea salt

Sherry's Secrets

I love the purity of flavor and texture of a properly made granita. The vivid taste of the fruit should burst through the ice, which should have a very clean taste. *Do not* use tap water. I prefer sparkling water for my granitas. It introduces a little more salt into the mixture, which pushes the flavor through all the more.

The other important thing you need to know is that granitas mustn't have too much sugar. If they have as much sugar as, say, a sorbet, ice crystals won't form, and the ice crystals are what make granita a granita.

PASSION FRUIT SORBET AND COCONUT GELATO FLOAT WITH GINGERED SODA

■ ■ ■

Each element in this tropical-flavored dessert complements the other: the sorbet has a floral acidity that is soothed by the creamy coconut gelato, which is in turn accented by the heat from the gingered soda. I made this dessert for a benefit hosted by the Women Chefs and Restaurateurs. The menu was Asian-inspired, and the tropical flavors in this dessert followed suit.

1. **MAKE THE SORBET:** Place a 1-quart freezer container in the freezer.

2. Bring the water to a boil in a small saucepan and add the tea leaves. Turn off the heat and let steep for 10 to 15 minutes. Strain into a medium bowl. Add the sugar and corn syrup and stir until the sugar has dissolved. Whisk in the remaining sorbet ingredients. Cool over an ice bath or chill in the refrigerator. Transfer to an ice cream maker and freeze according to the manufacturer's directions. Transfer to the freezer container and place in the freezer for at least 2 hours.

3. **MAKE THE COCONUT GELATO:** Place a 1-quart freezer container in the freezer.

FOR THE PASSION FRUIT SORBET

- ¾ cup water
- 1 teaspoon jasmine tea leaves
- ⅔ cup sugar
- 2 tablespoons light corn syrup
- 2 cups passion fruit puree (page 204)
- ½ cup fresh orange juice (from 1 large orange)
- 2 tablespoons fresh lemon juice
- 1 tablespoon Grand Marnier
- ¼ teaspoon vanilla extract
  Pinch of salt

FOR THE COCONUT GELATO

- 2 cups unsweetened coconut milk
- ⅓ cup sugar
- 1 cup milk
- 2 tablespoons dark rum
- 1 tablespoon fresh lime juice
  Pinch of salt

FOR THE GINGER SODA

- 1 16.9-ounce bottle (2 cups) sparkling water
- 1 1-inch piece fresh ginger, peeled and thinly sliced

4. In a medium saucepan, bring the coconut milk to a boil and boil to reduce to 1 cup. It will be very thick. Add the sugar and milk, stir together, and bring to a simmer over medium heat. Remove from the heat and stir until the sugar has dissolved. Whisk in the remaining gelato ingredients and mix together. Allow to cool over an ice bath or chill in the refrigerator. Freeze in an ice cream maker following the manufacturer's directions. Transfer to the freezer container and place in the freezer for at least 2 hours.

5. MEANWHILE, START THE SODA: Insert the ginger slices in the sparkling water. Close tightly and allow to infuse for at least 2 hours.

6. To serve, place 1 scoop of coconut gelato in each ice cream soda glass and top with a scoop of passion fruit sorbet. Pour on the sparkling water and serve.

Sherry's Secrets

For sorbets, ice creams, and gelatos, always put the container you are going to store your dessert in into the freezer before you process the base in your ice cream maker.

Special Events

A HUGE PART OF MY CAREER IS DEVOTED TO CHARITY
work. Which is why you will find me once a year out on the Santa
Monica Pier serving up Deep, Dark, Decadent Doughnuts and Pistachio Gelato to more than 1,000 people at the Special Olympics, or
in my bakeshop as the sun comes up, slapping a final layer of
chocolate onto an enormous truffle destined for 2,000 people at a
Meals on Wheels benefit.

Whatever the event—a Women in Entertainment gala for
breast and ovarian cancer research, a benefit for Careers Through
Culinary Arts Program to raise money for scholarships for culinary
students, an appearance on *Iron Chef*, or any one of the scores of
banquets that I donate my labor to every year—the dessert makes
it special.

The creations in this chapter are master combinations of basic
cakes, mousses, ice creams, and sauces. My chocolate doughnuts,
for example, have scoops of pistachio ice cream nestled in their
holes and are served with chocolate sauce in Pistachio Tuile Cups
atop the ice cream. Floating islands are served with yuzu curd ice
cream and huckleberry sauce, then topped with spun sugar. But
don't be intimidated: Though these desserts look exquisite and
elaborate when they're plated, they can be as simple as you want.
Feel free to deconstruct them. Their building blocks are easy to
make at home, yet absolutely unforgettable.

STRAWBERRY SPOOMS

■ ■ ■

Aclassic spoom is a fruit- or wine-based ice or sorbet to which meringue is added. These always make me think of Sidney Poitier, who eats lunch at Spago so often, he's become part of the family. He loves this nondairy dessert.

FOR THE STRAWBERRY SORBET
- 2 pints strawberries, hulled
- ½ cup water
- ¼ cup sugar
- 2 tablespoons fresh lemon juice
- 2 tablespoons Grand Marnier

FOR THE MERINGUE
- 3 large egg whites, at room temperature
- ⅛ teaspoon cream of tartar
- ¼ cup sugar

1. **MAKE THE SORBET:** Place a 1-quart freezer container in the freezer.

2. Quarter 1 cup of the strawberries and reserve them for garnish. Puree the rest. You should have 2 cups puree.

3. Combine the water and sugar in a saucepan and bring to a simmer, stirring until the sugar has dissolved. Remove from the heat and allow to cool.

4. Combine the syrup with the strawberry puree, lemon juice, and Grand Marnier. Freeze in an ice cream maker following the manufacturer's directions. Transfer to the freezer container and freeze while you make the meringue.

5. **MAKE THE MERINGUE:** Place the egg whites in the bowl of a stand mixer fitted with the whisk attachment, or use a large bowl and a hand mixer. Begin beating at medium speed. When the egg whites begin to foam, add the cream of tartar and 1 tablespoon of the sugar. Continue to beat on medium speed until the egg whites form soft peaks. Slowly stream in the remaining 3 tablespoons sugar, a tablespoon at a time, beating at medium speed. Continue to beat until the mixture forms stiff, shiny peaks, 4 to 5 minutes.

6. Fold one third of the meringue into the soft sorbet, mashing the sorbet a bit at first if necessary. Fold in the balance of the meringue and return the sorbet to the freezer. Serve within 2 hours, while still light and foamy and fresh.

7. Scoop into glasses and garnish with the reserved quartered strawberries.

BOCA NEGRA
Chocolate-Whiskey Pudding Cake

SERVES 16

■ ■ ■

One day I found this message in the bake-shop: "Dear Abby called. She needs your advice." Thinking it was a joke, I didn't return the call. But Abigail Van Buren called again and posed her question: "When baking with alcohol, does the alcohol cook out?" "No," I told her. "There will always be trace elements of alcohol in a baked product."

While this rich, sexy chocolate-whiskey pudding cake won't make you drunk, it is intoxicating. The recipe is my version of a dessert I came across in Dorie Greenspan's *Baking with Julia.* It should be served up in very small portions. When I made this for the Women's Cancer Research Fund benefit, I served the cakes on a Pâte Sucrée (page 373) base and garnished the tops with tuiles (page 162).

- 8 ounces (2 sticks) unsalted butter
- 12 ounces bittersweet chocolate, finely chopped
- 5 large eggs
- 1 cup plus 2 tablespoons sugar
- 1/2 cup Jack Daniel's or bourbon whiskey
- 1 1/2 tablespoons all-purpose flour
- 1/2 cup crème fraîche, slightly whipped (see page 363), for garnish

1. Place a rack in the middle of the oven and preheat the oven to 325°F. Butter a 9-inch springform pan and line the outside with aluminum foil. Set in a baking dish.

2. Melt the butter and chocolate together in a microwave-safe bowl at 50 percent power for about 2 minutes or in a heatproof bowl set over a saucepan of simmering water. Stir the mixture with a rubber spatula until smooth. Set aside.

3. In the bowl of a stand mixer fitted with the whisk attachment, or in a large bowl with a hand mixer, whisk together the eggs and the 1 cup sugar until light and fluffy. Whisk in the melted butter and chocolate and the whiskey. Combine the 2 tablespoons sugar and the flour in a small bowl and whisk into the batter.

4. Pour the batter into the springform pan. Fill the baking dish with enough hot water to come halfway up the sides of the pan. Bake for 35 to 40 minutes, just until the cake is set.

5. Remove from the oven, allow to cool slightly, and remove the sides of the springform pan. Serve warm, with the crème fraîche.

WHIPPED CHOCOLATE SABAYON
WITH RASPBERRIES

SERVES 6

■ ■ ■

Every year I do the desserts for the Entertainment Industry Foundation/Women's Cancer Research Fund benefit dinner. It follows close on the heels of the Oscars and is just as star-studded, with the likes of Tom Hanks and the Spielbergs, and always features a fantastic performer—one year it was Tom Jones, my hero—and I'm not so far in the background that I don't get to see the performance and meet the star. Best of all, I get to send my parents, Ann and Bill, to the gala event, all dressed up in formal attire. They come out to California every year to help me at the Oscars, and this is their special night out in return.

This dessert, which I originally served at the fund-raiser, is perfect for a special event. Raspberries are piled into martini glasses, topped with frothy chocolate sabayon, and garnished with a chocolate cookie. The recipe calls for a wonderful fortified wine from Languedoc-Roussillon called Banyuls, a wine that marries exceptionally well with chocolate. If you can't get it, use port mixed with equal parts Syrah or Zinfandel.

- 2 ounces 64% bittersweet chocolate, such as Valrhona Manjari (see Sources), finely chopped
- 1 cup heavy cream
- 4 large egg yolks
- ½ cup sugar
- 1 cup Banyuls (see headnote)
- ¼ cup water
- 2 pints raspberries
- 6 chocolate wafers

1. Melt the chocolate in a microwave-safe bowl at 50 percent power for about 2 minutes or in a heatproof bowl set over a saucepan of simmering water. Stir until smooth and set aside in a warm place. The temperature should be about 100°F.

2. Whip the cream to soft peaks. Set aside.

3. Fill a medium saucepan one quarter of the way up with water. Bring the water to a boil, then turn the heat down to low. Using a whisk, preferably a balloon whisk, whisk together the egg yolks, sugar, wine, and water in a medium heat-proof bowl. Place it on top of the saucepan, making sure that the bottom doesn't touch the water. Immediately begin to whisk continuously, lifting the whisk out of the mixture with each pass to incorporate as much air as possible. Whisk until the egg yolks have tripled in volume and reached 160°F, 3$\frac{1}{2}$ to 4 minutes.

4. Remove the sabayon from the heat and fold half of it into the melted chocolate. When thoroughly combined, fold in the balance, turning the bowl and folding from the center to the sides. Allow to cool slightly, then fold in the whipped cream.

5. Distribute 1 pint of the raspberries among six martini glasses and pour in the sabayon. Garnish with the remaining 1 pint raspberries and the chocolate wafers and serve.

VARIATION

This sabayon also makes a great boozy chocolate tart, baked in a Pâte Sucrée (page 373) or Chocolate Pâte Sucrée (page 375) crust. Pour the batter into the shell and bake at 350°F for about 20 minutes, until slightly oozy in the center and just about firm on top.

DEEP, DARK, DECADENT DOUGHNUTS

MAKES 9 DOUGHNUTS

■ ■ ■

Many local restaurants contribute to a huge breakfast buffet on the pier in Santa Monica at the benefit for the Special Olympics. Since it's breakfast, I make different types of doughnuts. These chocolate doughnuts have always been a favorite. I use chocolate truffle cake batter for them. This may sound strange, but it works beautifully. I freeze the batter, then cut out the doughnuts while the batter is frozen, coat them with panko (Japanese bread crumbs), and quickly fry them. They can be done in advance, which is really useful when you're serving more than 1,000 people, and reheated just before serving.

I serve these with Pistachio Gelato (page 318), and Pistachio Tuile Cups (page 317) filled with "Ten-Year" Chocolate Sauce (page 345).

Batter for Chocolate Truffle Cakes
   (page 80)
Vegetable oil for deep-frying
2 large eggs
1½ cups panko bread crumbs
   (available at gourmet markets
   and some supermarkets)
1 cup all-purpose flour

1. Line an 8-inch square baking pan with parchment paper. Pour the chocolate truffle batter into the pan. Cover directly with plastic wrap and place in the freezer. Leave until frozen solid, at least 4 hours.

2. Remove from the freezer and remove the plastic wrap. Dust a work surface lightly with flour, run a knife around the edges of the pan, and flip the frozen batter over onto the work surface. Peel off the parchment. Dust the batter lightly with flour, and using a 2½-inch doughnut cutter dipped in flour, cut out 9 doughnuts. Place the doughnuts on a half sheet pan and return them to the freezer if not cooking right away.

3. Preheat the oven to 375°F. Heat about 3 inches of oil in a deep skillet, saucepan, or wok to 350°F on a deep-fry thermometer.

4. Meanwhile, in a medium bowl, whisk together the eggs. Set aside. Place the panko bread crumbs in a medium bowl. Place the 1 cup flour on a piece of

parchment. One at a time, dust each doughnut generously with the flour. Dip into the eggs and tap off the excess. Place in the panko and coat evenly.

5. Using a slotted spoon, carefully place one doughnut at a time in the oil. Deep-fry for 1 minute, then flip the doughnut over. Fry for 30 seconds, remove from the oil, and place on a paper-towel-lined rack set over a 12-x-17-inch half sheet pan. Make sure to allow the oil to come back up to 350°F between batches. (You can fry the doughnuts 2 to 4 hours ahead and reheat just before serving, as directed in Step 6).

6. To serve, place the doughnuts in the oven and heat through for 6 to 10 minutes, depending on how hot they were to begin with. The outside should be crispy and the inside should be oozing.

SERVING HOT AND COLD DESSERTS

I have a set routine for sending desserts out to our guests. Precise orchestration is essential, especially with a dessert like these hot doughnuts that are served with cold ice cream, warm chocolate sauce, and a delicate tuile.

I communicate with the manager to get the exact time that the first plate will go out. At that time (the "pickup time"), waiters will be lined up like soldiers at attention (no talking allowed), ready to sweep up the assembled plates. If the pickup time is 9:05 P.M., for example, my team begins plating at 9:00.

SETUP (this happens hours before pickup time)

- All the plates are laid out with the pattern in the same direction.
- Sheet trays are placed in the freezer.
- The ice cream is prescooped (this can be done 2 hours ahead) and set on the sheet trays.

PLATING

- One person picks up the hot doughnuts and places one in the center of each plate.
- Using a spatula, the next person transfers a prescooped ball of ice cream from the chilled sheet tray to the center of the doughnut.
- The next person flattens the top of the ice cream ball slightly with a spatula and sets a tuile cup on top.
- The next person fills the tuile with chocolate sauce.
- The waiter picks up two plates at a time and carries them out.

Of course, if you're making the doughnuts at home, you won't have the extra hands, but then you won't be trying to get this out to 1,000 people either. Take the time to prescoop the ice cream balls and follow the steps anyway, to get your dessert out in the most efficient manner.

PISTACHIO TUILE CUPS

MAKES 12 COOKIES

■ ■ ■

These delicate tuiles are shaped by draping the warm cookies over espresso cups so they take on their shape. I like to serve them with Pistachio Gelato (page 318). The trick to making the lacy cookies is to make sure they don't bake for too long, then to allow them to rest briefly on the baking sheet until they are warm enough to shape but not so hot that they fall apart when you lift them off the baking sheet.

2 ounces (¹/₂ stick) unsalted butter
¹/₄ cup sugar
¹/₄ cup light corn syrup
¹/₂ cup pistachios, lightly toasted
   and coarsely chopped

1. Place a rack in the middle of the oven and preheat the oven to 350°F. Line a 12-x-17-inch half sheet pan with a silicone mat. Place four espresso cups upside down on the work surface.

2. In a small saucepan over medium heat, melt the butter. Stir in the sugar and corn syrup and stir constantly until the sugar has dissolved, about 1 minute. Remove from the heat and stir in the pistachios.

3. Spoon 1 level tablespoon of the tuile batter onto the silicone mat for each cookie, allowing 2 inches on all sides for spreading. You can do up to four at a time, but it might be easier to do two at a time.

4. Bake for 6 to 8 minutes, until the tuiles are very lightly browned. Remove the pan from the oven and allow to sit for 2 to 3 minutes. With a metal spatula, preferably offset, carefully remove a tuile and drape it over an espresso cup. Continue with the remaining tuiles. Carefully remove from the espresso cups when cool. (The cookies can be stored airtight for 2 days.)

PISTACHIO GELATO

■ ■ ■

This is a very light gelato, with no eggs and just a bit of cream. I like to serve it with my super-rich Deep, Dark, Decadent Doughnuts (page 314). I put a scoop right in the doughnut hole.

- 3 cups milk
- ½ cup heavy cream
- ¾ cup sugar
- 1 cup powdered milk
- ¼ cup corn syrup
- 5 ounces (1 cup) pistachios, warmed and coarsely chopped
- 1 ounce (2 tablespoons) pistachio paste (available at gourmet markets, or see Sources)
- ¼ cup unsweetened coconut milk
- 1 tablespoon fresh lemon juice
  Pinch of salt

1. Place a 1-quart freezer container in the freezer.

2. Combine all of the ingredients except the lemon juice and salt in a large saucepan and bring to a boil. Remove from the heat, and using a handheld or a regular blender, puree until smooth. Pour through a fine-mesh strainer into a bowl.

3. Place over an ice bath to cool. Add the lemon juice and salt. Freeze in an ice cream maker following the manufacturer's directions. Freeze in the chilled container for 2 hours, or until firm.

Sherry's Secrets

Warming the pistachios helps release their aroma. Be careful not to toast them, or you'll lose their bright color.

THE WORLD'S SECOND LARGEST CHOCOLATE TRUFFLE (DOWNSIZED)

MAKES 24 (REGULAR) TRUFFLES

■ ■ ■

The recipe here is for truffles on a human scale, but they are adapted from my formula for The World's Second Largest Chocolate Truffle.

After years of catering charity galas, I decided one day to try making one huge item for a Meals on Wheels benefit for 2,000 people. I had T-shirts made with the ingredients printed on the back (600 ounces bittersweet chocolate, 600 ounces heavy cream, 60 sticks softened butter, 12 bottles Jack Daniel's), and on the front, "I made the world's largest truffle and all I got was this sweet T-shirt."

All night long, the night before the event, we worked on the giant truffle, slapping the ganache onto the growing ball. It was like making a huge clay sculpture. My assistant, Steve "Monkey Boy" Peungraksa, and I were covered in chocolate when we walked out of the kitchen to discover that the sun had come up. All went well until it was time to transport the thing to the event. It was 4 feet in diameter, and we couldn't get it through the main door of the restaurant. I had the guys open the double doors that led out of the private party room, and the refrigerated truck backed up onto the sidewalk so that we could roll the tray it was sitting on directly inside. Just as we were rolling it up the plank, a wheel fell off the cart and the truffle began to roll. It nearly flattened my tiny assistant Helen Arsen, but we managed to get the monster into the truck and to the event unscathed.

I thought we'd made the world's largest truffle until I found out a few months later that the French guys at Lenôtre Paris had made one that weighed 200 pounds more than mine.

FOR THE TRUFFLES

- 8 ounces bittersweet chocolate, finely chopped
- 2 tablespoons unsalted butter, softened
- 1 cup heavy cream
- 2 tablespoons Jack Daniel's or bourbon whiskey
  Cocoa powder for dusting

FOR THE COATING

- 1 cup cocoa powder, sifted, for dusting
- 8 ounces bittersweet chocolate, finely chopped

1. **MAKE THE TRUFFLES**: Place the bittersweet chocolate and butter in a heatproof bowl. Bring the cream to a boil and pour over the chocolate and butter. Tap the bowl on the work surface to settle the chocolate into the cream, then let the mixture sit for 1 minute. Using a rubber spatula, stir slowly in a circular motion starting from the center of the bowl and working out to the sides. Be careful not to add too much air to the ganache. Stir until the chocolate has completely melted, about 2 minutes.

2. Add the whiskey and stir to combine. Allow the ganache to cool until it is firm. This should take at least 4 hours in a 65°F room or 2 hours in the refrigerator.

3. Once the ganache is firm, it can be formed into truffle balls. Using a piping bag, a mini ice cream scoop, or a tablespoon, make 1-inch-diameter "blobs," then roll the blobs by hand into somewhat uniform balls. This is messy, no doubt about it. If the truffles begin to warm up and become soft, refrigerate for 10 to 15 minutes, until firm. (If you have hot hands or it is a hot day, it may feel as though you can't get a grip on the truffle: work near a sink, and if the ganache feels as if it's melting, cool your hands under cold running water, then dry them and dust with a little cocoa powder. Be careful not to get too much cocoa powder on the truffles, or they will taste of cocoa powder.)

4. **COAT THE TRUFFLES**: Place a parchment-lined 12-x-17-inch half sheet pan on your work surface. Place the cocoa powder on the bottom fourth of the parchment paper. Melt the bittersweet chocolate in a microwave-safe bowl at 50 percent power for about 2 minutes or in a heatproof bowl set over a saucepan of simmering water. Spoon a small amount of melted chocolate into the palm of your hand and roll one truffle at a time in it. Drop the truffle into the cocoa powder. Take a fork and roll the truffle from west to east, then north, to coat. Tap the truffles so that the cocoa isn't too thick. Place on the parchment to harden. The truffles should be stored in an airtight container in a cool place or in the refrigerator. (They will keep for 4 days.) If condensation forms on them when you remove them from the refrigerator, toss them in more cocoa powder before serving.

LIME-SCENTED FLOATING ISLANDS WITH YUZU CURD ICE CREAM

SERVES 6

■ ■ ■

One Tuesday morning, Wolfgang, Lee Hefter (the executive chef of Spago), and I sat down for a meeting with the *Iron Chef* producers. Wolfgang was to compete against the formidable Japanese chef Masaharu Morimoto, who had already won eighty *Iron Chef* battles, and we had just found out that the taping would be the following week!

The premise of *Iron Chef* is that the culinary teams are assigned a "secret ingredient," which will be the basis of a menu that must be created in exactly 1 hour. In one respect, we live "the *Iron Chef*" life every day at the restaurant, but we have a much bigger staff there than our team of three on that soundstage. My position on the team was not just that of pastry chef but also that of sous-chef to Wolf and Lee. We made five courses, many with four components each.

The secret ingredient was revealed: eggs. I thought fast: begin with lemon curd, the ultimate egg-dessert preparation, and then break it down into different components. This dessert is simple—remember, we had just 60 minutes to prepare the entire menu (and I had much less time for the dessert, as I was also the sous-chef). Each part of the dessert uses the basic curd, but in a different way. It serves as a base for the ice cream (since we had a

FOR THE YUZU CURD
- 1½ cups sugar
- 6 large eggs plus 9 large egg yolks
- 1 cup yuzu juice (see headnote or Sources)
- ½ cup fresh lime juice (from 3–4 limes)
- 2 ounces (½ stick) unsalted butter, cut into small pieces, softened

FOR THE YUZU SAUCE AND ICE CREAM
- 1½ cups milk
- 1 tablespoon sugar

  Spun Sugar (page 352; optional) for garnish

FOR THE MERINGUES
- 2 tablespoons softened butter for the ramekins
- ¾ cup sugar, plus more for dusting the ramekins
- 3 large egg whites, at room temperature
- ⅛ teaspoon cream of tartar
- 1 teaspoon grated lime zest

- ½ recipe Huckleberry or Blackberry Merlot Sauce (page 361)
  Sugar for caramelizing (optional)
- 1 cup huckleberries or blueberries for garnish (optional)

very powerful ice cream maker, we were able to make it much faster than normal), for the sauce that tops the meringues, and for the "sea" in which the islands of meringues float. I added a dimension of flavor and color to the plate with a huckleberry sauce, and drama—which is what *Iron Chef* is all about—by bruléeing the top with a kitchen torch and making spun sugar for the final, classic garnish. What people remember most is the spectacle of me wildly pulling the strands of hot spun sugar directly from the pan with my bare hands (don't try that one at home!). And yes, we won!

You can find yuzu juice at some Japanese markets; make sure not to buy the salty variety. Lemon juice or Meyer lemon juice may be substituted.

1. **MAKE THE YUZU CURD:** Prepare an ice bath to cool the finished curd: fill a large bowl with ice and a little water and have a medium heatproof bowl ready to set into the ice. Fill a medium saucepan one-quarter full with water and bring to a simmer over medium heat.

2. In the medium heatproof bowl, combine the sugar, eggs, and egg yolks and whisk together for 30 seconds. Place the bowl over the simmering water and immediately begin whisking vigorously. Whisk continuously for 15 seconds, or until the sugar has dissolved.

3. Add the yuzu juice and lime juice and cook the curd over the simmering water, whisking continuously, for about 5 minutes. Use the whisk to scrape the sides and bottom of the bowl so that no bits stick to the sides and overcook. Insert a thermometer and check the curd's temperature. The curd is done when it reaches the consistency of sour cream and has a temperature of 160°F.

4. Remove the curd from the heat. Add the butter, piece by piece, whisking after each addition until it melts. Once all of the butter has been added, whisk for an additional 30 seconds, or until the texture is blended. Set the bowl in the ice bath and stir the curd occasionally until it has cooled completely. (At this point the curd can be refrigerated in an airtight container for up to 1 week.) Transfer 1 cup of the yuzu curd to a bowl, cover with plastic wrap, and set aside in the refrigerator. You will use this to finish the dessert.

5. **MAKE THE SAUCE AND THE ICE CREAM:** Place a 1-quart freezer container in the freezer.

6. Stir the milk and sugar into the remaining curd. Mix well. Transfer 1¼ cups of this mixture to a container. This will be your yuzu sauce. Cover and refrigerate.

7. Freeze the rest of the curd mixture in an ice cream maker following the manufacturer's directions. (You can make the spun sugar, if using, while the ice cream churns.) When the ice cream reaches the desired consistency, transfer to the freezer container and place in the freezer for 2 hours, or until firm.

8. MAKE THE MERINGUES: Place a rack in the middle of the oven and preheat the oven to 325°F. Lightly butter and sugar six 6-ounce ramekins and place in a baking dish.

9. Place the egg whites in the bowl of a stand mixer fitted with the whisk attachment, or use a large bowl and a hand mixer, and beat on medium speed until they begin to foam. Add the cream of tartar and 1 tablespoon of the sugar, and continue to beat until the egg whites begin to form soft peaks. Slowly stream in the remaining 11 tablespoons sugar, a tablespoon at a time. Continue to beat until the mixture forms stiff, shiny peaks. Fold in the lime zest.

10. Spoon into the ramekins. Fill the baking dish with enough hot water to come halfway up the sides of the ramekins. Bake for 20 minutes, or until the meringues are set and their internal temperature is between 145° and 150°F. Remove from the oven and carefully remove from the ramekins. Place on a parchment-paper-lined baking sheet to cool.

11. ASSEMBLE THE DESSERT: Spread a spoonful of yuzu sauce over one half of each large, wide bowl or soup plate and a spoonful of the huckleberry sauce over the other half.

12. Scoop out the center of each meringue and place a small scoop of ice cream inside. Place in the middle of each plate. Top the ice cream with the 1 cup curd you set aside. If you wish, sprinkle sugar over the top of the curd and caramelize with a kitchen torch (see page 360). Garnish with the remaining huckleberry sauce and the huckleberries or blueberries, if using. Top with the spun sugar, if desired, and serve.

The Academy Awards

IT'S 4 P.M. ON A SUNDAY IN MARCH, AND I AM WORKING with utter concentration while helicopters flutter loudly overhead, chilling me and my staff with their downdraft. We are on the rooftop of the Hollywood and Highland Center complex in Hollywood, one floor up from the Kodak Theatre, where the Academy Awards ceremony will begin in an hour. The shouts and screams of fans rise from the street below as they applaud and cheer their favorite actors and actresses on the red carpet. We can see the red carpet but have to crane to see the stars. The helicopter whirring and the screams and cheers below get louder and louder, telling us that the 5 P.M. curtain time is approaching.

The awards gala will go on for almost four hours. Afterward, 1,700 people will take the escalator up to attend the Governors Ball in the rooftop ballroom. Wolfgang Puck Catering does the dinner for the star-studded event, and I've been creating the desserts since the year I joined the company. For me, it's the most dramatic, demanding event of the year. The desserts must be original and exquisite, and the advance preparation, on-site plate prep, and service organized and timed to perfection. In one hour, we serve a four-course meal to the hungry VIPs who attended the ceremony. Then they're off in their limos to the next Oscars after-party.

Everything from the plate to the very tip of the dessert is themed to match the ballroom decor. Chocolate is always part of the equation, and there is always an element that is molded in the shape of the statuette. We work for weeks designing and making the plate decorations, and on the day itself my team never looks up. We work in a large catering tent next to a hotel swimming pool. Some workers spray-paint the plates with chocolate or gold decorations, others turn the decorated plates so that they're all facing the same direction (that way, the waiters can set them down just the right way in front of the guests). Others stick gold-leaf suns onto handmade royal blue sugar boxes, and still others coat 1,700 hazelnut tortes with croquante. We don't stop until the corps of waiters finishes filing through the room and running the plates out to the tables.

*M*OM AND DAD are part of the team. Every year, they fly in from New York to help at the Oscars and take care of me. While they've never been chefs, over the years they have learned to bake off sheets of cookies, assemble desserts, and even temper chocolate. They plate up and rally with the rest of the gang, and when the pressure is really on, they're excellent at policing.

The countdown has begun, and with it the pressure intensifies. After one month of work, it is now all down to a few hours. Will the show let out on time? Will it run long? Timing is crucial. We work with a walkie-talkie system, and once the telecast is under way, I get regular updates through my headset as to how it's progressing. Starting at around 8 P.M., Wolf and Chef Matt Bencivenga will come in every fifteen minutes or so and announce the projected time for when the hors d'oeuvres will go out (the hors d'oeuvres are also plated in the pastry tent).

The clock is ticking. I hear over the headset that the guests are leaving the theater. We begin to work faster. The appetizers go out on scores of beautifully composed platters. The energy level rises in the kitchen as the cooks ready themselves for the main course, and we kick into high gear. It's time for the entrée, and the kitchen is roaring with calls from Chef Matt for pickups.

The tension builds. The ice cream can't be brought out and plated until the last minute. If you do it too early, the ice cream will melt, destroying the plate. Too late, and the wave of 400 waiters, who carry only two plates at a time, will bear down on us and compromise the entire pickup. It's like building an elaborate sand castle out of 200 pounds of chocolate, 1,600 eggs, 100 pounds of sugar, and as many pounds of butter. Then the waiters swoop down and make it disappear like a big wave, and the room is cleared in thirty minutes.

We ready the frozen sheet trays topped with scoops of ice cream, stacking them on rolling carts at one end of the room, and in a whirlwind put together the finishing touches. It is only minutes before the first waiter will come in. I look down each row of plates, proud of the flawless, precise lines. The desserts are like rows of soldiers at attention, in perfect formation, ready for battle.

There's little time to admire this awesome sight, as hordes of waiters wearing fresh white gloves have amassed at the door. As they come down the first aisle of tables, the pastry team keeps one step ahead of them, setting an ice cream quenelle on each plate just before the waiter sweeps it up. Back they come, again and again. When one row of plates is gone, we pull away the tables and the waiters start down the next aisle. The room clears of both tables and desserts, and in half an hour it's all gone, as if a cleaning machine had swept through. Whew!

The calm lasts only until the stars begin to exit the banquet on their way to the next party. Waiters are posted outside the dining room, baskets in hand, filled with small gilded chocolate statuettes sealed in acetate gift bags. No matter what happens during the awards ceremony, nobody leaves the Governors Ball without an Oscar. It may be made out of chocolate, but it's an Oscar nonetheless.

BANDED LAYER CAKES
(67TH OSCARS)

■ ■ ■

I created this for the 67th Oscars, my first Oscars. The individual layer cakes are chocolate-glazed, then "banded" with chocolate to create a ready-to-eat chocolate stand. I topped them with a sweet Oscar statuette.

NOTE ON SPECIAL EQUIPMENT: You will need ten 10-x-1¾-inch acetate banding strips (called "ribbons" in the pastry trade), available at pastry supply stores, or see Sources.

1 recipe My Favorite White Birthday Cake (page 7), baked in two 12-x-17-inch half sheet pans for 25–30 minutes and cooled
1 cup Simple Syrup (page 350)
1 recipe frosting from My Favorite White Birthday Cake

FOR THE CHOCOLATE BANDS
18 ounces bittersweet chocolate, finely chopped

1. Brush both sheet cakes lightly with simple syrup. Using a 3-inch cookie cutter, cut the cakes into 30 rounds.

2. Heat the frosting to 68° to 70°F. Make ten 3-layer cakes, placing 1 tablespoon of frosting between the layers, spooning it on, placing another round of cake on top, and pressing down. Leave the top layer unfrosted and set aside the remaining frosting. Place the cakes in the freezer for 10 to 15 minutes to set while you prepare the bands.

3. **MAKE THE BANDS**: Place a large piece of parchment paper on your work surface and lay 10 acetate banding strips on the parchment. Place another piece of parchment paper on a second work surface. Melt the chocolate in a microwave-safe bowl at 50 percent power for 2 to 3 minutes or in a heatproof bowl set over a saucepan of simmering water. Stir until smooth. Working with one strip at a time, using a small offset spatula, smear 3 tablespoons of chocolate evenly over the strip. Let set for 3 to 4 minutes, then lift the strip up off the parchment, leaving behind any chocolate that ran off the edges of the strip onto the parchment, and set the strip, chocolate side up, on the second, clean parchment-covered work surface. Let the chocolate band set until the chocolate is no longer shiny but the band is still flexible, 3 to 5 minutes.

4. **ASSEMBLE THE TORTES:** Set one of the cakes on your work surface. Using both hands, carefully lift up the still-flexible band by the edges and quickly wrap it, chocolate side facing in, around the cake. Peel back a little of the acetate on one end and press the other end over it. Repeat with the remaining bands and cakes. Refrigerate for 1 hour.

5. Heat the remaining frosting in a microwave at 50 percent power to 80° to 82°F. Spoon over the top layers of the cakes and tap against the table so it spreads evenly. Return the cakes to the refrigerator.

6. When ready to serve, peel away the acetate bands. Using a hot knife, trim off the excess chocolate where the ends of the bands join. Serve at once.

CHOCOLATE BOXES
(73RD OSCARS)

SERVES 6

■ ■ ■

When the Oscars were held downtown, we prepared everything for the Governors Ball in a huge catering tent erected on the plaza. We had to bring our trucks and rent ovens, refrigerators, and freezers. We called it the MASH Unit Catering Tent.

Made in the weeks leading up to the event, the dessert for the 73rd Oscars was a delicate chocolate box. On site, we filled the boxes with chocolate mousse and deep, dark chocolate cake and set them on plates that had been frozen. Using a power painter, we sprayed them with colored white chocolate to create a "red carpet." Each plate was garnished with raspberries and an edible envelope that read, "The Oscar Goes to."

That year the temperature in the tent ran high, and the chocolate began to soften. We pulled down some of the tent panels so that the outside air would blow in, and that 45°F air saved our chocolate Oscar boxes.

Julia Roberts won the Oscar for best actress that year, for *Erin Brockovich*. Partway through the Governors Ball, she came running through the kitchen to escape to the next party, but when she saw the desserts, she stopped, and Mom got to photograph her, Oscar in hand, beside me, with one of my Oscars chocolate boxes.

FOR THE CHOCOLATE MOUSSE
- 1 pound bittersweet chocolate, finely chopped
- ½ cup sugar
- ½ cup water
- 9 large egg yolks, at room temperature
- 2 cups heavy cream
  Brooklyn Blackout Cake (page 40), cut into ½-inch cubes

FOR THE CHOCOLATE BOXES
- 1½ pounds bittersweet chocolate, finely chopped

FOR THE RED CARPETS (OPTIONAL)
- 4 ounces white chocolate, finely chopped
- ¼ cup vegetable oil
- 2 teaspoons oil-based red food coloring (available at pastry supply stores, or see Sources)

FOR THE RASPBERRIES
- 2 tablespoons sugar
- 1 teaspoon fresh lemon juice
- 1 tablespoon fresh orange juice
- 1 pint raspberries

NOTE ON SPECIAL EQUIPMENT: You will need six 2-inch-wide, 4¾-inch-tall, clear plastic pencil holders for the molds; they are available at office supply stores. You'll also need a shower/tub liner if you are planning to make the red carpets; liners can be found at hardware stores.

1. **MAKE THE MOUSSE**: Melt the chocolate in a microwave-safe bowl at 50 percent power for about 2 minutes or in a heatproof bowl set over a saucepan of simmering water. Stir until smooth.

2. Combine the sugar and water in a small saucepan and bring to a boil. Reduce the heat and simmer until the sugar has dissolved. Remove from the heat and wait for the bubbles to subside. Meanwhile, in the bowl of a stand mixer fitted with the whisk attachment, or in a large bowl with a hand mixer, begin to beat the egg yolks on high speed. Slowly stream in the hot syrup, making sure to pour it down the sides of the bowl and not over the beaters, and continue to beat on high speed for 2 to 3 minutes, until the mixture is thick and has doubled in volume. It should still be warm.

3. Fold half of the egg yolk mixture into the melted chocolate. When thoroughly combined, fold in the rest.

4. Whip the cream to soft peaks. Fold into the chocolate mixture. Fold in the cake pieces. Cover with plastic wrap and refrigerate until the mixture has set, about 2 hours.

5. **MAKE THE CHOCOLATE BOXES**: To make the chocolate boxes, you must temper the chocolate. If you are not familiar with tempering chocolate, please see page 379. I give you the microwave method here, but you can use a double boiler, following the directions on page 380, if you wish. Make sure your molds are ready and your rack is in place before you begin.

6. Line a 12-x-17-inch half sheet pan with parchment paper and place a rack over the parchment. Place 18 ounces of the chocolate in a microwave-safe bowl and microwave at 50 percent power for 1 minute. You need to gradually heat the chocolate to 115°F (120°F maximum). Remove from the microwave, stir, and return to the microwave. Microwave for another minute at 50 percent power. Stir the chocolate again. Then zap at 30-second intervals, at 50 percent power, stir-

ring between each interval and being careful to scrape the chocolate from the sides of the bowl, where it risks burning, to the center. When all the chocolate has been melted and is smooth, insert an instant-read thermometer. Continue to zap for 10-second intervals, at 50 percent power, until the chocolate reaches 115°F.

7. When the chocolate has reached 115°F (it will be smooth and flow freely), allow it to sit for 10 minutes at room temperature.

8. Add the remaining 6 ounces chocolate, a handful at a time, stirring to cover it with the melted chocolate. Add and stir until the mixture is smooth and reaches 85°F. You may not use all of the chocolate. Now very gently reheat the chocolate at 3- to 5-second intervals, until it reaches 89° to 90°F, no higher. If it goes higher than 97°F, you will have to begin the process again (Step 6).

9. Don't put your bowl of melted chocolate on a cool surface, or the chocolate will cool down. On the other hand, don't fill the molds in too warm a spot or under a hot light, or the chocolate won't set. Line up your molds on the rack. Fill one mold with chocolate, all the way up to the top. Tap with the handle of a wooden spoon to release any air bubbles, then invert the mold over another mold so that the chocolate runs into the second mold. Tap out the chocolate using the wooden spoon, holding the corner of the full mold over the center of the empty one. When all of the chocolate has flowed out of the first mold, leaving a coating adhering to its insides, place the mold upside down on the rack. Pick up the second mold and tilt it to coat any uncovered surfaces with the chocolate, then tap out over the third mold, and so on, until all of

Sherry's Secrets

MOLDING CHOCOLATE

One of the reasons pouring and molding chocolate works so well is that the chocolate will always mirror the surface upon which it is poured, and it will retract when it cools. If you pour tempered chocolate onto a smooth, shiny surface—like the surface of the plastic pencil boxes we used—it will cool and retract, making it easy to remove from the mold. And the surface of the sides will be as smooth and shiny as, well, plastic.

the molds have been coated. By the time you get to the fourth mold, you will need to add some warm chocolate from the bowl. Tap out the chocolate from the sixth mold back into the bowl. The whole process of coating the molds should not take more than 5 to 7 minutes. (Note: There will be lots of leftover chocolate, in the bowl, on the parchment paper, and on the rack. Wait until it hardens, then detach and keep in an airtight container. Use again as you would any chocolate.)

10. After 5 minutes, as the chocolate on the edges of the molds begins to harden onto the rack, lift up the molds and shift them to another spot on the rack. After 10 minutes, once the chocolate has just about set but is still soft, scrape away the excess bits hanging off each mold with a paring knife, so that the edges are clean and even (reserve these chocolate scraps with the rest of the extra chocolate); hold on to the molds by the corner edges so that your hands don't warm the chocolate. Place the molds, right side up, in the refrigerator for 15 minutes, or freeze for 10 minutes. The chocolate will retract from the plastic molds. You can tell when the chocolate boxes are almost ready because the outer surface of the clear plastic will be mostly cloudy, with small shiny spots where the chocolate is still adhering.

11. Remove from the refrigerator or freezer and gently tweak or squeeze the molds to completely dislodge the chocolate. Place one hand on the inside of the mold, and with the other hand, holding the corner edges with your fingertips, gently ease the mold and the chocolate apart. The sleek chocolate boxes should slide out pretty easily. (The boxes can be stored in a cool, dark place for up to 1 week.)

12. MAKE THE RED CARPETS IF USING: Combine the white chocolate with the vegetable oil and melt in a microwave-safe bowl at 50 percent power for about 2 minutes or in a heatproof bowl set over a saucepan of simmering water. Stir until smooth. Add the food coloring and stir until the chocolate is bright red. Cut a red carpet template for the plates from a shower/tub liner and, with a pastry brush, paint a red carpet onto each plate.

13. PREPARE THE RASPBERRIES: Stir together the sugar, lemon juice, and orange juice. Lightly toss the raspberries with the mixture to give them a nice shine.

14. Fill the chocolate boxes with the mousse. Set upside down atop the red carpets, if using, on the plates, garnish with the raspberries, and serve. Guests should crack the boxes with their forks to get the surprise inside.

Sherry's Secrets

KNOW YOUR FOOD COLORING

Some food colorings are water-based, while others are oil-based. Water-based food coloring should be used only for sugar work (such as royal icing, colored sugar, candy, and macarons). Oil-based food coloring is best used in applications that involve fats, such as chocolate work or buttercream.

CHOCOLATE TRUFFLE TARTS WITH CHOCOLATE CRÈME BRÛLÉE DIAMONDS AND SEVEN-BEAN VANILLA ICE CREAM (75TH OSCARS)

SERVES 8

∎ ∎ ∎

For the seventy-fifth anniversary of the Oscars, I researched what was served for dessert at the first Oscars. It was chocolate and vanilla ice cream with cherries. My incarnation of this was a molten chocolate tart topped with diamond-shaped chocolate crème brûlée, served with port-wine-poached sour cherries and an extravagant Seven-Bean Vanilla Ice Cream. It's a perfect dessert for a diamond anniversary. You can substitute sun-dried cherries for the poached sour cherries.

1. **MAKE THE CRÈME BRÛLÉE:** Place a rack in the middle of the oven and preheat the oven to 325°F. Line a 9-x-13-inch baking pan with a silicone baking mat.

2. Place the bittersweet chocolate and the unsweetened chocolate in a medium heatproof bowl. Combine the cream, milk, and sugar in a saucepan and bring to a simmer while stirring with a heat-resistant spatula. Stir gently until the sugar has dissolved. Pour half of this over the chocolate and tap the bowl on your work surface to settle the chocolate into the cream. Let sit for 1

FOR THE CRÈME BRÛLÉE

- 4 ounces bittersweet chocolate, finely chopped
- ½ ounce unsweetened chocolate, finely chopped
- 2 cups heavy cream
- ¾ cup milk
- ½ cup plus 2 tablespoons sugar
- 4 large egg yolks

FOR THE POACHED SOUR CHERRIES

- 4 ounces sour cherries, pitted
- 4 cups port wine
- ⅓ cup sugar
- 1 vanilla bean, split, seeds scraped out; seeds and bean reserved

- 8 3-inch tartlet shells made with Chocolate Pâte Sucrée (page 375), prebaked
- ½ recipe Chocolate Truffle Cakes (page 80) batter
  Sugar for dusting

  Seven-Bean Vanilla Ice Cream (recipe follows)

minute, then whisk gently until the cream and chocolate are blended.

3. In a separate bowl, gently whisk the egg yolks. Slowly ladle ½ cup of the remaining hot cream into the yolks. Whisk in the rest of the cream, combine well, and add the melted chocolate mixture. Stir to combine thoroughly.

4. Pour the mixture through a fine-mesh strainer into the lined pan. Place the pan in a larger baking pan, and add enough hot water to the larger pan to come halfway up the sides of the smaller pan. Place in the oven and bake until the crème brûlée is set, 30 to 35 minutes. Remove from the oven and the water bath and allow to cool, then cover tightly with plastic wrap and freeze overnight or up to 2 weeks.

5. Remove the crème brûlée from the freezer and place a sheet of parchment paper on your work surface. Run a knife along the edges of the baking pan and flip over the frozen crème brûlée onto the parchment. Peel back the silicone mat. Working quickly, cut the brûlée into 3-inch-long, 1-inch-wide diamonds. Transfer the parchment paper gently to a baking sheet, cover with plastic wrap, and return to the freezer. (You will have leftover crème brûlée; keep frozen, tightly covered, for up to 2 weeks.)

6. MAKE THE POACHED SOUR CHERRIES: Place the cherries, port, sugar, and vanilla seeds and bean in a saucepan and bring to a simmer over low heat. Simmer very gently for 30 minutes, until the liquid is thick and the cherries are plump. (The cherries will plump up like meatballs in sauce. The longer you leave them, the more liquid they will soak up. That's why you need only 4 ounces of cherries.) Remove the vanilla bean from the cherries.

7. ASSEMBLE THE TARTS: Place a rack in the middle of the oven and preheat the oven to 375°F.

8. Fill the tartlet shells with the cake batter, filling them all the way to the top.

Sherry's Secrets

When making crème brûlée in a large pan, make sure both the pan you're baking it in and the pan you use for the water bath are perfectly flat. If either one is warped or dented, the sheet of crème brûlée will not be uniform.

9. Bake for 12 to 15 minutes, until the cake is just set and slightly oozing in the center. Remove from the oven and allow to cool for 10 minutes.

10. Remove the chocolate brûlée diamonds from the freezer and place one on top of each tart. Dust each with ½ teaspoon sugar, and using a kitchen torch, caramelize the sugar (see page 360).

11. Transfer the tarts to dessert plates. Spoon about 2 tablespoons of the cherries onto each plate and place a ball of ice cream alongside. Serve immediately.

Seven-Bean Vanilla Ice Cream

MAKES 1 QUART

2 cups milk
2 cups heavy cream
7 vanilla beans, preferably Tahitian, split, seeds scraped out; seeds and beans reserved

¾ cup Vanilla Sugar (page 349) or regular sugar
6 large egg yolks
Pinch of salt

1. Place a 1-quart freezer container in the freezer. Prepare an ice bath: fill a large bowl with ice and a little water and nestle a medium bowl in the ice.

2. In a medium nonreactive saucepan, combine the milk, cream, vanilla seeds and beans, and half the sugar. Place the pan over medium heat and bring the mixture to a boil. Turn off the heat, cover tightly with plastic wrap, and allow the milk and cream to infuse for 20 minutes.

3. While the milk and cream are infusing, combine the egg yolks and the remaining 6 tablespoons sugar in a medium bowl and whisk them together until lemony yellow.

4. After infusing the cream mixture, remove the plastic wrap and return the mixture to the heat. When the milk and cream come to a simmer, remove from the heat and slowly whisk ½ cup into the egg yolks. Once the cream is incorporated into the yolks, whisk the yolks back into the cream. Be sure to scrape all the yolks into the pan with a rubber spatula.

5. Place the pan over low heat and immediately begin to stir the custard. After about 2 minutes, the custard will begin to thicken. Keep stirring until the con-

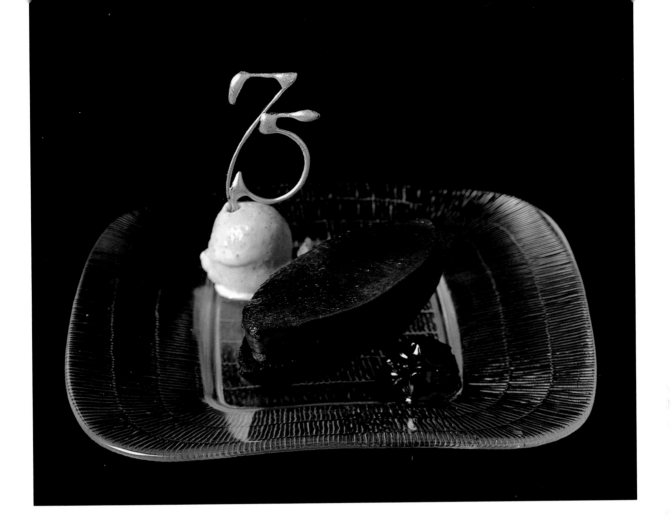

sistency is like thick cream. The custard is done when the temperature reaches 180°F. Test for readiness with your spatula: dip it into the custard, pull it out, and run your finger across the back of the spatula. Your finger should leave a clear trail and the rest of the spatula should remain coated with custard. If the custard does not run into the finger trail, it is thick enough and can be taken off the heat. If it does run, cook the custard for another minute, or until the consistency is right.

6. Remove the custard from the heat and immediately pour through a fine-mesh strainer into the bowl in the ice bath. (Rinse the beans and save for Vanilla Sugar, page 349.) Stir occasionally for 5 to 10 minutes, until the temperature of the custard drops to room temperature. Stir in the salt. If you have the time, chill in the refrigerator for a couple of hours. Otherwise, continue to stir over the ice bath until the temperature drops to 40°F. Transfer to an ice cream maker and freeze according to the manufacturer's directions. Transfer to the freezer container and place in the freezer for 2 hours, or until firm.

SIX-LAYER DOBOS TORTES WITH COFFEE ICE CREAM AND OSCAR TUILES (76TH OSCARS)

SERVES 6

■ ■ ■

For the seventy-sixth Governors Ball, the theme was the Palace of Versailles. Decorator Cheryl Cecchetto created a ballroom complete with hand-painted periwinkle blue draped-cloth ceilings, which gave the effect of a smaller room. Each table had golden rose bouquets holding as many as 200 flowers per vase. The white plates and crystal stemware were ringed in gold, and the utensils were gold. For this opulent event, I created round periwinkle blue sugar boxes with gold-leaf trim to cover my twelve-layer chocolate Dobos tortes. The boxes were topped with gold tuile-shaped bowls, which would be filled with neat scoops of coffee ice cream when they were served. As the announcer said, "Presenting Oscar the Seventy-Sixth," tuxedo-clad white-gloved waiters went out to the tables, set down the plates, and lifted the sugar boxes to reveal the rounds of caramel-dusted cake. Then they set the ice cream in its "bowl" next to the cake. That year, Oscar was a delicate tuile.

Twelve-Layer Flourless Chocolate Dobos Torte (page 240) made through Step 13
1/2 cup Croquante (page 355), pulverized
Coffee ice cream (page 132)
6 Chocolate-Dipped Tuiles (page 162), ganache omitted, made through Step 4, brushed with edible gold dust (see Sources)
2 cups golden raspberries (optional)

1. Cut the cake lengthwise in half. Stack one half on top of the other. Cool and freeze.

2. Line a 12-x-17-inch half sheet pan with parchment paper. Using a 3-inch cookie cutter as a guide, cut the cake into 6 rounds. (You will have leftover cake, which you can cut into small squares or diamonds and freeze for another use.) Place the rounds on the sheet pan and return to the freezer until shortly before serving.

3. Place the cakes on dessert plates. Sprinkle with croquante, sprinkling some around the cakes. Place a scoop of ice cream next to each cake. Garnish each plate with 1 tuile and golden raspberries, if using, and serve at once.

Basics

"TEN-YEAR" CHOCOLATE SAUCE

MAKES 2 CUPS

■ ■ ■

It took me ten years to perfect my ideal chocolate sauce, and now it is a mainstay at Spago. I was looking for a chocolate sauce that was shiny and substantial, with unforgettable texture and great depth of flavor. I achieved this by using simple syrup, rather than heavy cream, to melt the chocolate, though there is a small amount of heavy cream in the sauce. Crème fraîche adds tang, and Tia Maria contributes flavor and a little mystery. When Wolfgang heard what I'd named this sauce, he said, "I should name my lamb chops Twenty-Year Lamb Chops!"

2 ounces unsweetened chocolate, finely chopped

6 ounces bittersweet chocolate, finely chopped

2 tablespoons unsalted butter, cut into small pieces, softened

½ cup Simple Syrup (page 350)

2 tablespoons heavy cream

½ cup crème fraîche

2 tablespoons Tia Maria or other coffee liqueur

1. Combine the unsweetened chocolate, bittersweet chocolate, and butter in a medium heatproof bowl.

2. Bring the simple syrup to a boil. Pour over the chocolate and butter. Tap the bowl against your work surface to settle the chocolate mixture into the syrup, then stir with a whisk until homogeneous. (If necessary, place over a pan of simmering water briefly or heat in a microwave-safe bowl at 50 percent power to melt all the chocolate.) Add the heavy cream, crème fraîche, and liqueur and whisk together. Serve warm. (The sauce will keep, covered, for up to 2 weeks in the refrigerator. To reheat, warm gently in a double boiler, stirring occasionally, or heat in a microwave at 50 percent power.)

GANACHE

MAKES 2 CUPS

■ ■ ■

Ganache is a simple, heavenly mixture of chocolate and cream. It's the basis for many desserts and dessert components—tart and cake fillings, icings, truffles, and Chocolate Whipped Cream (page 362). It couldn't be simpler to make.

8 ounces bittersweet chocolate
1 cup heavy cream

1. **TRADITIONAL METHOD**: Using a serrated knife, chop the chocolate into small pieces, about ¼ inch in size, and place in a medium heatproof bowl.

2. Pour the cream into a small saucepan and bring to a boil over medium heat. Watch carefully—boiling means the cream will actually rise up in the pan and may threaten to boil over. You can also bring the cream to a boil in a microwave. Immediately pour the boiling cream over the chopped chocolate. Tap the bowl on the work surface to settle the chocolate into the cream, then let sit for 1 minute.

3. Using a rubber spatula, slowly stir in a circular motion starting from the center of the bowl and working out to the sides. Be careful not to add too much air to the ganache. Stir until all the chocolate has melted, about 2 minutes. It may look finished after 1 minute of stirring, but keep going to be sure it's emulsified.

4. Let the ganache sit at room temperature and allow the temperature to drop to 70°F. In a 65°F room, this will take approximately 4 hours. You can speed up the process by pouring the ganache out onto a clean baking sheet (a thinner layer will cool faster). Once the ganache is at 70°F, it is stiff enough to spread and is ready to be used. (At this point, it can be covered and stored in the refrigerator for up to 2 weeks.)

1. **FOOD PROCESSOR METHOD**: Break up the chocolate and place in a food processor fitted with the steel blade. Pulse to chop into small pieces.

2. Pour the cream into a small saucepan and bring to a boil over medium heat. Watch carefully—boiling means the cream will rise up in the pan and may threaten to boil over. (Or bring the cream to a boil in a microwave.) Immediately pour the boiling cream into the food processor, on top of the chocolate, and let sit for 1 minute.

3. Pulse the machine 3 times. Scrape down the sides with a rubber spatula and pulse 3 more times, or until all the chocolate has melted.

4. Transfer the ganache to a bowl and allow it to cool to 70°F (see Step 4 of the traditional method). Once the ganache is at 70°F, it is stiff enough to spread and is ready to be used. (At this point, it can be covered and stored in the refrigerator for up to 2 weeks.)

Sherry's Secrets

I prefer using a serrated knife for chopping chocolate. It's safer—the blade doesn't slip off the hard surface of the chocolate. And I find that it's also easier to get small chunks if I use a serrated knife.

CHOCOLATE PUDDING

■ ■ ■

Use this rich chocolate pudding as a filling for cakes, or serve it on its own for dessert, with whipped cream.

4 cups milk
1½ cups sugar
¼ cup plus 2 tablespoons unsweetened cocoa powder
¼ cup plus 2 tablespoons cornstarch
2 ounces unsweetened chocolate, finely chopped
2 tablespoons unsalted butter, cut into small pieces
1 tablespoon vanilla extract

1. In a large saucepan, combine the milk and ¾ cup of the sugar and bring to a boil over medium heat. Remove from the heat.

2. In a medium bowl, whisk together the remaining ¾ cup sugar, the cocoa powder, and cornstarch. Whisking constantly, stream this mixture into the hot milk. Return to the heat and whisk constantly for 4 minutes, or until thick.

3. Remove from the heat and whisk in the chocolate, butter, and vanilla. Whisk until the chocolate has melted and the mixture is smooth. Pour into a pan or wide bowl and place a sheet of plastic wrap directly over the surface. Place the pan or bowl in an ice bath to cool, or refrigerate. (It can be stored in the refrigerator for up to 2 days.)

VANILLA SUGAR

MAKES 2 CUPS

■ ■ ■

Whenever you have leftover split vanilla beans, air-dry the pods and add them to sugar to make vanilla-scented sugar. You can also stick unused vanilla beans into a jar of sugar, but the beans must first be dried. Split them and leave them in a warm spot to dry for 48 hours, or dehydrate them in a dehydrator if you have one. I go a step further and make an intensely fragrant vanilla sugar by grinding up the dried beans in a spice mill and adding the powder to my sugar.

1 vanilla bean
2 cups sugar

1. Split the vanilla bean and leave it on a rack on a baking sheet in a warm, dry place (such as on top of the stove or in an oven with a pilot light) for 48 hours. Place in a jar, cover with the sugar, and seal tightly.

2. For a more intense vanilla sugar, break up the dried bean and place in an electric spice mill or clean coffee grinder. Pulse the machine until you have vanilla powder. Pass through a fine-mesh strainer. Place any large pieces back in the spice mill, pulse again, and strain; discard any remaining pieces of vanilla bean.

3. Place the sugar in a bowl, add the vanilla powder, and whisk together. Store in a tightly sealed jar.

SIMPLE SYRUP

■ ■ ■

You can keep simple syrup in the refrigerator for a couple weeks, and it's convenient to have around. If you aren't going to use it for pastry, use it for sweetening iced tea, or add a little coffee to it and use it for your coffee. Or use it for mixed drinks like lemon drops and Pisco sours.

1 cup water
1 cup sugar

In a heavy saucepan, whisk together the water and sugar over medium heat; bring to a boil, stirring to dissolve the sugar. Remove from the heat and allow to cool to room temperature; you can do this quickly over an ice bath. (The syrup can be stored in a covered jar in the refrigerator for up to 2 weeks.)

CARAMEL

■ ■ ■

Caramel is at the base of many of my desserts. Here is my basic caramel technique.

¼ cup water
1 cup sugar
2 tablespoons light corn syrup

1. Wash and dry your hands thoroughly. In a medium saucepan, combine the water, sugar, and corn syrup. Stir them together with very clean fingers, making sure no lumps of dry sugar remain. Brush down the inside of the pan with a little water, using your fingers to feel for stray granules of sugar.

2. Cover the saucepan and place it over medium heat for 4 minutes. After 4 minutes, remove the lid, increase the heat, and bring to a boil. Do not stir from this point on. Keep an eye on the pan. It will be very bubbly. When stray sugar crystals appear on the sides of the pan, brush them down with a wet pastry brush.

3. As the sugar cooks, the bubbles will get larger and the sugar will turn golden brown. Insert a candy thermometer. When the temperature reaches 300°F, lower the heat to medium, which will slow the cooking. Continue to cook the sugar until it reaches 325°F, about 3 minutes more. Remove the pan from the heat and let sit for about 2 minutes, until the bubbles subside.

SPUN SUGAR

MAKES ENOUGH FOR 30 TO 40 NESTS

■ ■ ■

Spun sugar, gossamer strands of golden caramel, adds a special touch to almost any dessert. Traditionally it is set atop floating islands (see page 322) and the French dessert called croquembouche. This recipe is for the industrial-strength spun sugar we make at the bakeshop. It has more corn syrup than most recipes, and that helps it to stand up to humidity. However, it can't be stored for more than a few hours. If keeping it for longer, wrap some silica gel (see Sources) in cheesecloth and place it with the spun sugar in a tightly sealed container.

¼ cup water
1 cup sugar
1 cup light corn syrup

1. Wash and dry your hands thoroughly. In a medium saucepan, combine the water, sugar, and corn syrup. Stir them together with very clean fingers, making sure no lumps of dry sugar remain. Brush down the inside of the pan with a little water, using your fingers to feel for stray granules of sugar.

2. Cover the saucepan and place it over medium heat for 4 minutes. After 4 minutes, remove the lid, increase the heat, and bring to a boil. Do not stir from this point on. Keep an eye on the pan. It will be very bubbly. When stray sugar crystals appear on the sides of the pan, brush them down with a wet pastry brush.

3. As the sugar cooks, the bubbles will get larger and the sugar will turn golden brown. Insert a candy thermometer. When the temperature reaches 300°F, lower the heat to medium, which will slow the cooking. Continue to cook the sugar until it reaches 320°F, about 2 minutes more. Remove the pan from the heat and allow the caramel to cool for about 8 minutes, until it drops to 300°F. It should be thick but still liquid, like honey.

4. Cover your work surface and floor with tablecloths or parchment paper. Place three saucepans on the edge of the work surface with the handles facing out. Now you are ready to spin.

5. Scoop up a forkful of the caramel and let it fall back into the pot. It should flow in a smooth, steady stream. If the sugar drips as it falls, it is still too hot. If it's thick and unwieldy, reheat until it is the consistency of honey. Dip your fork into the warm caramel and pull it out, hold it above the saucepan handles, and begin to move the fork back and forth, fanning it over the handles and waving the strands carefully back and forth. After two or three forkfuls, stop and gather up the spun sugar with your hands, then begin again. If the caramel becomes too cool, reheat it over medium heat for 5 minutes, without stirring. Do not let the temperature exceed 310°F.

6. Wrap the spun sugar around a cake, fashion it into a nest, or loosely gather it into balls. Or store it in an airtight container, layered between sheets of parchment paper, with a small cheesecloth sachet of moisture-absorbent silica gel or limestone. Spun sugar can be stored for only a few hours, less if the environment is humid.

Sherry's Secrets

WORKING WITH CARAMEL

When making caramel in production, I pour out the hot caramel onto a clean flat sheet tray lined with a silicone mat. When it's cool, I break it into pieces and store it airtight. Then when I need it, I place pieces in a saucepan over low heat and stir the caramel until it has the consistency of honey. From there I can use the caramel for spun sugar, for Croquante (page 355), or for sauce.

CREAMY CARAMEL SAUCE

MAKES 1¼ CUPS

■ ■ ■

This is one of my favorite sauces, and I keep it on hand at all times in the bakeshop. It can be served hot or cold, used as a filling or as a base for caramel whipped cream, or used to flavor truffles and ganache.

¼ cup water
1 cup plus 1 tablespoon sugar
2 tablespoons light corn syrup
½ cup heavy cream, warmed to 100°F
¼ cup crème fraîche
½ teaspoon fresh lemon juice
Pinch of salt

1. Wash and dry your hands thoroughly. In a medium saucepan, combine the water, the 1 cup sugar, and the corn syrup. Stir them together with very clean fingers, making sure no lumps of dry sugar remain. Brush down the inside of the pan with a little water, using your fingers to feel for stray granules of sugar. Cover the saucepan and place it over medium heat for 4 minutes. After 4 minutes, remove the lid, increase the heat, and bring to a boil. Do not stir from this point on. Keep an eye on the pan. It will be very bubbly. When stray sugar crystals appear on the sides of the pan, brush them down with a wet pastry brush.

2. As the sugar cooks, the bubbles will get larger and the sugar will turn golden brown. Insert a candy thermometer, and when the temperature reaches 300°F, lower the heat to medium, which will slow the cooking. Continue to cook the sugar until it reaches 335°F, about 4 minutes more. Remove the pan from the heat and let sit for about 2 minutes, until the bubbles subside.

3. Add the heavy cream to the caramel. The mixture will bubble up vigorously, so be careful. Stir in the crème fraîche, the 1 tablespoon sugar, the lemon juice, and salt. Serve warm. (The sauce will keep for up to 1 month stored airtight in the refrigerator. When cold, it has the consistency of peanut butter. Reheat in a microwave at 50 percent power.)

CROQUANTE

■ ■ ■

Croquante is caramel with almonds—a version of praline. It can be cut into squares and dipped in chocolate, but I usually grind it up and use it to dust pastries. It makes a wonderful topping for cakes and parfaits.

⅓ cup water
1 cup sugar
½ cup light corn syrup
½ cup sliced blanched almonds, toasted (see page 378) and still warm

1. Line a baking sheet with a silicone mat or parchment paper. Coat the parchment with a very thin film of butter or pan spray.

2. In a medium saucepan, combine the water, sugar, and corn syrup and stir to dissolve the sugar. Dip your clean fingers in water, then wipe down the sides of the pan to make sure there are no stray sugar crystals. Place over high heat and boil until the mixture turns amber brown and the temperature reaches 325°F on a candy thermometer, about 10 minutes.

3. Remove the pan from the heat and wait until the bubbles have dispersed, then stir in the warm toasted almonds. Immediately pour the croquante out onto the lined baking sheet. Using an oiled metal offset spatula or an oiled rolling pin, flatten the croquante to ¼ inch thick. If it hardens and is too thick, reliquefy by placing it in a 350°F oven for 1 to 2 minutes. The heat will cause the croquante to melt and spread.

4. Quickly, while the croquante is still hot and pliable, score it into 2-inch squares with an oiled chef's knife. When the croquante cools, the squares will snap apart easily. (The croquante can be stored at room temperature for up to 2 weeks in an airtight container.)

NOTE: To pulverize croquante, break apart the squares and place, a few at a time, in a food processor fitted with the steel blade. Pulse gently until pulverized.

ALMOND SEATS

MAKES 1¼ CUPS

■ ■ ■

Plated desserts require all sorts of tricks to keep them in place between the time the waiter picks them up in the kitchen and the time they are set in front of the guests. To keep ice cream or sorbet from sliding on the plate, for example, I serve the balls on a base, like these shiny toasted sliced almonds. The almonds have many other uses. You can chop them and fold them into a mousse filling or sprinkle them over parfaits, as I do in Biscuit Tortoni (page 30). You could also roll ice cream balls in them.

¼ cup sugar
3 tablespoons water
1¼ cups sliced blanched almonds

1. Place a rack in the middle of the oven and preheat the oven to 325°F. Line a baking sheet with parchment paper and spray the parchment with pan spray.

2. In a small heavy saucepan, combine the sugar and water and bring to a boil. Remove from the heat and stir until the sugar has dissolved.

3. Place the almonds in a bowl, pour on the syrup, and stir until coated. Pour out onto the baking sheet and spread in a thin layer.

4. Bake for 5 minutes, then stir the almonds. Bake for another 5 minutes and stir again. Bake for another 5 minutes, or until the almonds are an even golden brown. Allow to cool on the pan and store airtight at room temperature. (The almond seats will keep for up to 2 weeks.)

Hazelnut Praline Paste

MAKES 2 CUPS

■ ■ ■

This rich, nutty paste makes a great flavoring for buttercream. It has a place in chocolate desserts as well.

1¼ cups hazelnuts
¼ cup water
¾ cup sugar

1. Place a rack in the middle of the oven and preheat the oven to 350°F.

2. Place the nuts on a baking sheet and toast them until they are dark golden brown, 10 to 12 minutes. They should fill the room with a toasty nut smell. If the nuts have skins, remove them (see page 379). Leave the baking sheet on top of the stove to keep the nuts warm.

3. Line a baking sheet with a silicone mat or parchment paper coated with a very thin film of butter or pan spray. In a medium saucepan, combine the water and sugar. Stir to dissolve the sugar. Dip your very clean fingers in water, then wipe down the sides of the pan to make sure there are no stray sugar crystals. Place over high heat and boil until the mixture turns dark brown and the temperature reaches 350°F on a candy thermometer, about 10 minutes. Remove from the heat and let sit until the bubbles subside.

4. Stir the warm nuts into the caramel. Pour out onto the lined baking sheet. Using an oiled metal spatula, preferably offset, or an oiled rolling pin, flatten the mixture to ½ inch thick. If the mixture hardens and is too thick, reliquefy by placing in a 350°F oven for 1 to 2 minutes. Allow to cool, then break into pieces.

5. In 2 batches, process the cooled hazelnut praline in a food processor fitted with the steel blade until fine and liquefied. At first this will be very noisy; it will take 5 to 7 minutes.

BUTTERCREAM

MAKES 2 CUPS

■ ■ ■

Buttercream, the classic marriage of meringue and butter, is the most sensuous of fillings and icings. My method here is quite simple. I warm the egg whites and sugar together in a double boiler, then whip the combination to a meringue and gradually beat in the butter, a little at a time.

2 large egg whites, at room temperature
1/2 cup sugar
6 ounces (1 1/2 sticks) unsalted butter, softened

1. Combine the egg whites and sugar in the bowl of a stand mixer or in a metal bowl and whisk together. Place the bowl over a saucepan of simmering water, being careful not to let the bottom of the bowl touch the water. Insert a thermometer and whisk until the mixture reaches 100°F (warm to the touch). Remove the bowl from the saucepan and place on the stand mixer, fitted with the whisk attachment, or use a hand mixer. Beat on high speed until the egg whites form soft, thick, shiny peaks.

2. Make sure your butter is soft and lump-free. Then add to the meringue a tablespoon at a time while beating at high speed. Don't worry if the mixture looks broken, with little grains of butter, after you've added all of the butter. Just continue to beat on high speed and the buttercream will smooth out. It's best to use the buttercream right away. If it firms up before you can use it, though, you can whip it just until it's warm and fluffy again, or warm it ever so slightly in a double boiler.

Sherry's Secrets

For those of you who use a kitchen scale, the buttercream ratio is 1-2-3: 1 egg white (or 1 ounce), 2 ounces of sugar, and 3 ounces of butter.

VARIATION

COFFEE BUTTERCREAM: Beat 1 tablespoon Trablit coffee extract (available at pastry supply stores, or see Sources) into the finished buttercream.

CRÈME BRÛLÉE

SERVES 8

■ ■ ■

There is nothing like that click of a spoon on the crisp, bittersweet caramel topping that reveals the silky cream of a crème brûlée. This cream sighs and yields with each caramel-and-custard-containing mouthful. It is pure decadence.

4 cups heavy cream
2/3 cup sugar, plus 1/2 cup sugar for caramelizing
1 vanilla bean, split, seeds scraped out and reserved
6 large egg yolks

1. Place a rack in the middle of the oven and preheat the oven to 300°F. Place eight 8-ounce ramekins in a large baking pan. (Be sure the baking pan is at least 1/2 inch deeper than the ramekins.)

2. In a large saucepan, combine the cream, the 2/3 cup sugar, and the vanilla bean and seeds and bring to a simmer over medium heat. Turn off the heat, cover the pan with plastic wrap, and allow the mixture to steep for 15 minutes. After steeping, the cream mixture should be at 165°F.

3. Whisk the egg yolks lightly in a large bowl. Gently whisk the cream mixture into the egg yolks. Pour the custard through a fine-mesh strainer into a bowl or large Pyrex measuring cup.

4. Fill each ramekin to the brim with custard. Fill the baking pan with enough hot water to come two thirds up the sides of the ramekins. Cover the baking pan loosely with aluminum foil and bake for 1 hour to 1 hour 15 minutes. The custards are done when they are set but still have a slight jiggle. They should not be allowed to brown or rise. Remove from the water bath. Let cool at room temperature for 30 minutes, then chill the custards for at least 2 hours before serving. (They will keep, covered, for up to 2 days in the refrigerator.) Do not caramelize the tops until just before serving, as the caramelized sugar will begin to melt after 1 hour.

5. **CARAMELIZE THE CRÈME BRÛLÉE:** You will be coating the tops of the custards in two thin layers of caramelized sugar. Coat the top of each cus-

tard with sugar in a thin, even layer. Wipe off any sugar that sticks to the rim of the ramekin. Melt the sugar by moving the flame from a propane or butane kitchen torch, following the manufacturer's directions, back and forth across the top of the custard, from a height of not less than 8 inches. As soon as the sugar melts and starts to color, dust lightly with a second layer of sugar and continue to melt and caramelize the sugar. Turn the ramekin every few seconds for even coloring. Within 1 minute, the sugar will begin to melt, bubble, and then turn into golden caramel. Stop when the sugar is a dark golden color. (Even though the name of this custard is French for "burnt cream," try not to burn the sugar.) Allow the caramel to cool and harden for 2 minutes before serving.

6. Place the ramekins on plates lined with napkins or doilies.

Sherry's Secrets

The amount of sugar required for caramelizing the top of the crème brûlée depends on the circumference of the ramekins used. In the restaurant, we use shallow, wide crème brûlée dishes. At home you will probably use deeper ramekins with a smaller surface area. These require less sugar for a thin layer and you may have some sugar left over.

HUCKLEBERRY
OR BLACKBERRY MERLOT SAUCE

MAKES 4 CUPS

■ ■ ■

I keep this berry sauce on hand in the bakeshop at all times. It's a wonderful formula and the sauce has many uses. I poach figs in it (page 205) and pears, and I use it as a base for sorbets, soufflés, and jellies.

1½ pounds fresh huckleberries or fresh or frozen blackberries
1 orange, peeled and sliced
1 lemon, peeled and sliced
½ cup plus 2 tablespoons sugar (½ cup if using frozen berries)
½ vanilla bean, split, seeds scraped out; seeds and bean reserved
2 cups Merlot
½ cup water
1 3-inch cinnamon stick
3 tablespoons Chambord
Pinch of salt

1. Bring the huckleberries or blackberries, orange, lemon, sugar, vanilla seeds and bean, Merlot, and water to a boil in a large saucepan over medium heat. Microwave the cinnamon stick on 100 percent power for 10 seconds to release the oils, or heat in a small dry skillet over medium heat until fragrant. Carefully remove it and add to the sauce. Reduce the heat to low and simmer for 10 minutes, or until the liquid has thickened and coats the back of a spoon.

2. Remove the sauce from the heat, cover with plastic wrap, and let the flavors infuse for 30 minutes.

3. Prepare an ice bath by filling a large bowl with ice and a little water. Pour the sauce through a fine-mesh strainer into a medium bowl and firmly press out the juices. Do not puree, or the sauce will turn cloudy. Place the bowl in the ice bath and allow the sauce to cool completely. Add the Chambord and salt. (The sauce can be refrigerated in an airtight container for up to 3 days or frozen for up to 3 months.)

RASPBERRY SAUCE

MAKES 2 CUPS

■ ■ ■

This luxurious, clear red sauce makes a plain bowl of vanilla ice cream special.

1 cup dry red wine
1$^1\!/_2$ pounds fresh or frozen raspberries
$^3\!/_4$ cup sugar
2 tablespoons fresh lemon juice
$^1\!/_2$ orange, peeled and sliced
$^1\!/_4$ teaspoon balsamic vinegar

1. Combine the ingredients in a large saucepan, stir, and bring to a boil. Reduce the heat to medium and cook, stirring occasionally, for 15 minutes. Remove from the heat, cover with plastic wrap, and infuse for at least 2 hours, or overnight.

2. Pour through a fine-mesh strainer and firmly press out the juices to release the pectin. Chill in an ice bath or in the refrigerator. (The sauce can be refrigerated in a covered container for up to 3 days or frozen for up to 3 months.)

CHOCOLATE WHIPPED CREAM

MAKES 2 TO 2½ CUPS

■ ■ ■

Chocolate whipped cream makes a great filling for cakes, tarts, and cream puffs. Be careful not to overwhip the cream.

1$^1\!/_2$ cups heavy cream
1 tablespoon sugar (optional)
4 ounces bittersweet chocolate, finely chopped

1. Nestle the bowl of a stand mixer, or a metal mixing bowl if using a hand mixer, in a bowl of ice. In a heavy saucepan, bring the cream and sugar, if using, to a boil. Remove from the heat, add the chocolate, and whisk until the chocolate has melted and is just combined. Pour into the bowl set in the ice and allow to cool or chill in the refrigerator for at least 4 hours, or overnight.

2. Whip the cold chocolate cream to soft peaks. The cream will thicken as it cools. Use at once, or store in the refrigerator in a covered container for up to 2 days.

WHIPPED CRÈME FRAÎCHE

■ ■ ■

This is a tangy version of whipped cream. It's great with fruit, and it also contrasts nicely with sweet desserts. Be careful not to over-beat the cream, as it will thicken more in the refrigerator.

1 cup crème fraîche
2 cups heavy cream
2 tablespoons sugar

Combine all of the ingredients in a bowl and whip to just past soft peaks. Refrigerate in a covered bowl. (The whipped crème fraîche will keep for 2 to 4 hours.)

WHIPPED CARAMEL CRÈME FRAÎCHE

MAKES 3 CUPS

■ ■ ■

I use this incredible cream for many of my desserts. It's great as a filling for napoleons and cakes, and it also makes a wonderful base for a caramel mousse. Or just serve it as is, with fresh berries.

1 cup heavy cream
1/2 cup crème fraîche
1 teaspoon sugar (optional)
1 cup Creamy Caramel Sauce (page 354), chilled until cold

1. Combine the cream, crème fraîche, and sugar, if using, in a bowl and whip for 3 minutes, or until stiff peaks form.

2. Using a rubber spatula, carefully fold in the caramel sauce. Place plastic wrap directly over the surface and refrigerate until ready to use. (It will keep for a day in the refrigerator.)

FAT RAISINS

■ ■ ■

I use these any time I want to add raisins to a dessert. I prefer golden or Red Flame raisins because they're not as sweet as the dark ones and they're prettier.

1 cup golden or Red Flame raisins
½ cup dry white wine
2 tablespoons fresh orange juice
1 tablespoon dark rum
2 tablespoons sugar

1. Combine the raisins, wine, orange juice, rum, and sugar in a small heavy saucepan, bring just to a boil over medium heat, stirring all the while. Lower the heat so that the liquid is at a bare simmer and poach for 20 minutes.

2. Remove from the heat, cover the pan with plastic wrap, and allow to cool to room temperature. Transfer to an airtight container and store in the refrigerator. (The raisins will keep for up to 2 weeks.)

VARIATIONS

FAT APRICOTS: Substitute chopped dried apricots for the raisins and follow the directions in the basic recipe.

FAT CHERRIES: Substitute dried cherries for the raisins and red wine or port for the white wine and follow the directions in the basic recipe.

GINGER JUICE

MAKES 1 TABLESPOON

■ ■ ■

Ginger juice adds a fresh flavor to any dessert. Use it as you would vanilla extract.

1 3-inch piece fresh ginger, peeled

Shred the ginger on a grater. Wrap the shredded ginger in cheesecloth and squeeze out the juice into a small bowl. Discard the fibers.

APPLE COMPOTE

■ ■ ■

Nothing compares to homemade apple-sauce, which is what apple compote is. Commercial applesauce is too watery to use in most of my recipes unless you cook it down first.

3 tablespoons unsalted butter
1/2 vanilla bean, split, seeds scraped out; seeds and bean reserved
1/4 teaspoon freshly grated nutmeg (optional)
1 1/2 pounds Braeburn or Pink Lady apples, peeled, cored, and cut into eighths
1/2 cup sugar
2 tablespoons Calvados (apple brandy)
1/4 cup heavy cream
2 teaspoons fresh lemon juice

1. In a large skillet, melt the butter over medium heat. Add the vanilla seeds and bean and the nutmeg, if using, and allow the butter to brown. It should give off a slightly nutty aroma. Add the apples and toss to coat with the butter. Sprinkle in the sugar, turn the heat to medium-high, and sauté the apples until lightly caramelized and tender, 20 to 25 minutes, turning them often so that they cook evenly.

2. Remove from the heat and stir in the Calvados. Add the cream and lemon juice and return to the heat. Cook, stirring, for 2 minutes. Remove from the heat and allow to cool for 10 minutes. Remove the vanilla bean. Puree the apple mixture in a food processor fitted with the steel blade until smooth. Allow to cool, then cover and refrigerate until ready to use. (The compote will keep for up to 1 week in a covered container in the refrigerator.)

BANANA SCHMUTZ

■ ■ ■

Don't throw your dark brown bananas away—use them for schmutz! I always keep this caramelized banana concoction on hand in my bakeshop. *Schmutz* is the Yiddish and German word for "mud," which is what this sautéed banana puree looks like. I use it in several of my banana desserts, like the banana—chocolate chip soufflé that is the essence of the Banana Salzburger Nockerln on page 236, and Caramelized Banana Tarts (page 85).

2 tablespoons unsalted butter
1/2 cup sugar
1/2 cup packed light brown sugar
3 large very ripe bananas, cut into 1/2-inch pieces
1/4 cup dark rum
Pinch of salt
1 tablespoon fresh lemon juice

1. In a large skillet, heat the butter over medium heat until the milk solids separate, sink to the bottom, and begin to brown and the butter is a dark golden color, 3 to 5 minutes. Add the sugar and brown sugar and stir until dissolved.

2. Add the bananas and sauté, stirring constantly, for about 2 minutes, until softened and caramelized. Remove from the heat and carefully add the rum and salt. Stir to combine, place the pan back over low heat, and cook, stirring, for 1 minute more, or until most of the liquid is gone. Remove from the heat and stir in the lemon juice.

3. Immediately, working in 2 batches, puree the bananas in a food processor fitted with the steel blade. Be very careful, as the mixture will be extremely hot. Use at once, or allow to cool, then transfer to an airtight container. (The schmutz can be refrigerated for up to 3 days or frozen for up to 1 month.)

APRICOT SCHMUTZ

MAKES 2 CUPS

■ ■ ■

I use apricot schmutz as a filling for my Rainbow Cookies (page 15), on my Topfenknödel (page 229), and in many other desserts. You can substitute strained apricot preserves, but this tastes much more special. You can also swirl it into ice cream (see page 377).

1 cup dried apricots

1 cup fresh orange juice (from 2 large oranges)

$1/2$ cup water

$1/4$ cup dry white wine (or omit, and use $3/4$ cup water in all)

2 tablespoons sugar

2 tablespoons Vanilla Sugar (page 349; or omit and use $1/4$ cup sugar in all)

1 $1/4$-inch slice fresh ginger, peeled

1. Combine the apricots, orange juice, water, white wine, sugar, vanilla sugar, and ginger in a medium heavy saucepan, place over medium heat, stir together, and bring to a simmer. Cook, stirring occasionally, for 10 minutes. Remove from the heat and let sit for 30 minutes.

2. Remove the ginger. Put the mixture through a food mill while still warm, or process in a food processor fitted with the steel blade. Allow to cool, then cover and refrigerate. (It will keep for up to 2 weeks.)

LINZER DOUGH

■ ■ ■

This nutty, spicy hazelnut dough is a favorite cookie dough in Austria. It's also wonderful as a tart shell, especially with fruit tarts, like the Caramelized Banana Tarts on page 85. It's a very moist dough and requires some time in the freezer before you can shape it. I like to use Vietnamese cinnamon, which has exotic, spicy floral overtones. I buy it from Penzeys Spices (see Sources).

1 cup all-purpose flour
1 cup cake flour
1/4 teaspoon salt
6 ounces hazelnuts, toasted, skinned (see page 379), and ground
8 ounces (2 sticks) unsalted butter, cut into 1/2-inch pieces, softened
1/2 cup sugar
1 teaspoon ground cinnamon, preferably Vietnamese (see headnote)
1 teaspoon Chinese five-spice powder
1 tablespoon honey
1 large egg
1 tablespoon grated orange zest

1. Sift together the all-purpose flour, cake flour, and salt. Stir in the ground hazelnuts and set aside.

2. In the bowl of a stand mixer fitted with the paddle attachment, or in a large bowl with a hand mixer, cream the butter on medium speed until lemony yellow, about 2 minutes. Scrape down the sides of the bowl. Add the sugar, cinnamon, and five-spice powder and continue creaming the mixture on medium speed until it is smooth and lump-free, about 1 minute. Stop the mixer and scrape down the sides of the bowl and the paddle.

3. Add the honey, egg, and orange zest and beat on low speed for 15 seconds, or until they are fully incorporated. Do not overbeat. Scrape down the sides of the bowl and the paddle. On low speed, add the flour and hazelnut mixture. Beat slowly until the dough comes together. Scrape down the sides of the bowl, then mix for 15 seconds, until an even-textured dough is formed.

4. Remove the dough from the bowl. Divide into 2 equal pieces. Wrap in plastic wrap, pressing the dough into a square, and refrigerate for 30 minutes. (The dough can be refrigerated for up to 2 days.)

5. See directions for Pâte Sucrée (page 373) to roll out and prebake.

MERINGUE TRIANGLES AND CIRCLES

MAKES TWO 12-X-17-INCH HALF SHEET PANS

■ ■ ■

Meringue triangles and circles make useful platforms for sorbet and ice cream, as well as bases for baked Alaska. In the bakeshop, I use stencils to get perfect circles: I cut them out of shower and tub liners I buy at Home Depot. These flexible sheets of sturdy plastic are perfect for the job. I cut out circles and triangles, smear the meringue all over the liner, and then lift off the template.

- 4 large egg whites, at room temperature
- 1 cup sugar
- 1/2 cup confectioners' sugar

1. Place a rack in the middle of the oven and preheat the oven to 250°F.

2. Combine the egg whites and sugar in the bowl of a stand mixer or in a heat-proof bowl and whisk over a saucepan of simmering water (do not let the bowl touch the water) until the mixture reaches 100°F (warm to the touch; this happens quickly). Place the bowl on the stand mixer fitted with the whisk attachment, or use a hand mixer, and beat on medium speed until the meringue is stiff and cooled. Reduce the speed to low and slowly sprinkle in the confectioners' sugar.

3. **FOR FREEHAND TRIANGLES:** Line two 12-x-17-inch half sheet pans with parchment paper and spray with pan spray. Put a dab of meringue under each corner of the parchment to stick it to the pan, so it doesn't slip (or fly up if you're using a convection oven). Fit a pastry bag with a #4 plain tip and pipe 1-x-1-inch triangles onto the parchment.

    FOR FREEHAND CIRCLES: Line two 12-x-17-inch half sheet pans with parchment paper and spray with pan spray. Put a dab of meringue under each corner of the parchment to stick it to the pan, so it doesn't slip (or fly up if you're using a convection oven). Fit a pastry bag with a #4 plain tip and pipe 3-inch circles onto the parchment-lined sheet pans.

    FOR PERFECTLY UNIFORM CIRCLES OR TRIANGLES, USING A STENCIL: Prepare the sheet pans as directed above. Make a template using a sheet of gray shower/tub liner from a hardware store, cutting out the desired shapes with an X-acto knife. Lay the cut-out liner on one of the parchment-lined sheet pans and smear an even, delicate layer of meringue into the shapes with an offset spatula. Scrape off the excess meringue, then carefully lift off the template. Repeat the process on the second baking sheet.

4. Bake the meringues for 1½ hours. Remove a test piece to check for doneness. It should be stiff and crisp to the bite after a 5-minute rest. If it is still moist in the middle, bake for another 30 minutes. When the meringues are done, turn off the oven and leave inside for 1 hour more.

5. Remove the meringues from the oven and allow to cool completely, then pack carefully in an airtight container. Store at room temperature until ready to use. (The meringues can be stored for up to 4 days in a dry environment.)

Sherry's Secrets

PASTRY TOOLS FROM HOME DEPOT

Going to Home Depot is a real treat for me. There I find many of the tools that make my work easier and give it a precise, professional look—often at a fraction of the price I'd pay at a kitchen shop.

POWER PAINTERS: I use them as spray guns for airbrushing plates and for chocolate coatings.

SHOWER/TUB LINERS: I use these sheets of gray matting to make templates. I cut out intricate or simple designs, lay the templates on parchment-lined baking sheets, smear batter, such as tuile batter or meringue, over the tops, then lift off the templates and bake.

CEMENT SCRAPERS: These are useful for cleanup. After scrubbing down a station, I use them to push the water off the surface.

PAINTBRUSHES: These are less expensive than pastry brushes and offer great quality.

3-INCH AND 4-INCH PVC PIPING: Have the salesperson cut you 2-inch lengths, and you will have molds for semifreddo, cakes, and mousses.

X-ACTO KNIVES: These are essential for cutting out molds and templates.

LEVELERS: I find them great for stacking wedding cakes.

SPRAY BOTTLES: I use them for spraying syrups, oils, and clarified butter.

PLASTIC SCRAPERS: These are great for cleaning out bowls.

PÂTE BRISÉE
Flaky Pastry

MAKES TWO 9- OR 10-INCH PIECRUSTS

■ ■ ■

This is my standard pie dough. It is marvelously flaky and extremely easy to work with.

8 ounces (2 sticks) unsalted butter
2½ cups all-purpose flour
2 tablespoons sugar
1 teaspoon salt
About ½ cup ice water
½ teaspoon champagne vinegar or white wine vinegar

1. Cut the butter into 1-inch pieces and place it in the freezer to chill for 15 minutes.

2. TO MIX WITH A STAND MIXER: Sift together the flour, sugar, and salt into the bowl of a stand mixer fitted with the paddle attachment. Add the partially frozen butter. Turn the machine on low and beat for 2 minutes, or until the butter is broken down to the size of walnuts. Stop the machine, and by hand, pinch flat any large pieces of butter that remain. In a small bowl, combine the ice water and vinegar. Turn the mixer on low speed and add the liquid all at once. Beat just until the dough comes together, about 15 seconds. The dough should be tacky but not sticky (see Note).

TO MIX BY HAND: Sift together the dry ingredients into a large bowl. Add the partially frozen butter, and using a wire pastry cutter, incorporate it into the flour until the butter is broken down to the size of walnuts. Or use your fingers, rubbing and pressing the butter and flour between your thumbs and first two fingers to create flattened broken walnut-sized pieces. Combine the ice water and vinegar and add the liquid all at once; mix lightly with a fork until the dough just comes together.

3. Remove the dough from the bowl, divide into 2 equal pieces, and wrap each piece in plastic wrap. Do not squeeze the dough together or overwork. Chill the dough in the refrigerator for at least 1 hour before rolling it out. (The well-wrapped dough can be kept in the refrigerator for up to 3 days or frozen for up to 2 weeks. If I am going to freeze the dough, however, I prefer to roll the 2 pieces of dough out into circles, place them between pieces of parchment

paper, wrap them airtight in plastic, and freeze. You can also line the lightly sprayed pie or tart pans with the pie dough, wrap airtight, and freeze.)

4. Roll out the dough on a lightly floured work surface and line two lightly sprayed 9- or 10-inch pie or tart pans or a 9-inch springform pan.

5. **TO BLIND-BAKE (PREBAKE) A PIE SHELL:** Place a rack in the lower third of the oven and preheat the oven to 425°F.

6. Prick the bottom of the pastry a few times with a fork. Line the pastry with parchment paper or large coffee filters. Fill the lined shell to the rim with dried beans, uncooked rice, or pie weights and gently press the "faux filling" into the corners. Bake for 10 minutes, then turn the heat down to 350°F and bake for another 7 minutes. (If you are prebaking the dough in a springform pan, increase the amount of weights so that they reach the top of the rim.)

7. Remove from the oven and remove the weights and the liner. Return to the oven for 10 minutes, until the center turns golden and looks dry. There should be no sign of moisture. Remove from the oven and allow to cool on a rack.

NOTE: The amount of water can be variable. It is better to have a slightly wet/tacky dough than one that is too dry; add a little water if your dough seems dry.

PÂTE SUCRÉE

Sweet Pastry

■ ■ ■

Confectioners' sugar makes this dough melt-in-your-mouth tender.

- 2½ cups all-purpose flour
- ¾ cup confectioners' sugar
- 8 ounces (2 sticks) unsalted butter, cut into ½-inch pieces, chilled
- 2 cold large egg yolks
- 2 tablespoons very cold heavy cream

1. **TO MIX WITH A STAND MIXER:** Combine the flour and confectioners' sugar in the bowl of a stand mixer fitted with the paddle attachment. Beat on low speed for 1 minute. Add the cold butter and beat on medium-low speed until the pieces of butter are barely visible, about 3 minutes. Add the egg yolks and beat on medium-low speed just until the dough comes together, about 1 minute. Turn the machine down to low and stream in the heavy cream. Stop the machine and scrape down the sides of the bowl and the paddle. Continue to beat on low speed for 1 minute.

   TO MIX BY HAND: Sift together the flour and confectioners' sugar into a large bowl. Add the cold butter and incorporate into the flour by taking up handfuls of the butter and flour mixture and rubbing briskly between the palms of your hands until the butter is barely visible. Using a fork, beat together the egg yolks and cream in a small bowl and add to the flour mixture. Mix together with the fork until the dough just comes together.

2. Remove the dough from the bowl and divide into 2 equal pieces. Place each one on a piece of plastic wrap and flatten into a disk about ½ inch thick. Wrap tightly and refrigerate for at least 4 hours, or overnight.

3. Place one piece of dough at a time in a stand mixer fitted with the hook attachment. Work the dough on medium-low speed just until pliable. If you don't have a stand mixer, soften the dough by pounding it with a rolling pin on a lightly floured work surface. Roll out each piece with a rolling pin on a lightly floured work surface to a 12-inch-wide, ¼-inch-thick circle. Place between pieces of parchment paper, wrap tightly in plastic wrap, and refrigerate for a minimum of 4 hours. Alternatively, line lightly sprayed pie or tart pans with the dough and

wrap tightly. (The dough can be stored in the refrigerator for up to 3 days or in the freezer for up to 3 months.)

4. **TO BLIND-BAKE (PREBAKE):** Place a rack in the lower third of the oven and preheat the oven to 350°F. Lightly spray two 9- or 10-inch pie or tart pans with pan spray and line with the dough.

5. Prick the bottom of the pastry shell a few times with a fork. Line the pastry with parchment paper or large coffee filters. Fill the lined shell to the rim with dried beans, uncooked rice, or pie weights and gently press the "faux filling" into the corners. Bake for 15 minutes. After 15 minutes, carefully remove the weights using a dry measure and transfer them to a container. Gently pull up on the liner. If it sticks, return the covered pastry shell to the oven for another 3 minutes, or until you can easily lift off the liner. Bake for another 10 minutes, or until the pastry is a deep golden brown. Remove from the oven and allow to cool on a rack.

VARIATIONS

FOR INDIVIDUAL SHELLS: Use lightly sprayed 3-inch ring molds set on a lightly sprayed, perfectly flat baking sheet, or use lightly sprayed 3-inch tartlet pans. Roll out the dough on a lightly floured surface to a 1/8-inch thickness. Cut 4-inch circles. The dough should be cold enough for the edges to stand up without flopping over (chill if necessary), but not brittle. To ease into the molds, take a circle, set it over the mold, then with your thumb and forefinger, pinch in the east and west edges, then the north and south edges, so that the circle will slip inside the edges of the mold. Gently ease into the bottom of the ring, making sure the bottom of the circle is flush against the bottom edge of the ring rather than curving up the sides.

TO BLIND-BAKE (PREBAKE): For tartlets, it is not necessary to use pie weights when you prebake. Place a rack in the lower third of the oven and preheat the oven to 350°F. Bake for 15 to 20 minutes, until deep golden brown.

FOR DISKS: Cut 3- or 4-inch circles, depending on the desired size. Place the disks on parchment-paper-lined baking sheets and bake at 350°F for 15 to 18 minutes, until golden.

FOR WAFER COOKIES: See page 376.

CHOCOLATE PÂTE SUCRÉE
Chocolate Sweet Pastry

MAKES TWO 9- OR 10-INCH PIECRUSTS OR SIXTEEN 3-INCH TARTLET SHELLS

■ ■ ■

This pastry makes delicate short crusts and crispy, tender tart shells. You can also roll it into a log shape and make cookie-like wafers (see Variations).

2³/₄ cups all-purpose flour
¹/₂ cup unsweetened cocoa powder
¹/₂ cup sugar
8 ounces (2 sticks) unsalted butter, cut into ¹/₂-inch pieces, chilled
2 cold large egg yolks
3 tablespoons very cold heavy cream

1. **TO MIX WITH A STAND MIXER:** In the bowl of a stand mixer fitted with the paddle attachment, combine the flour, cocoa powder, and sugar. Beat on low speed for 1 minute. Add the butter and beat on medium-low speed until the pieces of butter are barely visible, 2 to 3 minutes. Add both the egg yolks at once and continue to beat for another 30 seconds. Add the cream in a slow stream and continue to beat until the dough comes together. Scrape down the sides of the bowl and the paddle and continue to beat on low speed for 1 minute.

   TO MIX BY HAND: Sift together the flour, cocoa powder, and sugar into a large bowl. Add the butter and incorporate into the flour by taking up handfuls of the butter and flour mixture and rubbing briskly between the palms of your hands until the butter is barely visible. Using a fork, beat together the egg yolks and cream in a small bowl and add to the flour mixture. Mix together with the fork until the dough just comes together.

2. Remove the dough from the bowl and divide into 2 equal pieces. Place each one on a piece of plastic wrap. Flatten into a disk about ¹/₂ inch thick and wrap tightly. Refrigerate for at least 4 hours, or overnight.

3. Cut one of the pieces of dough into 8 pieces and place in the bowl of a stand mixer fitted with the hook attachment. Beat on low speed just until pliable. If you don't have a stand mixer, soften the dough by pounding it with a rolling pin

on a lightly floured work surface. Gather the dough and roll out on a lightly floured work surface to a 12-inch-wide, ¼-inch-thick circle. Place between pieces of parchment paper, wrap tightly in plastic, and refrigerate for a minimum of 2 hours. Repeat with the other piece of dough. (The dough can be frozen for up to 2 months. You can also line the pans and freeze, wrapped airtight.)

4. **TO BLIND-BAKE (PREBAKE):** Place a rack in the lower third of the oven and preheat the oven to 350°F. Lightly spray two 9- or 10-inch pie pans with pan spray and line with the dough.

5. Prick the bottom of the pastry shell a few times with a fork. Line the dough with parchment paper or large coffee filters and fill to the rim with dried beans, uncooked rice, or pie weights. Gently press the "faux filling" into the corners and bake the shell for 15 minutes. After 15 minutes, carefully remove the weights using a dry measure and transfer them to a container. Gently pull up on the liner. If it sticks, return the covered pastry shell to the oven for another 3 minutes, or until you can easily lift off the liner. Bake for another 10 minutes, or until the pastry shows no sign of moisture; it will be a dull dark brown. Remove from the oven and allow to cool on a rack.

VARIATIONS

FOR TARTLET SHELLS AND DISKS: See page 374.

FOR WAFER COOKIES: If you have extra dough after cutting out tartlets, gather it up and shape into a 1½- to 2-inch-thick log. Wrap tightly in plastic wrap and chill for at least 2 hours. Place a rack in the lower third of the oven and preheat the oven to 350°F. Cut thin wafers ¼ to ⅛ inch thick and place on a parchment-paper-lined baking sheet. Bake the wafers for 10 minutes. Allow to cool on a rack.

■ ■ ■

Making Swirled Ice Cream

MAKES 1 QUART

You can easily make your own swirled ice cream by layering fruit schmutz, such as Apricot Schmutz (page 367) and Banana Schmutz (page 366), or other sauces with vanilla ice cream or other flavors. You can also use Creamy Caramel Sauce (page 354) or "Ten-Year" Chocolate Sauce (page 345).

    1 quart ice cream
    2 cups schmutz or sauce (see headnote)

1. Chill a 2-quart metal bowl or freezer container in the freezer for 30 minutes.

2. Beginning with the ice cream, layer the ice cream and schmutz or sauce in alternating layers in the chilled bowl. Place a sheet of plastic wrap directly over the top and return the ice cream to the freezer immediately.

Making Granita

Granita is an Italian ice made by stirring up a liquid as it freezes in a shallow pan. As soon as it's scooped onto a plate or into a bowl, granita begins to melt, so make sure your serving plates or bowls are cold—put them into the freezer for a while before serving.

1. Place a large flat-bottomed pan in the freezer before you make your base. A roasting pan or rectangular cake pan works well for this. Make your base and allow it to cool completely, then pour it into the pan and place it in the freezer.

2. Fluff the granita with a fork every 20 minutes. Bring the frozen crystals that form around the edges of the pan into the center. This forces the unfrozen liquid to

the edges to freeze. The crystals are delicate, so don't overstir. Set a timer for the 20-minute intervals. If forgotten, the mixture will freeze into a solid block, and the freezing process must be started over. If this should happen, place chunks of the frozen granita in a food processor fitted with the steel blade and pulse until the granita is liquefied.

3. The granita is ready when all the liquid has frozen into small ice crystals, which should take about 2 hours. Once the ice crystals are formed, the granita can be stored in the freezer, wrapped airtight, for up to a week. Serve it directly from the freezer, because it melts fast! If the granita freezes solid, use a food processor fitted with the steel blade to break it up. Pulse until slushy and serve immediately.

Toasting Spices

I toast all whole spices, such as cinnamon sticks, star anise, cardamom pods, and Szechuan peppercorns, before adding them to a recipe. Heating the spice releases its oils and wonderful fragrance. Hot spices should be added to warm or hot ingredients.

1. Place a rack in the middle of the oven and preheat the oven to 300°F.

2. Place the spice in a pie pan and toast in the oven for 5 minutes, or until it smells slightly toasted. Remove from the oven and use as directed in the recipe.

Toasting Almonds and Walnuts

Place a rack in the middle of the oven and preheat the oven to 350°F. Place the nuts on a baking sheet and bake for 5 to 10 minutes, or until they smell toasty and have turned a darker shade of brown. Remove from the oven and transfer to a bowl to cool.

Toasting and Skinning Hazelnuts

1. Place a rack in the middle of the oven and preheat the oven to 350°F.

2. Place the nuts on a baking sheet and toast them until they are dark golden brown, 10 to 12 minutes. They should fill the room with a toasty nut smell.

3. If the nuts have skins, remove the skins by wrapping the nuts in a damp kitchen towel and rubbing them or by placing them in a pasta pot insert and rubbing them against the surface.

Tempering Chocolate

Chocolate must be tempered before it is molded or used as a coating. Tempering makes the chocolate shiny and gives it a crispy snap. If it isn't tempered properly, it will taste just as good, but it will be dull and streaky.

There are three steps to tempering:
1. Carefully melting and heating the chocolate to 115°F.
2. Cooling the chocolate to 85°F.
3. Slightly warming the chocolate—to 89° to 90°F for bittersweet and semi-sweet chocolate, to 84° to 86°F for milk chocolate and white chocolate.

The above steps must be done gradually and under the right conditions:
1. Start with chocolate that has been wrapped tightly and stored away from strong-smelling foods in a moisture-free environment, about 65°F (no warmer than 70°F).
2. The room temperature should be 65° to 70°F. Do not try to temper chocolate in a hot kitchen or near an oven that is turned on.
3. You need a good instant-read thermometer, preferably a digital thermometer, with a 40° to 140°F range.
4. You need a clean, dry microwave-safe bowl.
5. Not essential, but I like to wear plastic surgical gloves when I temper chocolate so my fingers don't leave marks on the surface.

1. **TO TEMPER 1 POUND OF CHOCOLATE:** With an offset serrated knife, cut the chocolate into small, even pieces, about ¼ inch.

2. **USING A MICROWAVE:** Place two thirds of the chocolate in a microwave-safe bowl and microwave at 50 percent power for 30 seconds. Remove the chocolate from the microwave and stir gently; you don't want to create air pockets in the chocolate. Stir the chocolate from the edges of the bowl into the center.

3. Place the chocolate back in the microwave and, again at 50 percent power, zap in 10-second intervals, stirring and taking the temperature frequently, until all of the chocolate has melted and is smooth and the temperature is 115°F. Let sit for 10 minutes.

4. Begin the cooling process. Add the remaining chocolate, a handful at a time, to the bowl and stir gently until all of it has melted and is smooth (if necessary, return the chocolate to the microwave and zap for 10 seconds at 50 percent power). At this point your chocolate should be 85°F or 80° to 81°F for milk chocolate and white chocolate.

5. Begin the warming process. Return the chocolate to the microwave and zap at 50 percent power in 3- to 5-second intervals, stirring each time, until the temperature rises to 89° to 90°F or 84° to 86°F for milk chocolate or white chocolate. *Do not allow the temperature to go any higher than 97°F, or you will have to begin all over again with Step 2.*

2. **USING A DOUBLE BOILER:** Take care not to let steam from the bottom of the double boiler come in contact with the chocolate. Moisture will work its way into the chocolate and make it too thick and cause it to seize.

3. Choose a medium heatproof bowl that fits perfectly over a saucepan. Fill the saucepan about one-quarter full of water; the water should not touch the bowl. Bring to a boil and turn off the heat. Place two thirds of the chocolate in the bowl and place over the water. Stir gently until the chocolate has melted and reached 115°F.

4. Begin the cooling process. Remove the bowl from the saucepan. Add the remaining chocolate, a handful at a time, and stir until melted and the temperature is 85°F.

5. Begin the warming process. Return the bowl to the saucepan and stir until the chocolate reaches 89° to 90°F or 84° to 86°F for milk chocolate or white chocolate.

6. TESTING THE TEMPER: Dip the corner of a piece of parchment paper into the chocolate, remove it, and let it sit undisturbed for 2 to 3 minutes. The chocolate should harden and be dry and shiny, and it should have a snap when split in half. Once it is tempered, proceed with your recipe, stirring the chocolate frequently and gently to maintain the temper (see Sherry's Secrets). If the tempering has been unsuccessful, the chocolate will have a gray cast. If the temperature went too high, the chocolate will be grainy and you will have to start over.

Acknowledgments

I'VE BEEN BLESSED AND HONORED OVER THESE LAST twenty years to work with and feed the most amazing characters. This book is essentially a big thank-you note to all of you.

My thanks go out especially to the incomparable Wolfgang Puck, for putting up with this ballsy Brooklyn gal. He gave me a stage to perform on and the autonomy to explore my wildest ideas. Danke schön! for your continuous guidance and blessing—albeit with the occasional "ai yi yi" shake of your head.

My gratitude to the brilliant writer Martha Rose Shulman cannot be measured. Her integrity and unassuming approach are unmatched. Without her, this book would not have come to fruition. I am honored to call her my friend. Thanks, too, to her son, Liam, for being the best taster ever.

My editor, Rux Martin, cheered the book and shepherded it to completion. Thank you for making this such a wonderful experience.

Thanks to my agent, Janis Donnaud. I will always admire you for your savvy candor and for not letting me be "too cute."

Suzanne Griswold, the multitalented pastry chef and mind reader, who can do everything from recipe testing to creating a life-sized chocolate car to being my production manager on photo shoots, was indispensable to this project, as were the recipe testers and set assistants Ashley Rodriguez, Katherine Sacks, Echelle Morales, and Jenny Machias.

Special thanks to Ari Rosenson and the gang at CUT Restaurant for letting me use their beautiful space for the photography.

Thanks to the photographer Ron Manville. Photography can be grueling, but Ron always made it interesting, fun, and an adventure. To Harry Langdon, the legendary Hollywood photographer, who took the picture on the cover of this book, and to Michaela Sullivan, for making me a cover girl. To Anne Chalmers, for the elegant and lovely interior design.

I also need to single out Sixto Pocasangre, the executive pastry chef at Wolfgang Puck Catering. He has been there with me since I walked into Spago Hollywood fourteen years ago. He always indulges my passion for creating the "best bite" with a beautiful smile and plain old hard work.

To my current and former Pastry Angels, thank you for your devotion: Gustavo Escalante, Julian Saldana, Juan Pocasangre, Ian Flores, Isla Vargas, Kenny Magana, Nicole Lindsay, Artemio Sanchez, Fredy Garcia, Jorge Lopez, Cesar Loya, Suki Sum, Frank Bonventre, Helen Arsen, Steve "Monkey Boy" Peungraksa, Leslie Quinn, Katherine Sacks, Katherine Hamilton, Zairah "Cupcake" Molena, Cecilia Leung, Jennifer Palombo, Elizabeth "Doc" Ko, Sherri Richardson, and Jennifer Shen.

To Lee Hefter, Spago's brilliant leader. He never ceases to amaze me with his steel-trap memory, his knowledge of all things culinary, and his chutzpah. Lee truly lives the mantra "It's not a passion, it's an obsession."

To the Spago institution, "a string with no ending and no beginning," and the visionary Barbara Lazaroff, for giving me years of wonderful memories I could never have dreamed of. Thanks to the supremely talented members of this family, chefs Thomas Boyce and Chris Hook; sous-chefs Josh Brown, Hugo Bolanos, Tetsuro Yahagi, Burton "Way" Yi, and Justin Bamberg. To Tracey Spillane, our general manager, who with grace and style has whipped and polished us into a lean, mean fighting machine. Great appreciation goes out to the hardworking Spago family of managers, runners, waiters, bartenders, busers, and, last but not least, stewards.

To the farmers and their farmhands who grow the most amazing produce under the sun. And to our purveyors, Rick Fisher and Rhonda Rago of LA Specialties, who fulfill my every need at a moment's notice.

I'd also like to thank my sister and brother bakers, friends, and contemporaries for making the world a sweeter place to bake in: Florian Bellanger, Sebastien Cannone, Janet Rikala-Dalton, Jim Dodge, Stephen Durfee, Robert Ellinger, Elizabeth Falkner, Claudia Fleming, Pierre Hermé, Martin Howard, David Lebovitz, Emily Luchetti, Leslie Mackie, Sam Mason, Joe McKenna, Ewald Notter, Susan Notter, Pichet Ong, Jacquy Pfeiffer, Nicole Plue, Michael Recchiuti, Michel Richard, Surbhi Sahni, Suvir Saran, Mindy Segal, Biagio Settepani, Nancy Silverton, En-Ming Hsu, Donald Wressell, and Bill Yosses. Like firefighters of the kitchen, you are always there with advice and inspiration. I truly admire every one of you and feel fortunate to share the same passion for pastry.

I'd also like to tip my hat to some people who, over the years, have given me guidance and changed my life along the way. They include Drew Nieporent, Barbara Fairchild, Carolyn Bates (for saving my career with a few typed words), Flo Braker, Maida Heatter, Suzy Heller, Russ Parsons (for introducing me to Martha Rose Shulman), Jacques Pépin, Jan Birnbaum, and the late Johnny Apple (for just loving food and inspiring me to make more). Also the food writers from *Bon Appétit*, Michael and Ariane Batterberry from *Food Arts, Chocolatier, Pastry Art & Design, Food & Wine, Gourmet*, the *New York Times*, the *Los Angeles Times*, and *Saveur*.

Finally, to my nearest and dearest:

Mom, who served up frozen dinners with unconditional love and support.

Dad, who worked two and three jobs and still found time to come home to barbecue kielbasa in the dead of winter.

My sisters, Terry, Laurie, and Lynne, who put up with the Sherry Shrine.

My fairy godson and computer guru, Blake.

My niece and nephews, Erica, Sean Flin, and Will Yum Yum (the best bagel chef ever!).

My West Coast dad, Teddy Goldstein, for the occasional push, and his talented pastry chef wife and best buddy, Jackie.

My friends from childhood to present: Stephanie Sozomenu, Martha Gramlich, Christine Perasso, Debra Dimino, Barbara Binkes-Keller, Marissa Guerlich, Jill Miller, Lorri Wressell, Melissa Prentice, Clare Davis, Jon Hirsch, Heidi White, and Shelly Balloon.

Sources

Amazon.com
www.amazon.com
Feuilles de brick.

Bavaria Sausage, Inc.
6317 Nesbitt Road
Madison, WI
(608) 271-1295
(800) 733-6695
www.bavariasausage.com
Kuchle Back-Oblaten (wafer papers) for making Austrian wafer cookies.

Beryl's Cake Decorating & Pastry
Supplies
(800) 488-2749
www.beryls.com
Specialty pastry tools and equipment and edible gold dust.

Chefs' Toys
3001 South Main Street
Santa Ana, CA
(800) 755-8634
www.chefstoys.net
Professional kitchen supply store, with a mobile unit that serves southern California, driving tools right to your door. Tell them Sherry sent you!

Chocosphere
(877) 992-4626
www.chocosphere.com
Features the best chocolates from all over the world, including Michel Cluizel and Valrhona.

The Cook's Library
8373 West Third Street
Los Angeles, CA
(323) 655-3141
(866) 340-2665
www.cookslibrary.com
Los Angeles's premier cookbook store.

Dean & DeLuca
(800) 221-7714
www.deandeluca.com
Great for tools, as well as specialty items such as chocolate, spices, and produce. Check the Web site for retail locations around the country.

eBeeHoney.com
1318 Township Road 593
Ashland, OH 44805
(419) 289-6701
www.ebeehoney.com
Beeswax.

Home Depot
(800) 553-3199
www.homedepot.com
> Great for tools like paintbrushes and scrapers and for toolboxes. Find the nearest location on the Web site.

JB Prince
36 East 31st Street, 11th floor
New York, NY
(800) 473-0577
www.jbprince.com
> High-quality chefs' equipment and tools.

King Arthur Flour: The Baker's Catalogue
135 Route 5 South
Norwich, VT
(800) 827-6836
www.kingarthurflour.com
> Stocks all your baking needs, from equipment and tools to great flour and ingredients, including tapioca flour, maple sugar, and praline paste.

Kitchen Arts & Letters
1435 Lexington Avenue
New York, NY
(212) 876-5550
www.kitchenartsandletters.com
> Ten thousand books in stock: store owner Nach Waxman will locate hard-to-find books.

L'Epicerie
(866) 350-7575
www.lepicerie.com
> Dehydrated raspberry and strawberry powder, passion fruit puree, and other hard-to-find pastry items.

New York Cake Supplies
56 West 22nd Street
New York, NY
(212) 675-2253
www.nycake.com
> Acetate rolls.

Pastryitems.com
(443) 417-8854
www.pastryitems.com
> Specializes in pastry and baking equipment and ingredients, including acetate banding strips, bombe molds, oil-based red food coloring, and sanding sugar.

Penzeys Spices
(800) 741-7787
www.penzeys.com
> Great spices, cocoa powder, and vanilla. See the Web site for retail locations around the country.

Sinclaire Company
(866) 523-6523
www.sinclairecompany.com
> Chocolate cups.

Surfas Chef's Paradise
8824 National Boulevard
Culver City, CA
(310) 559-4770
(866) 799-4770
www.surfasonline.com
> Cooking and restaurant equipment, such as bombe molds, and specialty foods, including almond flour, oil, and paste, Lyle's Golden Syrup, oil-based red food coloring, peppermint oil, pistachio paste, all-butter puff pastry, rose water, salts, Trablit coffee extract, verjus, and yuzu juice.

Sur La Table

(800) 243-0852

www.surlatable.com

Well-made baking equipment and utensils, including cornstick pans; sanding sugar, Trablit coffee extract. Find the nearest location on the Web site.

Sweet Celebrations

(800) 328-6722

www.sweetc.com

Unique cake-decorating and baking equipment. Check the Web site for retail locations.

VeriTemp

(310) 288-0475

www.veritemp.com

Silica gel.

Whole Foods Market

(512) 477-4455

www.wholefoods.com

Rose water, salts, malt syrup. Find a location on the Web site.

Williams-Sonoma

(877) 812-6235

www.williams-sonoma.com

Well-made baking equipment and utensils. Find the nearest retail location on the Web site.

Wilton Industries

Wilton Homewares Store

7511 Lemont Rd.

Darien, IL

(630) 985-6000

(800) 794-5866

www.wilton.com

Complete online bakeware store for home cooks and professionals.

WorldPantry.com

(415) 401-0080

(866) 972-6879

www.worldpantry.com

Specialty foods, Forbidden Rice by Lotus Foods.

Also check out these Web sites:

www.alinea.fr

www.baking911.com

www.bonappetit.com

www.chow.com

www.cooksillustrated.com—get a Web membership!

www.davidlebovitz.com

www.eggbeater.typepad.com

www.egullet.com

www.epicurean.com

www.fauchon.com

www.foodandwinemagazine.com

www.laduree.fr

www.lagrandeepicerie.fr

www.meilleurchef.com

www.pastryartanddesign.com

www.pastryscoop.com

www.pichetong.com

www.pierreherme.com

www.sammasonnyc.com

www.starchefs.com

www.yvesthuries.com

Index

Page numbers in *italics* refer to photographs.

C

gelato, 306
    butterscotch, 274–77, *276*
    coconut, 304–6, *305*
    Meyer lemon, 214–15
    pistachio, 318
    stracciatella, *280,* 281
gelée parfaits, pussycat café, 21–23, *22*
giant gingerbread cookies, 130–31
ginger
    -almond fortune cookies, 286–88, *287*
    aqua d-kula (lemon-mint tea), 187
    cream tartlets with poached figs and Persian mul-
        berries, 205–7, *206*
    juice, 364
    soda, passion fruit sorbet and coconut gelato float
        with, 304–6, *305*
gingerbread cookies, giant, 130–31
gingersnap toaster-oven tarts with peach filling,
    127–29, *128*
Girardet, Fredy, 269
Girl Scout cookies, 164
glazes
    chocolate, 15, 18, 74, 75, 82, 84, 96, 97, 244, 245
    custard, 228
    honey, 282
golden syrup, in treacle tart, 109
Governors Ball. *See* Academy Awards desserts
Grandma's A&P strawberry sodas, 19–20, *20*
granita
    aqua d-kula (lemon-mint tea), 187
    making, 303, 377–78
    mandarin, *302,* 303
Grant, Hugh, 167
grape. *See* Concord grape
Greenspan, Dorie, 310
Griswold, Suzanne, 240
grunt, apple-butterscotch, 146–47

H
half sheet pans, baking cakes in, 41
Halsey, Professor, 87–88
Harvey Nichols (London), 100
Hayden, Gerry, 82, 85
hazelnut(s)
    Campton Place bar nuts, 143

    linzer dough, 368
    praline paste, 357
    toasting and skinning, 379
Hefter, Lee, 182, 282, 322
herbed flatbread, crispy, 179–81, *180*
Home Depot, pastry tools from, 370
Honey Crisp Farms (Calif.), 189
honey-glazed Spago corn bread, 282–83, *283*
hot and cold desserts, serving, 316
Hotel Sacher (Vienna), 217, 244, 246
huckleberry Merlot sauce, 361

I
ice cream, 306
    almond seats for, 356
    baked Alaska, 66–69, *68*
    black currant tea, 258–60, *259*
    Calvados, 148–49
    caramelized banana tarts with, 85–86, *86*
    coffee, 132–33
    coffee stracciatella, 176–78, *177*
    meringue triangles and circles for, 369–70
    peach melba, 110–11, *111*
    roasted banana, Brazil wet walnut sundae with,
        135–37, *136*
    strawberry, 19–20
    swirled, making, 377
    vanilla, seven-bean, 340–41, *341*
    yuzu curd, 322–25, *324*
ice milk, almond, 301
ices
    aqua d-kula (lemon-mint tea) granita, 187
    granita, making, 377–78
    lemon, Italian, *24,* 25
    mandarin granita, *302,* 303
icings. *See also* frostings
    buttercream, 358
    buttercream, coffee, 358
    lemon, 94, 95
    vanilla and chocolate, *32,* 33, 34
ingredients, notes on, 1
Iron Chef, 322–23
Italian desserts. *See also* gelato; granita
    biscuit tortoni, 30–31